*An exceptionally talented w
by the sense of a teacher wa.......
semblance of control and total collapse.*

— Emma Finn, Conville and Walsh

*Hugely accomplished prose, both in its precision of
observation and outstanding dialogue. It is rare to read
such a vivid cacophony of voices.*

— Lucy Morris, Curtis Brown

*An unflinching yet humane account. Beautifully written and
tenderly imagined, this novel will stay with you for a long
time.*

— Dr Mary Bousted, NEU

Born into a Yorkshire vicarage, Kester Brewin has taught
mathematics in South East London schools for over twenty
years and writes regularly for the national education press.
The author of a number of celebrated books of non-fiction,
notably *Mutiny* — an exploration of the impact of pirate
culture, and *Getting High* — a history of the human quest for
flight, he has twice presented at the UK's premier TEDx event
and spoken on his work across the US and Europe.

An excerpt from *Middle Class* was shortlisted for The Bridport
Prize in 2020, and his story *The Rot* was shortlisted for the
Dinesh Prize for Short Fiction in 2022.

He lives in London with his two teenage children.

Middle Class

Kester
Brewin

Vaux Books

Also by Kester Brewin:

*The Complex Christ / Other
Mutiny / After Magic
Getting High*

Published by Vaux Books
www.vaux.net

978-0-9935628-5-3

For every class,
CBC Wine Club,
and E, I & H
x

'They chose their pastors
as they chose their horses:
for hard work'

— R. S. Thomas

We are beyond 'crisis'.
We are in a state of distress.

*— 2019 report into mental health
of teachers in England.*

1

It is just before 9 am when Sally calls, the soft hum of phone vibrations shaking Jo from her thoughts.

'Hey,' Sally says. 'Just wanted to say good luck today.'

'Aww Sal, thank you.' She smiles. To be thought of is a wonderful thing. 'Where are you?' There's noise in the background, a pause before Sally answers.

'Sorry,' she says. 'Caught me mid-slurp. I'm actually going into work. Bit of a shock but "save Pret," you know.'

On Jo's desk is a mug of ditch-water instant balanced atop a pile of papers, the actual furniture barely visible under the stacks of paper that have already accumulated. Risk assessments. Instructions for quarantining worksheets. Homework timetables. Symptom checklists and action plans bumping up against fifty pages on the new school inspection framework, the 'three Rs' metastasising into long acronyms which will apparently help children to become more efficiently educated. She lifts her coffee, takes a sip and pushes the pile an inch or two further away.

'You're going to do great Jo,' Sally tells her, changing her tone to solemn, and though she's never seen Jo teach and has no metric by which to make this judgement, there's even warmth to be taken from naive encouragement.

Sometimes it hardly seems possible to Jo that the same literature degree landed her and Sally in two such different places and with such a vast difference in the quality of their beverages. But she knows better than to say this because: job security. Plus, she's just had six weeks off and — though Sally wouldn't ever say it so bluntly — knows that she has hardly put in a proper day since March. Things posted online. Worksheets and videos. Poems to for students to self-destruct, if they had access to the internet. If she can survive six weeks

1

of this new madness back in school there'll be another week off as reward. So yes, the readily available caffeine is terrible but no, she mustn't be heard to complain.

'Thank you,' she says again.

'I'm sorry I haven't been there more,' Sally begins, but Jo quietens her. No one has been allowed to be there, that has been the point. Kill the bug off by keeping people apart. Death by separation. The ghastly chorus of her personal collection of socially distanced horrors rises and limps across the stage. Unable to visit her dying mother. Forced to miss the funeral. Dad left alone. Ben using the convenience of lockdown to finish with her.

But — again she mustn't wallow — each has had their own private accretion of painful experiences. Sally marrying without her friends around her. Maria bringing a baby into a world so reduced and narrowed. At least Sally has made the effort to call. 'It's been hard for everyone,' Jo says with a wince. Her moods have swung hard recently; she is wary of any nudges that might send her towards descent.

But Sally hasn't got where she is without the courage to speak words into hard places. 'You're due to see him today?' she asks.

That she doesn't even need to mention the name is instructive. Darren. Of course she means Darren. The wince becomes a grimace. Jo presses thumb and finger to eyelids and tries to push her head back somewhere positive. 'Yes,' she says with a dark laugh. 'His class is due any minute. Very first lesson since lockdown and would you believe it it's them'

Sally giggles. 'Well... If you don't tell him to "fuck off" you're already winning.'

'That's not funny Sal!' Jo tells her. But she is smiling now.

'Sorry Jo,' she says. 'It's not.' Then pauses for another slug of coffee before giggling again. 'Except it is.'

Except, Jo doesn't want to have to point out, it nearly cost her her job. And coming up for forty going into a pandemic would hardly have been the ideal time to try to convince someone that a just-sacked English teacher was just who they ought to be hiring.

Sally thinks that she should be ennobled, that tough West London schools like Cromwell need more teachers like Jo. In the staffroom she'll now forever be the woman who told a rude, indolent boy to get the fuck out of her room, who finally said what everyone had been dying to say. But — Dad had told her in no uncertain terms — whatever her colleagues might feel, however much you want to tell a boy like Darren that he's a depraved human being he is ultimately a child, one who had deserved better.

'Don't beat yourself up. It'll probably end up being the best thing that's happened to him, you'll see.'

Just FUCK OFF Darren.

A shadow across Jo's face and the smile evaporates into a residue of grave doubts. Sally doesn't know all the ways Jo had tried to quieten him, all the grammar she'd tried to instil before a single syllable of old Germanic had finally slapped him into stunned silence. She loves her to bits, knows that Sally surely has tough days at work too, but probably has no idea how much she had taken before finally breaking.

Darren had goaded Nishaan again and again and she'd asked him politely, again and again, to stop.

He'd made disgusting remarks to Hayley and she'd stiffly, patiently chastised him.

He'd yawned, complained that Jo's breath stank, slapped Ade, threatened to bang Charlie up, got up to shout out of the window, refused to take his cap off, leant back on two chair legs, chewed gum, screwed up his first worksheet on *An Inspector Calls*, splayed his tag all over the back of the replacement.

Concern about the virus had already seeped under the doors, begun clinging to each surface and hanging in the air between them, but all of this she had taken, each thing Darren did further sucking her reserves, each incident tightening her nerves, the pitch of their trembling rising, desperately trying to push on with the lesson, to communicate something – *anything* – to them about the tension between the social classes in an industrial town a century or so ago, this pretty young girl who has taken her life...

'Not as fit as you,' he'd leered at Hayley. Hayley had not even turned round, just flicked a bird over her shoulder. 'Spin on my finger? Yeah, bet you'd love to.' The other boys shaking their heads, the girls united in disgust. 'No? What about your mum then? She's peng enough.'

Snap. Two words and Jo had exploded. *Your mum.* It was like blade he'd pulled from nowhere and thrust hard into her chest, releasing a gush of long-caged expletives.

Just FUCK OFF Darren. Get the fuck out of my classroom.

An injured look as if she'd hit an ill-healed wound, but she hadn't cared, had stormed on, pointing with the book she was meant to be teaching and continuing to shout at him, all that she'd kept pent up spilling out onto him and burning. A mild March day, but the classroom oven-hot with this scalding, the salad cream walls sweating as her voice had begun to crackle. Fury, love and hurt combusting together, and he'd risen in raging obedience.

She shifts in her chair and glances up at the clock. He'll be here again soon. There isn't much time.

'I don't know Sal.' She needs levity. Good humour a better weapon than rage in this place, but it takes a lightness of mind, a nimbleness of thought, and she can feel herself dragging. 'Not sure screaming expletives at him is going to turn him into Gandhi.'

Sally laughs. 'Well if anyone can, it's you Jo.'

Stock phrases like this, sometimes Jo wonders if the gradual accumulation of them over time is how she ended up going into teaching. The problem being, it's only now that she's realising how far teaching has gone into her, so far that she's not sure how she might ever pare herself from it. It has entered her, consumed her, taken over her days and infected her nights, and if the past months away from this place have taught her anything it's that she is desperate to wrestle back control. To do it, but not to *be* it. Yes, she thinks, to have an actual life apart, to have some independence, and if I cannot do that I might have to leave, to break it off, finish it. Then the "but." *But someone has to think of the children.* And so she stays. So she comes back. Because what else does she actually have?

A gentle ping of an elevator door comes through the phone into one ear and, as if in cosmic mockery, into the other comes the obscene clanging of the school bell, ringing in the start of the lesson with all the volume of an emergency situation. With Darren on the way it might well be.

'I'd better go,' she says, posture and expression shifting quickly.

'OK. Me too. Take care Jo. Chat soon.'

She thanks her again.

Take care. Be careful. Mind where you tread. Yes, Jo thinks, Sally is right about that at least. Pitfalls everywhere, mines that children keep buried just below the surface, knives everyone worries are concealed under a jacket or down a sock just a short angry grab away. Press them gently on some matter or another and suddenly you've triggered an explosion, a frenzied slaughter.

She pumps a squirt from a bottle and wrings her hands clean. Stay positive. Stay up. Don't swing now. So many deaths this year already, but she cannot think like that. Mustn't. All she wants is her mother's arms cradling her but it is too late for that now. *And it always was,* she can't help telling herself, her mind getting in a last word before she tells it to belt it. Too late. She and mum should have broken their silence sooner.

No, she mustn't start with complaints now; the bell has sent the building into its hourly writhing, there's no time for those thoughts. It trembles with the mass of children shouting and leering, cursing mothers and commenting on footwear and calling out greetings and — despite everything they've been told — still wrestling one another, hugging and landing punches. The hard thud of bodies slamming against walls and doors, bubbles broken as their arms lay around shoulders and trainered feet moon along corridors, the school flexing and shaking as they begin to close around her.

She scans the room. New exercise books have been fished out of the cupboard. She has her mask and her sprays. The desks are in reasonable lines. The interactive board is plugged in, next to it the old whiteboard on its runners, not clean exactly, but — she concludes happily — no marks that could easily be turned into a phallus. The floor pretty is much clear of the cans, cartons, or any other sizeable detritus that they could toe-punt, hurl, pop or splat. It will do.

Charlie is thumping on the door, Danny next to him. No sight of Darren. There's a rumble from somewhere below, another crash of chairs above, a shrill scream from a group of girls, corridors broadcasting on all frequencies. Forget novels and poems; if she can't grab their attention she knows that it's her that they'll critique in fine detail, offering strong opinions and different perspectives, tearing into her for an hour before tossing her aside and moving on to another colleague.

The pressure is building around the door. Two metres? Either their Maths is worse than she'd thought or they have agreed to be one very large household. She spurs herself, tells herself *I can do this,* and digs these words into her rib. Like a horse impelled she suddenly brightens, exaggerates a smile and strides over to welcome them, pre-flight check on the way: blouse buttons, skirt front and back, a sweep of the nostrils. Everything else might go awry, but this trinity of rites remained sacred. A stray bogey, sight of the underside of workaday bra, a piece of Sellotape stuck to a backside — avoid those three things and she had a fighting chance.

They know the drill. She holds the key up, shoos them back to stop them pushing on the door. Danny is yanked by the collar by someone and thrown backwards, disappearing from the frame of the window like a cartoon character. Jo laughs, actually laughs at this, is reminded that no matter how shit this job can be she still works with teenagers, children who in the throes of a global pandemic will still find ways to be entertaining, ridiculous or hilarious. All of these things, and then horribly cruel and this is interminable *chiaroscuro* of the job. Light and shadow always together, so laugh, yes, but keep your eyes open lest someone takes your feet out from under you, jumps up and throws a chair. She places the key in the lock, pauses a moment, blinks and repairs her face, swallows hard. No sign of Darren.

When she turns the lock they are meant to file in one by one, but instead the door breaks open and it all crashes over, a crescendo of noise, a torrent of bodies, some shoved in who shouldn't be, others just shoving because shoving is what is done around doors. English timetabled, but it is a whole chemistry lesson of violent reactions, bouncing, thumping, flaming, crashing, shouting, laughing, moaning, slapping, yanking, tripping and yelling.

She steps back and pulls her mask up over her mouth as she manages to resurface. 'Oi!' she splutters into the crowd, picking out Charlie who is now trying to charge back out. 'Come on. Once you're in, you're in!'

'Miss, man,' he says, pointing to someone ducking and weaving up the corridor, 'he's got my pen!'

She can't see who "he" is, but granted, Charlie will need a pen.

He takes Jo's permission before she's given it, dashes up the corridor and wrestles his friend to the ground amid a chorus of cheering, trainers flying in on both of them. A little lull round the doorway because of this, Jordan and Michael diverting to join the melee. They're big lads, have all put on inches over the summer, filled out in every dimension.

Hayley approaches with some of her friends and it's the same for them too: each less girl than when Jo had last seen them, and more woman. Their skirt-tops are rolled over and over how they like them, landing the hem mid-thigh, all them trilling hello, Hayley fussing at the cuticles of the nails that are done to the max.

'See you've got your priorities right,' Jo says, nodding at the little stick she's using to push the flesh back, and Hayley pulls her selfie face, holds them up as if for a photo and laughs, 'yeah, right hand first, then left.' Such a nice kid.

'Very droll,' Jo tells Hayley, 'I hope you've sanitised, right?' She funnels them in through the door then turns and calls, 'right, hurry up!' at no one in particular, and no one in particular listens. Neither Jordan nor Michael react, so — rules be damned — she launches out from the doorway to approach them. Michael turns and scowls before carrying on talking to a girl Jo can't recognise, an expanse of glistening Lyrca pulled around almost all of her face. Almost nobody else is wearing one, and Jo doesn't know what she is meant to feel about this, tries out different emotions — worry, relief, anger, empathy — but finds that none really feel true on their own. She opens out an arm to guide them in.

'Don't touch me, man,' Michael spits. 'Do. Not. Touch me.'

'Innit,' Jordan concurs with faux menace, knowing damned well that she'd never dare, this new panic of new rules nonetheless giving them a new means of baiting her, insisting that for their safety she cannot come too close. But before she can think of a way to turn this sneer — to use its own energy and send it back with enough spice to earn a smiling nod from Jordan that yes, she still had it — a battle erupts, a group of boys turning and forming, morphing and twisting like a rolling Hepworth, hard as bronze. Jesus, she thinks, even if they were wearing full PPE could they get any further from the idea of social distancing? Inside the womb of this scrum Jo can just see a boy, shoved this way, then that, baseball cap off, half of him trying to reach it while half struggles to break free. He emits a yelp like a fox as the hard toes of a trainer fly towards him, all the time working to get himself back up to his feet.

Please God, she prays, don't let Darren be among them. She needs to start positive, can't have an attempt to discipline him the first thing she does this year when it was the very last thing she did last. No, mustn't be moaning on the very first day, so she doesn't go straight over, forces a laugh instead and calls, 'come on, that's enough! Two metres please.' Silly boys, too much testosterone, wrestling and jousting. Jump in and they'd probably say she'd spoiled their fun.

There is laughter, but some of the kicks are really going in, and she recoils a little as she sees two punches land hard. Darren isn't among them, she's sure of that now, but — snoods round mouths and noses — neither does she recognise them or know any of their names. Function of a big school, it happens. Over two hundred children in each year, half of them with hoods permanently raised, a kind of brutal monastery, anonymity prized.

The boy in the middle of it all has made his way back to his feet and a couple of them have pinned him up on one whitewashed wall of the corridor, just beyond a large display board that's got photos of the lovely Year 7 trip to Canterbury last February. The *only* trip last year, as it turned out. She's annoyed to see that people have already brushed their bags up against it and the backing paper has begun to rip. Someone from management will doubtless be up to nag.

Then she sees the actual terror on the boy's face. One of them has cocked his fist at him, drawing it back like an archer, aiming head high.

'Stop it!' she shouts, suddenly back in the present. 'Stop that!'

But they don't seem to hear and she looks unsure, doubts whether her voice actually sounded. Lock yourself away alone in your flat for months and it turns out that this can actually be a question, but before she has time to answer it the boy's eyes widen in panic, then slam shut in anticipation of pain.

Just at the last a door swings open and the approaching fist pulls out. Mr Jackson.

'What do you think you're doing?!' he yells, and Jo comically smarts like he's telling her off too, which he might well do —

standing in a daze while these boys went about beating someone up. As soon as they see the Head they melt, tight grips turning fluidly to pats on the boy's shoulder, the solid caps of trainers transformed instantly to slowly oozing steps, turning, relaxed, away from the scene.

'Alright Sir,' they say. 'Just messing.' Lowering their coverings to flash wide smiles while the boy now kneels, picking up his cap, breathing quickly, unsure if it is really over.

'Messing with the bubbles we are trying to maintain to keep you lot safe! Get to your lessons,' Jackson orders, and they look him up and down a bit, take some measurements and then troop off.

'What was that about?' Jo asks the boy sympathetically, more loudly than she might need to, but trying to recover some sense of agency. He doesn't say anything, just offers a crumpled look, an almost imperceptible shake of the head as he pulls his hat firmly down. He gets up, attempts to straighten himself out, looks at a creased timetable, then the number on Jo's door, winces as he feels for a rib and ducks through it.

Shit. She tries to hide her wide-eyed surprise. She hasn't actually checked her class list for changes; it's their GCSE year, she hadn't thought she'd even need to. Jackson turns inspector, peers a moment at her door and the noise coming out of it before looking further along at a corridor that has miraculously cleared. His suit has a lustrous, firm weave that holds its shape in a way that a young staff member's cheaper cloth never would.

After the mess with Darren, Jo has become convinced that he wants to find a way to be rid of her.

'I'm an embarrassment,' she'd said earlier that morning to Cara, who teaches in the room opposite.

Cara had told her that she was being ridiculous. 'You've got experience,' she'd pushed back. 'Right now that's invaluable in a school like Cromwell.'

'Yes but you say "experience" to Jackson and you can see him auto-replace it with "expensive".'

Cara had laughed but Jo knows that there's some truth in her worries. Budgets had been strangle-tight even before this, and now things could only be worse, so the last thing he needed was a fight kicking off first day back from lockdown, a fight right next to the teacher who went viral in March, hollering for a student to fuck off out of her classroom.

'Bitch!' Darren had screamed back. 'I fucking will leave! School is *dead*, man!' finally obeying one of Jo's instructions, getting up to go, *fucking off out of her classroom*, nearly knocking the door off its hinges. That was it. *In loco parentis* and she had gone loco, had totally lost it with him.

It had made it to YouTube before Jackson had even heard what had happened. Scores of views before he'd called her in to explain herself, him furious, baying for blood, thinking first of reputation, threats of action against her for putting the school's image at risk, Jo breaking down, finally telling all. *I'm so sorry, my mum has been terribly ill, she's actually dying, and I...* he'd been shocked into silence, into a spluttered expression of condolence, and Jo had gone running and sobbing to get her things, rushing from the building, racing to see her mother while there was still time.

There hadn't been much, not nearly enough to say all she'd wanted to. A week, then the hospital had curled into battle-mode, all visits banned. Another week or so and she was gone. April. Not even allowed to the funeral.

So yes, if it's the first day back and already the Head is interrogating her again she feels she has some cause for worry. Sally's "you're going to do great" feels optimistic at best.

'Everything under control Miss Barker? Are you sure you can manage?' Jackson's questioning snaps her back into the now. She can't see his mouth, feels that half of the information she'd normally work with has been taken away. Stripped of any moderating smile the words land fully loaded, a subtle flash of the steel he is carrying, concealed for now but she's sure he won't hesitate to use it.

She tells him that she is fine. 'Tens of thousands dead, no vaccine, back in front of classes.' Her voice chokes like a faulty engine, refuses to go further. She restarts, more serious. 'But yes, everything under control.'

But he is not a man of humour, nor much grace. Taught Physics once (not well, apparently) so his universe is hard laws. He nods as if pondering slowly, looking over the English department corridor as if it were a troublesome galaxy. 'A big year,' he says, though he neglects to add who for.

Jo gathers herself to speak again, as if this were perhaps the right moment to remind him of her long service. But he pulls his eyebrows up, stretches his half-face into a picture of impatience.

'A chance to redeem yourself,' he says.

Her actual face is a poor mask. It slips and folds, creases and furrows under the cloth round her mouth as she collapses behind it all, trying to hide the smarting pain of him repeating words her mother had challenged her with.

Running out of school and up to the hospital, she'd told her mother what had happened with Darren, hoping for pure sympathy. But that wasn't the Barker way, and instead she was told that she shouldn't have, that the boy was just a child, that she had to look for a way to make things right.

Something had blown inside. 'Jesus mum, I just needed a bit of sympathy.' A shake of the head, a scoff that had rung its message clear: *why are you always like this.*

Mum had apologised then, and blamed a wave of pain. She'd reached out and asked Jo to start again, to tell her, to really explain how it had all happened. She'd taken her mother's hand and they'd looked at one another — *really* looked, perhaps for the first time in god-knows how long, both withered, both exhausted — and something had begun to shift.

But then the enforced separation, then the final blow, leaving Jo full of echoes, locked away all summer looking for an answer to this hanging question of how to achieve her redemption. Even though some saner part of her knew it was her father's religion speaking, her only conclusion had been a redoubled commitment to hard work. All of the sermons she'd grown up hearing him deliver had remixed themselves into this single problem: having lost a child, how was she going to make it better again?

She knows her mother had stood at church fetes, bragging 'yes, my daughter is an English teacher, in *such* a tough school and she just loves it,' had said nonsense like this without ever knowing the true brutality of her work, the sheer numbers of children that Jo was expected to carry without ever stumbling. Yet work was what she knew best, and this would be the forge from which she fashioned a restored reputation. In the waves of August heat, turning in her bed, peeling morning sheets away, she had settled on this decision: an atonement for her mistake with Darren, then she could allow herself to visit Dad and scatter Mum's ashes with him in good conscience.

She drags her attention to the present, finds it's thankfully only been a moment she's been away. You spend a whole summer holiday in another world, she thinks, it can be hard to stay in real life, have to do what other people need you to.

'I won't let you down,' she tells Jackson. No need to tell him of the doubled-down vow to herself to work harder than ever, because this is about showing her mother, not him.

'Get me those grades,' Jackson says, nodding towards her classroom, and though no one knows by what method grades will be awarded, or if they even will be, she plays the dutiful servant and promises him that she will.

Darren has not still arrived. She quickly scans the corridor for him. No sign.

'Oh, and Jo?' Jackson hasn't finished. 'These displays need touching up.' She looks back to see him flicking a torn corner of a photo of the Wife of Bath before marching away, leather soles squeaking on polished lino. She flicks V's behind his back, sticks her tongue into her bottom lip, then hurriedly checks that no one saw. But no, she is alone on the corridor, gaping door in front of her, the sound of a raucous mob flowing through it.

No Darren, but all the others she had told her mother about: Jordan, Ade, Michael, Nelson, Danny and Charlie, each with the power to ruin a lesson, all now in Year 11, all waiting for her to march in and begin.

Her hand moves, two fingers towards her mouth before she remembers to pull them back. As August had emptied itself she had chewed on worries about seeing them, worries about controlling them, worries about controlling herself, worries about failing them in their GCSE year, worries that she has already been marked out as a failure, worries about managers who will worry only about data. She pulls her hair round over her shoulder — dark strands on a cream blouse, a little crumpled where her ironing has missed it. Perhaps the girls will comment. Lauren, Hayley, Chanel, Nourin.

She steps towards the door thinking that she must now wash her hands again. Where the hell is he?

She needs some kind of positivity spell but there are no stone staircases, steam trains, or steaming puddings. No magic here, just infernal hard work in a room full of desks, windows down one side, display boards down the other, strip lights above and industrial strength carpet below. Everything hard-wearing, and everything hard-worn.

Her colleagues are in adjacent boxes. Most of them are new. Almost everyone who was here when Jo began has moved on, quit, retired. Ten years she has done when hardly anyone gets beyond three. Did her mother understand that? Likely not, always hoping instead that she'd be rescued, airlifted out to a better opportunity, a partner with a big salary. Cara across the corridor is the only one who has survived from last year, the other components of the English department either blown, failed or given up. No one believes that Jackson cares much. Teachers are machines to communicate information, if one breaks you just put a cheaper one in their place.

But no, Jo thinks, I cannot afford to fail, can't afford melancholy. Yank some happiness from somewhere, anywhere, win them over with humour.

She marches into the room. The boy from the fight has thrown himself down where Darren should be sat. He is hiding his head in folded arms, putting on show an ill-fitting uniform, shirt cuffs riding high up his wrists. He hardly moves; Jo stands skittish, eyeing the door, then the occupied desk, worrying about what will happen if Darren now shows up. She has rehearsed her apology to him, asking to see him one-on-one so that he won't be embarrassed in front of others, her showing him real contrition then turning this towards motivation, an offer to help him work a miracle and achieve a good grade.

Jordan and Michael are leant on their tables, torsos dancing by the line of girls, a phone drilling a beat out into the room that they hammer along to with raised arms. Beside them, Nelson is fingering his own handset. 'Boys!' she calls as firmly as she can, 'boys stop that music and sit at your desks now please.' They carry on gyrating as if they've not heard a word she's said. 'Boys!' she hollers, ripping the mask from her face, and only then do they spin round, silence the tune as they shake their heads, laugh even as they complain in acronyms. WTF Miss. WYD. KYS. Then Jakob actually drops a few expletives, but Jo laughs it off and pretends not to have heard, feeling vulnerable to the counter: *can't tell me to mind my language when last term you tongue-whipped some kid.*

She knows that they would have a point — less Achilles heel than a whole bare leg — but she lets it slide behind her because Nishaan has walked in late and begun turning the lights on and off and on and off. Some reflex triggers and she lifts her mask again.

'Come on Nishaan, sit down,' she says brightly, deliberately clear and direct, not playing up to him, not telling him that he really isn't supposed to be touching any fittings, not unless he sanitises after.

'Where shall I sit Miss?' he asks, stuttering, struggling. Jo closes her eyes a moment, breathing in patience.

She replies as calmly as she can, uses his name to help him focus his attention, 'Nishaan, sit where you sat last year,' and he turns, hears but doesn't hear, deliberately trips over a desk and crashes through a couple of chairs.

No one in the class reacts much; they've seen it a hundred times before though now there's the added problem of contamination. Some crossover in the wiring, perfectly manageable when there'd been Teaching Assistants to give him focused support, but cuts have bitten so hard now it's one adult versus countless different needs. Some dumped in the class because they find English really hard, some because they've not been speaking the language long anyway, others perfectly clever but sabotaged by poor behaviour — that or by poverty itself. All the little things in an upbringing that money can't buy, but actually does. Time. Quiet. A desk to spread work out and focus on homework.

Cara has the top set who are all keen to learn, this correlation one of the puzzles of education: do her class behave better because they are more clever, or are they more clever because they behave well? Always the doubt that maybe she is just a better teacher. If you swapped the staff of Eton and Cromwell, what difference would there be? What if you just swapped the buildings? Perhaps if I was somewhere else, she muses, I'd suddenly find myself judged brilliant. But here she is, and it is here that she must perform with what she has. They are not the bottom set. The middle set and not incapable, not by a long way, if only she could get them to make the most.

No one has commented on Darren's seat being taken. Jordan lands a playful punch in Ade's shoulder as he passes him, receiving a wounded 'Jesus' back, one that is quickly withdrawn as Jordan raises his fist with more menace, seeing Ade flinch before cracking up in laughter.

'Don't look so shook,' Jordan calls as he lowers himself into his chair. Jo checks that he is actually talking to Ade. 'Truss, I'm only having jokes.'

Trust. Another word that cracks like a whip. She looks at the clock. Fifty-three minutes left. The girls are talking to one another as if she is not there. A deep breath. A bright smile pushed to Hayley as Jo catches her eye, but then she realises it's got no further than the inside of her mask.

'Right,' she says, half to the class, half to herself. 'Really good to see you all.' A lie that she must try to make true. 'Now, listen please,' she shouts over them as she calls up the register on her computer.

No one listens.

'Quiet!' she yells, raising the volume but trying not to raise the stakes.

Lauren and Nourin look over with disdain, offer half a glance of disinterest before returning to what Chanel is telling them. Michael bursts out laughing at something Jordan has said.

'Please?'

'Just F-off,' Ade squeaks in falsetto, his back to Jo. 'Get the...' He leaves it there but doesn't have to continue; they are all hooting and screaming. Anxiety boils. She knows that this is them punishing her, payment for letting them down, disappearing in March then virtually abandoning them to death by worksheet over the months inside that followed.

But she couldn't make her own mother's funeral. There is a wild scream that lives in a cave far inside. She swallows, grips her desk as if yanking the chain to bring the beast to heal. She has to let them have this moment, cannot let what happened go unacknowledged. She undresses her face for extra sincerity. 'Yes, very funny Ade,' she says quietly with a tight smile, pushing every ounce of serenity to face frontwards and declare that she is calm and in control. 'Now, let's move on shall we?'

She runs through the familiar litany of names, then pauses where Darren should be.

Ade looks sharply, then laughs. 'What? Miss, you didn't know?' He turns to Michael, shakes his head slowly. 'Off-rolled. That is some cold sh...'

The others are quiet now, turning narrow stares onto her. She was about to chastise Ade for his language, but he stopped safe before the vowel did for him.

'Sorry, Ade. What?' Jo is blinking, seeing a truth dropped down on the floor in front of her, but shaking her head in disbelief.

'You know Miss.' He makes a pistol of his fingers to help Jo understand, lifts it and fires. 'Jackson smoked him. Wiped him.'

'Thank you, I'm aware of what off-rolling is.' Jo's face has paled even further, her mouth struggling to find words. 'But there must be some mistake. He's in Year 11. A Head can't. I mean...'

Their faces say different. 'Some legal BS,' Ade muses with a shrug. 'I don't know.'

Jo stares back at her register on the screen, at this brutal act of erasure, the other names now closed over the cut.

Our redemption from our sin, her father would thump from his pulpit, *required a body.* She looks aghast, wondering how her errors could now ever be atoned for, how she can ever fulfil her vow of resurrection if the child she had crucified has been taken away.

For a moment it is as if she is about to run back out, chase Jackson down and insist that he must undo this, that a school has to take responsibility for each child that they are given, even if they are as awful as Darren.

But she doesn't, knows that she cannot. What could be her complaint? She had screamed at the boy to leave.

Panic spreads beyond her face, the bonds she'd made in sleepless nights now laid to waste. She sees the municipal urn sat in Dad's hallway, her path to it blocked. The class shift impatiently. A chair creaks, plastic seat arguing with metal legs. Nishaan pushes out an elbow and the plastic tube of his pencil case begins to fall to the floor. She can't help throw an arm out to try to reach it, picturing instead a toppling jar, captive remains. It thumps into the carpet and Nishaan bends to lift it.

Jordan sighs loudly, fealty perhaps more to the mass of one another rather than any one individual. Darren was one of them but he was a pain in the backside too. Estate life. *People get trodden on,* his impatience seems to say. *You just keep going.*

She lifts her gaze to the ill-fitting windows, gathers the sky into her eyes. Outside, summer remains in golden light, though the evenings now cool more quickly. There aren't many leaves to mark the seasons here, just the carpet of blown litter round the vast estate. At certain hours in the coming winter afternoons, when the clouds are set just right and children are warming cold knees against the gurgling radiators, the sun descends and the tower block that so many of them live in blackens like a monolith, glowing red along its edges, casting an early twilight over the school before sunset bursts along one side, exploding reds and fire-orange pinks across the display boards on the far wall of her classroom. She thinks of telling this to Ben, before the ache reminds her that she now cannot. That he has no interest.

The slapping wave of bewilderment is followed by a surge of resolve. Come on, she thinks. Crucifixion is too strong, too much of her father. She'd shouted at the boy, yes. But not killed him. She mustn't take it all on herself.

They have all moved on already, fires of chatter breaking out all around the room. TV shows. He-said-she-said. Disputes over trainers.

'Right,' she says uncertainly, returning to the register, anxiously pushing a loose strand of hair behind her ear and cleaning her hands again. 'Forget Darren then,' saying this like it's the punchline to a joke. Leave the casualty behind. Pray that he forgives her. She swallows hard and the new boy dares a glance. Jo flushes and then unfolds herself. 'Right! Year 11. Let's push on.'

2

She beats her way through the rest of the names, fighting down the register until she sees that the boy from the fight, the child now in Darren's seat, must be Sami Karim. A moment of intrigued silence as the class focus on him, hearing his slightest flicker of response before Jordan says, 'speak up mate,' and they burst out into laughter.

'I'm Miss Barker,' Jo calls warmly over to him. But if he takes this in he doesn't show it. 'Where are you from Sami?' she asks, hoping that he doesn't take this the wrong way, trying to ascertain if English is actually something he has. He looks at her like he's trying to gauge the question, but before he can shepherd what words he has Charlie begins to share what people have already swept up: a recent arrival from Syria. Danny says he'd thought he was Italian because he looks like a footballer. Jordan says he's staying with some uncle in the Tower. None of this Sami disputes. He stares at his desk, shoulders hunched like the incident outside her door was just one more beating to add to the tally.

Jo is embarrassed to realise that she has no proper grasp of whether the situation in Syria was still ongoing, whether the recent uptick in media outrage about channel crossings meant that there had been an actual increase in channel crossings. Perhaps his summer has been even worse than hers, or Darren's. She pictures mortars and burned-out houses, diesel-choked inflatables and airless trailers. A virus, a parasite, unclean, unwelcome. A rutted track half-a-world long, smeared across deserts and seas, leading all the way to the estate out there then on through the school gate and up the stairs, across the floor, ending here of all places, his cap pulled down hard, sat bruised at one of her desks, his knee trembling.

Her embarrassment shifts, looking with fresh eyes at what he's fought so hard to get to. The painted walls of the classroom are cracked, splodged like acne by stamped-on ketchup sachets and exploding drinks. The windows are filthy and hardly fit in their frames, and how those stains have got onto the ceiling is anyone's guess. Poor lad. A treacherous journey only to land among children who have only known austerity. No youth clubs, funding cut and cut until there's no reserves left. Either way, he is hers now, she thinks, part of her congregation, another soul that she has the cure of for a while.

She has spent the last couple of training days mentally gathering fuel, her flints and powders, the books and spells that she felt so deft with. She knows that she just needs to find a way to ignite and burn again, harder still now that Darren's erasure has thrown cold water on the lesson before she'd even started.

'What you staring for?' Jordan spits at Danny, who is still eyeing Sami. 'Turn around man, stop looking at him.'

'Yeah hole it,' Ade adds.

'Was I talking to you?' Danny complains. 'Was I?'

'Stop chatting shit man.'

Each cuss slips free and flies around Sami's head, bowed and shell-shocked. The court of girls sit by the window, steam-rollered into silence by the aggression of the knights primping around them. Somewhere she must find the energy to begin again.

'I'll bang you in your dutty mouth.'

A certain poetry undeniable in their speech; her responsibility to forge it too good. Swords into... well, she thinks, will they have any clue what a ploughshare is? For a moment it looks as if the boys might erupt into a brawl, but then Jordan cracks up and they are all laughing and bumping fists. Like a feeble monarch she laughs too, knowing that as quickly as a fight became a joke, jokes could whip round into fights, no moment safely any one thing.

She must fan whatever small fires are still left in her. And as if to feed this she draws in a long breath, inhaling memories of the gorgeous banter from lessons past, the turns of phrase that would have Shakespeare weeping into Dickens' shoulder.

Do you bite your thumb at us, sir? Charlie stumbling through the opening of Romeo last Autumn. *No bruv,* Jordan throws down, raising up a single, straight prop, *just swivelling on this finger,* the class collapsing into the kind of jeers long missing from the theatre, Jo struggling to keep a straight face, debating to herself whether this word-perfect modernisation of the text should be censured.

Miss man, this room is bare frowsy. Hayley holding her nose as she rolls in late on a hot day, Jo's delight at this, interrogating the class, demanding to be told where this slang had come from, none of them knowing, but all of them a little surprised to hear that a long-buried piece of *Bleak House* had somehow resurfaced on a West London council estate. Them listening with as much awe as indifferent teens could muster as she'd read out the quotation, sat in the middle of them on the empty desk.

Darren's place. His the vacant table she'd so often commandeered in the centre of the room, his sporadic attendance playing havoc with her plans, his wild, feral liberty turning up when he liked, to vandalise, smash, tear down and disappear again.

But now he has gone. Gone for good and…

'RIGHT,' she shouts with a clap, sending the thoughts of her guilt away. Nearly a quarter of the lesson has gone and nothing to show Jackson for it. 'We *really* need to get started.'

But Jordan wants to know how her summer was, adding, 'I don't mean to be rude or nothing, but it looks like you went Siberia.'

'And sounds like you went to comedy camp,' she fires back quickly, drawing some appreciative ooooooos from around the room. 'Come on, let's not waste any more time.'

He's right of course. Teachers *should* be tanned in September. Tautened and recharged, skin ironed sharp like a knife again, oiled and bronzed. They look over her ghost-white arms, face lime-pale as Boleyn, creases in her blouse and the skirt that never made it to the dry cleaners. Even with the summer restrictions, something in the normal order of things has gone wrong. The weather wasn't that bad. Hadn't she even gone out? Was she infected?

The heat of a class-full of sixty focused eyes draws a bead of sweat that gleams and grows before she moves to adjust her hair and wipe it away. Less a mirror to see their own faults, more a screen for them prod, point and laugh at, seeing no depth, just a woman well past thirty, a model that could do with an upgrade, not slim as such but not *not* slim, brown hair that sits without great style, not one of the flashy young staff that are swooned over, no scandals likely to be noted.

'Seriously,' Jordan presses. 'Did you get it? Bare people died, you know. Bare.'

Confession. Central to atonement. Someone kisses their teeth.

Sometimes she thinks that she should have just told them. Used the trust she'd so patiently built and actually trusted them from the start, as soon as mum had been diagnosed. *Sorry. My mother has been taken into hospital.* But she'd been adamant, hadn't wanted to load them with it, had decided straight away that it wouldn't be fair to put that on them because they were just children, children with enough to deal with already.

She falls back again, disappearing into the afternoon when she'd found out. Multiple missed calls from Dad, finally calling him back at lunchtime, him in shock, telling her that something was wrong with Mum.

'No,' she'd said to Cara, who'd offered to sort some cover so she could leave straight away. 'No. I need to keep them in check,' adamant that she wouldn't leave until lessons were done.

Sweating, nauseous, she'd been absent anyway, standing trembling by the board waiting for the bell to release her. Darren hadn't even been there but Ade had got into a fight with Nelson, the class jeering them on, Jo inert, frozen until the hammer had struck, pushing past Charlie at the door, her bag knocking against the walls, shoes clicking loudly down the stairs, dashing to the station, calling Ben to tell him what had happened, Dad collecting her, explaining what was already known.

Further tests were being done and things were yet to be confirmed. 'Look,' she'd said, 'I really ought to get back.'

'Children come first,' Mum had said, and Dad had nodded in guarded support. He was a pastor. He understood. Untended sheep stray fast. She'd gone straight back to London that night though she and Mum would quickly find out: you can gather all of your energies but sometimes it is not enough; slowly your grip weakens, and things fall apart.

Back to work the next day she'd kept her news hidden, as if sharing might make it more real. Another hangover from her father: the idea that speech brought things into being: if words were an act of creation then by silence one might prevent reality dawning. But in this unspoken darkness chaos had mutated and swelled. Books unmarked, behaviour left unchallenged, incidents not written up: over the weeks that had followed she'd begun to crumble. Rushing out at the bell, arriving at the hospital but then not knowing what to say. Late nights, tired mornings. Ben sympathetic, then frustrated. Fuses shortening, anger simmering, beginning to boil over, no longer able to take it but unable to say why; Jackson circling, questions of competency following in tighter orbits. But no, she still would not tell them. Exhaustion. The malady spreads, increasing aggression, until you cannot hide it any more, until you suddenly collapse.

Your mum.

The trigger pulled, her tongue firing before she could stop it.

Just FUCK OFF Darren.

Mowing him down.

'Look, I'm sorry I wasn't there for you all more in lockdown,' she repeats more loudly. She can't wallow, can't keep disappearing back. These children just need her to be here in the present, don't need details about what's passed. 'Siberia was lovely, but Gulag Cromwell is so much nicer.' Jordan raises a hand in appreciation of her joke. She straightens some papers on her desk, bureaucracy signalling an end to any discussion.

'Thank you for getting jackets and hats off.' Standard teacher psychology, thanking children before they've even begun to do what you've asked. She catches Sami slipping his cap down onto the table, glad he understands this much at least, more obedient already than Darren had ever been.

'Come on Nourin,' Nelson says from the back, leaning his stomach onto his desk and reaching towards her headscarf. 'Do what Miss says.' Laughing in short grunts.

'Piss off Nelson,' she says with a basting of contempt, smoothing her hijab down at the back, checking.

'That is ENOUGH Nelson,' Jo barks and while the pack quietens she gulps down what optimism she can, drinks in the cleaned carpet, a new lesson planner lying crisp on her desk, as yet unsullied with violently red-circled notes and scrawled reminders about meetings and detentions, assessment deadlines and reports to be written.

She picks up a pair of scissors, presses the steel tips into the end of her thumb until she feels something, then releases, rips the blade through the cellophane wrapping and masks up. Nothing else for it; the risk assessments advise her against, but how else is she meant to get things to them? So she tenses, takes a breath, leaves her taped-off space and begins to walk among their desks, pacifying them with gifts of clean, unsoiled exercise books. She slings them down onto the newly scrubbed surfaces, thirty-two palimpsests, scratched compass-point markings of past classes, rubber bumpers pocked with ruler-sawn crevasses. Down the first aisle she goes, the edging of one desk gone altogether on one side, the smooth writing surface exposed as a thin veneer over a compressed mess of sawdust. The cleaners have done what they can on the tops, spraying and scrubbing, bottles and bottles of anti-viral decanted, though any wandering hand would doubtless find the slowly-building colonies of dried gum and snot still clinging to the shadows beneath, all sharp craters and rock-like slabs.

'Your final year of GCSEs,' she says as dramatically as she can from behind a muffling mask, signalling for the last remaining coats to be removed, for phones to be put away. Past Danny and Charlie, Ade and Jakob are slumped on the next desk back as if they'd been poured into their chairs and were slowly congealing with them. Five solid months playing games consoles and they're probably feeling withdrawal. Jakob takes one last look before reluctantly sliding a handset into his trousers. Their secret place. Their most sensitive place. Don't touch. Jo puts half an eye on Jordan, sat on his own at the back. She turns sharply before reaching him, as everyone seems to, never quite sure whether this bear of a boy is going to savage or startle. He's done both in the past, sullen silence suddenly broken by a flying verbal assault or some dazzling insight. She crosses back past Michael, an elaborate piece of graffiti already taking shape in his new planner, her telling the class that they need to get cracking straight away on the exam text that they're going to be reading this term. She stops a moment by Nelson's desk in the corner by the window, waiting until he opens his eyes, removes his hands from under his desk and slowly returns himself to vertical. Then turn for home, up to Darren's old desk, trying to take in as much of Sami as she can from the back, the marks on his neck, the matted line in his hair indented from his cap, the fraying threads of collar. The positions of the girls arrayed along the window are still engrained, Nourin-Chanel-Lauren-Hayley-Kelly-Safiya-Charis-Jenny. She gratefully approaches home ground, turning by Nishaan's table on the front row, him wondering if he should be taking notes, Radha sat next to him, a motherly look across to reassure.

'Fill in the front,' Jo tells them. Charlie sniggers, though no one is quite sure at what, and Jordan tells him to shut up, which he does because he is Jordan and has a heft that goes beyond his physical size.

'Now,' Jo says assertively, trying to summon a similar force, leaving the word to sit slammed on the desk. 'Now, rather than pick one of the really boring books on the exam board's list...' — a cheap line, and Radha smiles like she knows it — '...I have chosen something gritty, something for you to relate to.' Something she had chosen with Darren in mind, but here they are. 'A young London boy who starts off with nothing, whose life is transformed.'

Jordan sighs impatiently. 'Just give us the books Miss man.'

'Innit,' Charlie chirps, looking round for Jordan to welcome his support, quickly seeing that he cares nothing for it. Jo ignores them and takes aim at a new angle, throws talk out at them of a mysterious criminal and a prison boat, of drinking and spending and women. She is determined to push through, to not get bogged down admonishing them for every offence on the first day as she heads back out from her island to hand out copies of *Great Expectations,* this the final flourish she's pictured all summer as the moment of renewed lift off, this book the vehicle of their own ascension. She waits for the gasps of wonder, "surely you can't have been talking all this time about Dickens?!"

'The-fk-is-this?' Jakob slurs, vowels and consonants blurred just enough that he might plead innocence if challenged. She glares at him but just then Nishaan lets out a groan and violently pushes all of his books and pens to the floor, prompting jeers from Charlie and Danny just behind.

'Pick those things up now,' she barks, ignoring Jakob, and Nishaan bends down to do so while Radha turns round his exercise book, checks through the details he's only half filled in.

'My days, 'llow this,' Jordan begins.

Jo tries to bunt it back, add some humour. 'See everyone, why can't you be as keen as Jordan to get started?'

He frowns and shakes his head at Michael with a dismissive 'what?' like she's tried too hard. But she moves on, still fixing a face that confidently believes that she can win them with this. A feral child turned into a gentleman. Victorian poverty butting up against glittering riches. Violence. Social Mobility. The hope of transfiguration. What more could they want?

'This is hench!' Danny shouts, flicking back and forth, looking for pictures. 'I've seen them *Mice and Men* — it's half the size of this!' He's waving the buzzing swarm of nearly two hundred thousand words and she offers assurances that they weren't going to have to read the *whole* book — there would be videos and summaries — pretending that this wasn't so much a retreat as a clarification.

'So why you giving us these, Miss?' Charlie asks.

'To read you dumb twat,' Jordan snaps back impatiently, leaving Charlie scowling.

'Language Jordan,' Jo says, trying to model a gentle tone.

He stares her down for a moment and then shakes his head. 'Whatever Miss. I was just trying to help.'

She wants to thank him for his support *and* admonish him for his language, but as she tries to synthesise a phial of words that might combine these sentiments in just the right way, Ade slaps Danny in the shoulder with his book, and before she remembers that she shouldn't she's rushed between them to prevent retaliation. None comes because Kelly and Lauren and Hayley start kicking off about the school being so cheap all they could afford were these battered-up paperbacks, and what were they doing spending money on some big new sign by the gates and fancy chairs in reception when there's no decent books? Danny's not hot at maths but he calculates quickly enough here and lets Ade's slap go, taking the chance to back the girls up, joining in about the books, saying they've probably got virus all over them they're so old, then the rest do too and the noise rises, Jo saying 'listen, quiet now,' but hers just one voice lost in the cacophony, until she bellows

SILENCE then smiles. 'God, you lot,' she says. 'Can you not just put a sock in it for one minute?'

There are a few confused looks about what this might mean, so she rushes out a background worksheet for them to fill in, what London was like in Dickens' time, telling them not to worry as she hurries again around her route of desks, they'd been printed 2 days ago so were already quarantined.

Currents and counter-currents, gusts from all directions and she has to be stronger than 30 of them blowing together, hold her line through all of their storms. But, for no fathomable reason, they break out into still water. They do take the sheets and the girls get down to sticking theirs in their books (ultra-neat, first page, has to be.)

She sighs in resignation. She's already been around the class twice, so what extra harm could be done by launching out once more to check their work from an appropriate distance? She feels for the edges of her mask, accepts that she'll just have to wash her hands twice as hard after the lesson, but it seems important to make sure that Nishaan has got the gist, that Sami is at least able to access the task.

'OK?' she asks, trying to keep it simple, international, standing as erect as she can.

He's leaning back in his chair, legs stretching out a little from under the front of his desk, hands on the table, splayed out over the sheet, a cracked blue biro nestled between two fingers.

He twists his paper slightly towards her, revealing answers to the first multiple-choice questions.

She strains to see. 'Well done Sami, that's great.'

'Thank you,' he whispers happily, and leans forward, tongue poking from the side of his mouth, carefully following the words for the next section.

Calm descends and she lets it expand. Then into this relative tranquillity she drops a quiet reminder that, alongside the novel, they have more poems to study from their GCSE anthologies. 'So it'll balance out,' she reassures them. 'I know the book is long, but the poems I want to do are really short, really accessible.'

Hayley uncaps a puck of moisturiser, fingers it and glosses her lips, extracts a tissue from a plastic sheaf, wipes clean and tends to a split end before picking her pen, all of this done in silence, no thought for those around, just a ritual that must be observed before work can begin.

'When did you do your GCSEs, Miss?' Radha asks as she switches highlighter, six different colours she is using to mark up her sheet, a cypher that is beyond Jo.

'Gosh,' she says, now safely back in her teacher zone, 'that's hard to remember.' But perhaps not in the way that Radha might take it.

Sixteen and keen, ploughing through a revision timetable so carefully planned with her father, Mum hovering but never landing, as if fearing what she might say, that if examined she would be shown to have failed. So long ago, but still the sharp sense that the breach was already noticeable, increments as she'd grown.

She ought to give Radha something more but there is so much that is hard to remember, so much that she mustn't start remembering now, not here. Mustn't think of the books Mum had bought her in her teen years, these gifts messages that a mother couldn't find ways to speak herself. She mustn't start thinking about how she'd tried to return the favour when Mum had first fallen ill: gone to the ward with a selection of favourites, Jude the Obscure, Oliver Twist, pages that might somehow communicate what they'd never quite managed before.

She looks intently at the space where Darren used to be, head shaking slightly, lip bitten by a top tooth. Her hand drifts to the scissors but suddenly snaps away and she points Radha back to her work.

Jordan mumbles something Jo can't catch, and Michael next to him makes a noise like an exotic creature, *wa-waaaaa*, a sound that means nothing at all and definitely something. A mockingbird perhaps? Despite countless readings she's still no idea what sound a mockingbird makes. She walks down towards them to try to quell, to allow the calm to damp down again.

'Allow her 'tinkin breath,' someone murmurs as she turns and reaches the front line of tables again. She spins quickly enough but no one is looking, all eyes fixed on their work, laughing into their sleeves.

When she'd had enough of novels, Dad had read to Mum from the paper. A sigh at another stabbing — a kitchen knife plunged into a soft young chest — and Jo had jumped in to reassure. 'So *so* rare in school,' she'd said quickly, adding darkly that it wouldn't be that that killed her, more that her heart would be hewn off in tiny pieces. Stolen pencil cases, refusals to remove coats, the constant slapping of one another for no reason, the lost timetables, anger at scuffs on new trainers, the medication not taken, the arguments hanging over from home — all of these pocket-sized grenades lobbed each lesson, setting off reactions no one could predict or plan for, the constant anxiety of not knowing even where the battlefield was, let alone what the war was about. But this is the struggle, and underneath it all somewhere is the pure joy of working with children. Yes, in so many ways she is glad to be back.

'Miss. Shall I stick the sheet in?' Nishaan is asking, holding a glue-stick aloft like a torch. She tells him yes and walks past, wanting to sit at her desk just for a moment, but there's a scuffle and she turns and sees Nishaan twisting, rising out of his chair, lunging at Danny, shouting 'give it back!'

Danny says he only wants to borrow it, but shouts, 'have the bloody thing back,' then deftly sends the glue spinning upwards out of his hand, a stubby rocket that docks with a dull splat on the ceiling and remains suspended there.

Everyone gawps, Nishaan yells, then they laugh and point, hooting and leaning back in their chairs enjoying the show, all except Sami who frowns and returns his attention to his sheet.

Jo steps forward between Danny and Nishaan, but just then the glue commences re-entry. Her hand instinctively flaps up to protect her head but somehow manages to catch the barrel mid-flight.

There is a long ooooo and a moment's awed silence. She is holding the glue aloft like the Pritt-Stick Statue of Liberty, convenience adhesives the flame of virtue, face regal with the brief heat of this comic moment, the whole class finally focused, all their energy converging on this thin white wand she is brandishing.

Adrenaline surges, panic that she is out amongst them and holding a piece of unsanitised stuff. Her teaching mind is racing too though, this a moment that might bewitch them again if only she can conjure the right spell. She scrabbles together a quip about dramatic arcs and the burning lantern of enlightenment, but it's not cast quick enough, is drowned out by the clanging of the bell.

Jordan stands, aims a grin at Jo and raises his fist in a Black Power salute, shouting 'freedom!' before grabbing his bag and running for the door. 'Bye miss!'

'Wait,' she calls, 'please,' her hand still aloft, wanting more from this moment. But they do not wait and she holds her breath fast as they flow quickly past like the rushing tide in the Hudson, clutching bags and hats, pushing to disembark as quickly as they can, only Nishaan staying still, sticking around for his glue to be returned to him from its brief mission to the pocked white surface of the ceiling above.

The lesson chokes, splutters and burns out. She releases the air then looks a little faint, as if blood has fallen through her arm and chest and collected in her feet. She should have taken in their worksheets, should immediately be assessing what Sami has managed, getting work straight in, marking it now, making sure that everyone is heading off in exactly the right direction. But they've tumbled through the door, run right and left, heads tucked down against threat of recall.

No point trying to drag them back; she knows the limits of her majesty better than to try to be Canute. She sanitises her hands and sits instead, face shining briefly with elation. She almost had them. So close.

Only now does she notice that Sami has not run off, is stood between her desk and the open door, a crowd of boys standing outside.

'Well done Sami,' she says weakly. Both have survived. First lesson negotiated and it wasn't a total disaster.

'Thank you Miss,' he says smiling, edging nervously as if to ask something.

'The bell has gone Sami,' she says, as if he might not understand what bells do here. She wants time to come down, to gather herself again. She has the desks to wipe down, windows that she wants to open. 'Come on,' she says, 'out of here, off you go,' getting up to make sure that he does.

He takes a breath, turns and makes a run for it and seconds later a bunch of others lurch at pace down the corridor.

She walks to the door to close it off again, hears only echoes of an excited brawl, sees only a boy ambling by, looking at his phone. She tells him to turn it off.

He kisses his teeth and slides away along the scarred linoleum to catch up with his friend, who turns and makes to punch him in the bicep.

'Flinch,' he shouts, as if a point has been scored. But a hand comes back across his face, slapping him down.

'No man flinches at you, bitch.'

3

The room momentarily fills with noise, the heavy thump of something going to ground followed by a great cheer, a colleague in Science getting burned on the floor above. That, or some whizz-bang experiment that's got them excited. Easier to do that with test tubes and explosions than tenses and exclamation marks. But this is the job this is what she knows she must do: get a reaction going, set them alight, Darren or no Darren. Books as catalysts, she remembers from her kitchen table revision, improving reaction rates while remaining undestroyed. She picks up a discarded, battered copy of *Great Expectations* and rubs it with a thumb.

A few exercise books have been left behind. She pulls on a set of gloves, puts them onto her desk to sit for a time, stacks them next to the pile of policies still to plough through, ways to prevent radicalisation, to spot potential victims of genital mutilation, advice on helping parents bicker less, new rules holding her accountable for reporting those at risk of knife crime, self-harm, getting too fat or too thin, too moody or too wired.

The morning's assembly had been a video link set round, and Jackson had rolled out one of his favourite lines, "a school without children is a zoo without animals." He's a prick, Jo thinks, but he's right about this. She picks up a document and casts an eye down a long list of children with Special Needs. So many different species to manage, some nervous as dormice, others tall as giraffes, others sloths, wolves and snakes, slumbering lions and sharp vultures, but then wise owls too, wide-eyed kittens, faithful sheep and preening peacocks. There are cuckoos and sly foxes, collaborating sometimes, fighting at others, working in packs, building nests and setts.

Yes, this is exactly what a school is: a fence around all of this, trying to tame and train the young before releasing them into the wild. Her job to domesticate them, to prepare them for civil life. That, or be the ringmaster... except no whips now, just chairs. Get them to sit up and perform. But what to do if a truly wild creature wanders into this circus, prowls with no regard for boundary or property, heeding no call, obeying no one, both shocking and awesome, a challenge to all pretensions of control? Darren. She names him and smiles begrudgingly. Perhaps some children weren't meant to be cooped.

'Jo,' a voice says, knocking at the door and peering round. It is Mr Henderson.

'Hi Alex,' she says, and invites him to come in. 'Everything go OK with your Year 11?'

'They'll be fine,' he replies without great conviction. He is unmasked. His face is so young. She probably spends more on razors than he does.

She'd seen him earlier cajoling and ordering and trying to direct children without knowing any of their names, bouncing around with the kind of energy you only get from staff who've not hit 30.

'Why are you chatting at me when you don't know me,' a boy had shouted, but Alex had told everyone who'd listened that it didn't matter if he didn't know them because he was the new Head of English and he was giving them a clear instruction to get to their lessons.

'What happened to Burgess?' another had called, looking upset.

'He's left. And now I'm in charge.'

'No bruv.' Frowning eyes all that was visible, a speedy examination of Alex's person. 'You ain't no Burgess yet.'

No, he wasn't. Victor had been teaching when it had all kicked off with Darren and Jo had left the site thankful not to have had to see him, to witness the great weight of his disappointment, his protégé tearing a student to shreds. He has texted, offered to meet and talk, sent a beautifully crafted message of condolence about Mum, but it has mostly gone unanswered. A thank you. A thumbs up. All of it too humiliating to confront in full sentences.

He'd announced his retirement at Easter, made it clear to Jackson that whatever the future of education was going to be it was going to be without him. He'd found a way to wear a National Curriculum, put on the digital revolution like an ill-fitting coat; this latest remodelling would be a step too far. 'The Queen in Air Jordans,' he'd put in an email to the department. 'A fascinating prospect to some, I'm sure. But just *wrong*.' Underneath the humour, the feeling of constant failure. Jackson's targets too absurd. Always more for always less. A small pub gathering of farewell suited him fine; Jo had made her excuses, making up something about her father. But she misses him now, especially with all her new colleagues with sharp suits and glowing foreheads, clasping clammy class lists. She must make time to get in touch. Explain things, hope he'll understand. Comprehension, it was what they did.

'Once you get the names, and they get to know you,' she offers to Alex. She wants to try to be kind to him. It's the least the job deserves.

'Oh I'm not worried about that,' he snaps. 'I like to think it doesn't matter much what they think of me, or the other way round, as long as they get the grades.' His hands grip the brushed metal of a sleek laptop. 'I've just shared the new assessment policy with you,' he says, tapping the computer with his middle finger. 'Something to read and digest.'

She thanks him, looks over at her desk as if mentally adding it to the pile.

'And I noticed the display boards outside your room...'

Fingers into thumb, she holds up a hand and mimes a yakking mouth. 'Jackson beat you to it,' she tells him cheerily. 'Don't worry, I'll get it repaired.'

He deflates in relief and thanks her, relaxes his shoulders, the padding in his suit reluctantly following. 'Your experience is going to be vital. So much that is going to need doing. Big shoes to fill.'

Jo scans his face for signs of malice. He surely *must* have heard what had happened with Darren? Or if he hasn't, it won't be long before he has. He is looking around at the untidy mess of desks and the chairs toppled on their backs. She flicks a look up and sees a splodge on the ceiling still where the glue had temporarily docked. Yes, she thinks, he already knows.

'How are your 11's going to do?' he asks as he returns from his speedy appraisal.

She tips her head from side to side as if making an astute professional judgement. 'They'll be OK. You'll see when you meet them: there's some characters in here, but they're essentially good kids.'

'In figures I meant,' he says, and begins tapping. 'How many good passes are we looking at. Given the reduced content and the likelihood of later exams.'

She pauses long enough for him to stop his scan of the screen and fix on her instead.

'I hadn't analysed them in those terms just yet,' she says, pushing shoulders back and starting around the room, straightening out the desks, righting the chairs. Who even knew if they would even sit exams. They'd been out of school for so long she wanted time to settle them, work out where they behind. 'With Victor, in a normal year the strategy was always to focus on getting them fired up and only think about possible results after their January mocks.'

'Hmmm,' he says, ruminating. Then stops and makes the noise again, a nervous junior bureaucrat, the manmade fibres of his trim jacket creasing stiffly like baking foil.

She feels for this year-group, for Jordan and his peers, the pressure doubled overnight. Mocks used to be that: a joke, nothing deep, just see how it goes. Now, with the farce over last summer's results they will be fully loaded with anxiety. That could be it; an algorithm would do the rest.

'Why don't you tell me, Alex.' she says in warm conspiracy. 'How many good passes do you need from this group to hit your target?'

Not his target, obviously. The one he's been fed.

'Oh,' he says, wiping his brow with a jacket sleeve, 'I don't know.' He is attempting to be jaunty but his eyes are locked on something on his screen. He's nervous. It must be a number so impossible he's got to build up to disclosing it. A target so high no one could hit it. 'I should do a data-grab as soon as possible,' he continues, trying to justify himself. 'See what the numbers say.'

'So soon?' He's said her experience will be vital so she'll damned well give it to him. 'We don't want to scare them off.'

'Kids are kids are kids,' he scoffs. 'At the end of the day, in that exam hall all that'll matter is whether we've done enough to drag them over the line.'

'That's one way of looking at it. If, of course, they actually end up sitting the damn things.' She disagrees but plays along, bending down to pick up a crushed ball of paper, the department's wish-list of expectations still visible along one rumpled edge.

He looks just about to add to his brilliant insights when Jackson marches through the door.

'Ah, just the two people.' Jo swallows hard as he addresses her. 'Everything go OK?'

Inspection from all sides, a hint of coordination. But she holds ground, effects not to rise to it, just repeats that yes, it had done.

'Sami Karim?'

'Impossible to tell so soon what he's capable of...'

'But,' Jackson lowers his mask and flashes a conspiratorial smile, 'better than Darren.'

She folds her arms, perches on her desk, sends some sass out to confront him. There is a pause while both men wait to see if she has the gall to say it. She does. 'You've off-rolled him, haven't you?' Alex shifts uncomfortably between her and Jackson, scuttles to move a cursor around with his trackpad.

'That's a loaded term,' Jackson says, his gaze still locked on hers.

'With the same result. He's erased. The school abdicates...'

'No,' he spits, twisting the toe of his high-polished shoes into a stain on the carpet. 'No Jo, we simply made a strong recommendation of alternative provision.' He emphasises this with scare-quote fingers, a sure-fire signifier of bullshit.

'You *know* he won't take up a place somewhere else. It was hard enough getting him across the road into Cromwell. The nearest referral unit is miles away. I...'

But he looks back up and glares, slashes quickly across her. 'Darren was already on his last warning when, to refresh your memory, you howled at him to "fuck off and leave."' Alex's eyes nearly pop, and he blinks over and over to keep them inside his head, his face reddening as Jackson continues. 'And I will remind you of the conversations we had then.'

The riot act read. The bullet points of capability procedure, each one shot mercilessly across his desk, her crumpling, finally showing her wounds, cancer her last card, played in desperation. He'd pulled back then, hands twitching, withdrawing, offering narrow words of sympathy. But she can't start falling back now, can't have it all replayed again today.

'I haven't forgotten,' she says hollowly. 'I'm sure that this year...'

'I am sure that this year will be far better,' he says over her before activating a kind of cheery estate agent tone. 'Which is why I have asked Mr Henderson to keep a close eye.'

'I,' Alex says, this single apologetic syllable all he manages before spluttering out.

Quite the reversal, she thinks: a child will be monitoring my work. Alex looks so embarrassed Jo wonders for a moment if she actually spoke aloud. He then sees Jackson watching him and tries out a face that's probably meant to be efficient and stern.

Jo weighs her situation but knows already that she has no choice, no leverage. Payment for her sins will have to be made;

if there are any more missteps the procedural wheels will start again.

'Now,' the Head says, the apparition next to him dissolving, 'I asked Alex to share your target grades for this class with you?'

'I'd... we'd...' Mr Henderson's jaw is moving in odd directions, but he's not generating speech. He starts sliding a finger around his keyboard, then deftly turns it over into a tablet and holds up a list of names, scores, and grades.

A near top grade for Jordan. The same for Ade, Michael, and Hayley, Nishaan only one grade below. They're a middle-ability set, but these were wildly optimistic.

'This can't be right.' Jo's head is shaking as she processes. She pulls other columns into view, then lets out a laugh. 'I mean, in terms of predicted grades, each of these are at the miracle end of likelihood.'

'So not impossible then?' Jackson says. 'Not beyond what each is capable of.'

'Well, technically. But in terms of being realistic with all that they've been through and their engagement in their work.' She looks down the list again. 'I mean, I can give you something more reasonable once I've had time to assess them...'

'No,' Jackson interjects curtly, arms folded, mouth pulled tightly into a thin line. 'These will stand.'

'Come on,' she protests, trying to retain good humour. 'You know these kids. Alex, you don't know your class yet, but I promise you...'

'They stay unchanged.' Jackson pulls at a jacket cuff, brushes his hand down a sleeve. 'We need staff here who are ambitious Jo.' He lets this hang in the air, then claps his hands together. 'Like I said, a big year ahead.' He looks at a message that has just flashed up across his wrist. 'Right, I must get on. Alex — all clear I hope?'

Crystal, she thinks darkly. He is a calculating man who knows that the whole cohort's GCSE grades might end up calculated again this year. It is a bet, a gamble; over-inflate the prices now in the hope that he can cash in later. And if the exams go ahead... well, she is a moderately expensive employee who is considered a repetitional risk. Ask the impossible wait until she delivers less, or breaks in the process of trying.

Alex nods meekly as Jackson exits, looks to say something to Jo but then thinks better of it. 'I...' he says, then points his thumb over his shoulder, marches his bright leather shoes across to the door and follows Jackson through it.

She scrambles round to her desk, unlocks the drawer and whips out her phone, hoping she has time to alert Cara of Alex's imminent approach. 'Damn,' she curses, fumbling. He is already calling out brightly to her and Cara is calling back, asking if he wants a tea.

Jo unlocks the handset anyway — no missed calls, no notifications — raises a hand to her mouth, pressure of emotion building, but she knows that she must not show it. Not here. In front of her a mass of papers heavy enough to smother a fire.

I need air, thinks. Not the staffroom; she doesn't want to have to make polite chat with colleagues. Not the English office. Can't face the wide-eyed new staff dissecting early successes, bright and still luminous with dazzling lesson plans, unaware of how long they are going to have to burn. One of them will surely soon get round to asking why she hadn't stepped up when Victor had left, why — after all these years — she'd never risen into management.

She had her stock response of course: the higher up the pole, the less she would get to do the thing she actually cared about. To put it in her father's language: her *calling* was to teaching kids literature, not to meetings and pushing paper. Mum had naturally had her own opinions of a woman's ministry, worn out her knees praying that her only daughter would graduate from mother-to-hundreds to mum-to-one. Fat chance. That was further away than ever now. She looks again at her phone, thinks of the gamut of their relationship it holds inside somewhere. Pictures. Texts. Calls. Pleas and apologies. With all her journeys up to the hospital, Ben had claimed to be both neglected *and* penned in. Arguments had begun to crescendo; he had finished it as lockdown had fallen, abandoning her to a flat alone, to sobs that had stoppered further words, knocking them back down her throat into a crumpled chest. 'What's the matter, Jo? Tell me,' her father had pleaded, passing the phone to her mother. But what right did she have to demand sympathy? Someone was actually dying.

She stands and turns and looks out of the window, out onto the Tower and the estate beyond the playground. Well done, she tells herself mockingly. Her principles had survived another relationship intact.

There's a bench out there under the Tower, a paved open area, quiet and empty. Somewhere to sit for a moment. Outside. Away from bubbles and the smear of sanitiser. Fresh air. A few minutes to gather herself, to carefully repack her emotions.

Two kids shoot past the door shrieking, followed by a troop of howling others. She pauses and lets the noise fade before slipping out, locking her room behind her. She whispers for the display boards to go fuck themselves and makes quietly along the corridor, through the double doors onto the stairs, past the tables covered in cartons and ketchup, past the chairs strewn across the foyer, distant cries of other battles echoing down after her.

Words and all their meanings. Relationships, all built and broken by the tongue. This was why children had to become skilled in language: it was sword-craft for the sharpest weapon they owned. Different lengths and weights, each sentence a knife, every phrase a blade; each lesson about the power of speech and the burden of having it.

She walks towards the heavy steel gates. She *could* make them good enough to smash those targets if only they would shut up long enough to let her, if Jackson had actually told her that he trusted her. But, she thinks, she has run a knife through Darren's life-chances, she has spoken this world into being, and she must now find a way to survive in it. Work twice as hard; be twice as sharp. Yes, she vows to herself, do this and earn her reward come half term.

Her lanyard is wrapped around two fingers, tight like a tourniquet. She holds her new swipe-card against the reader and a magnet releases somewhere — a signal received and processed, permission given — and she heaves the gate open, breathing out and feeling lighter as she steps through.

4

She approaches the bench and the Tower rears up, leans in, a hundred panes peering. It is a single, brutal high-rise reigning over lower-lying barracks of three-storey blocks. Pebble-crushed roadways lie in tired, cracked panels, industrial-sized bins half-rolled into their right places. Only a few scrubs of grass, a little green on the ground to break the grey above. Security doors, cheap double glazing added a few years back, pretence at treatment. A cheap skin of plastic thrown around, slowly spreading, reaching up, floor by floor. The politics of facade.

The school building now looks unsure of its place. It must have seemed an oddity these past months. A vast physical space that needs heating and lights, sweeping and tidying; a heavy thing in a time of WiFi. Walking from one toward the other, the tower stands more defiant, knows its role more surely. The school empty, hollow and without purpose, the Tower perhaps came into its own, pivoted quickly into office and studio, classroom and salon.

Yes, she thinks, mass creates gravity, draws things to itself. Bleak House, Howards End, Satis House, buildings so heavy that they become characters in themselves. The Tower is a living thing. Stairwells rise to windowless doors, the smell of simmering spices, of burning toast and frying chicken, families sat on splintered sofas while others lay back in the softest beds. She's never been inside of course, has assembled this detailed collage from conversations overheard and descriptive writing tasks read. Stories from every storey, a whole world stacked up and pressed together: beautifully tended flats of fresh flowers and tumbling plants, others laden with wood carvings, others so thick with smoke that men only seem able to crawl slurring from them, the air moved by powerful speakers focused entirely on bass. Some have been here for generations while others are recent arrivals from each of the four corners, all of them bound together in the wait for the lifts and the struggle for repairs. Colleagues complain about class sizes but there are places around here packed with four families, one-time council flats sliced and resliced, half a window each. Rents rocketing; benefits pinned down. It cannot have been an easy few months for students locked down here and she worries what price she and her colleagues will have to pay, forced into proximity with young people who have been pressed together for so long and will now be looking for release.

Truth is, she cannot know how they are going to respond. 'You ain't Tower, Miss,' Jordan had reminded her when she'd offered critiqued of a homework of his last year. No. It didn't matter that the vicarage she'd grown up in was as run down as anywhere else: she remains middle class from fifty paces. God had called her father to a poverty-stricken Doncaster and Mum's role in this seemed to be to inoculate Jo against the hard knocks. Her chosen vaccine: books. Always more books. 'Culture, culture, culture... was she making a yoghurt or bringing up a kid?' Sally had joked back in their first year at university.

Hers has been another England, another London. But though she might not 'be Tower,' she knows that there is a grit that has never left, a flint buried in her heart. So when she looks up she still feels at home with what she sees. Everyone talks, everyone shares. A few roads over, the broken concrete and the plastic cladding gives way to beautiful red-brick edifices and white-washed stucco. Gated drives, video entry systems, panic buttons and sophisticated alarms, the fine line between space and isolation. But here there's always a buzz, always jokes. People hovering, dashing off and returning, flying in and out of the single narrow entrance on the ground floor.

Somewhere above is Chanel's window, father looking after chair-bound mother, waiting as government computers confer, determining whether they deem his wife fit to be sent out to work. Elsewhere, Charlie's flat, his Dad not strictly working but still the hope that some odds will come good soon, his mum fed up of promises, taking what shifts she can at the discount supermarket. Higher up is Michael, his elder brother not long back from some time in the Scrubs, ankle bracelet, chastened and anxious. Both parents elsewhere, so it's grandparents on duty for reasons he's never written down. Ade is not far away, his door open early, mum out before dawn and not back until dark. Same number of jobs as sons; three of each. Minimum wage requires maximum hours, but thankful for anything with so many out of work. Hayley's family are born and bred, her dad custodian of a stall in Shepherd's Bush, not that she's ever mentioned it herself, but Lauren has written of it, a few extra fruits to people he knows in the Tower; friends with benefits. And then Jordan somewhere up there too, his father also a minister, though not in the kind of church Jo had ever been to. Fire and wailing, fasting and praying, shouting up to heaven for blessings to be rained down, a long way from received Anglican manners.

All these just threads, getting to know them a little, trying to weave a picture. Understand them, and they might understand what you are trying to say. An exercise in comprehension. See what connects. *What makes Macbeth tick*, she'd asked Jordan's class once, and been met with blank faces. A few seconds before she'd realised: nothing ticks anymore. Insides all digital, unfathomably complex, sealed up behind glass. So she'd quickly changed the metaphor — *what presses his buttons* — adapt to survive, this the joy of it, the joy and the struggle.

Yes, she thinks, yes, there has been joy, but there is real struggle right now. Darren's 'crib' is behind one of those windows. That's what the boys called home, their *crib*. Bars around, a safe place for a child. Except for Darren it hadn't seemed to be. Clothes not washed, skin that seemed to yearn for fresh veg. Some shame about this, but more about the dated handset he'd had to put up with, screen cracked in a thousand places. No contact with his dad, little clues Jo has picked up that mum had given up on him, chalked him up as a mistake from her teens. Half siblings now the ones invested in, noise, plastic toys, screams, so gradually he'd spent more time out, building bonds with different brothers.

And doubtless Jo had made it all worse. Turfed out the boy who'd already felt excluded enough, pushed him out of the zoo to fend for himself. She sighs, tries to breathe all of this out of her, knowing that she has her own fight on her hands too, also needs to find a way to evolve, some animal advantage to ward off Jackson.

A window opens far above, a peripheral shift in the light. She thinks of Kayleigh, always waving across at her mum in the Tower, Jo fed-up of asking her to stop so getting the whole class to wave too, using it, turning it: getting them to write poems to relatives imagined stuck across an unbridgeable divide. One boy had come close to tears, Jo not far behind, reading what he'd written to his dad stuck in Kabul. She'd kept him behind, just checking if he was alright, saying he could come find her anytime. He never had, but still.

A clatter makes her start, a fox scampering out from behind a bin, limping, a tin can rolling noisily after. It pauses, makes an assessment, and trots away towards the school.

Like the Tower, Cromwell has its own ugly beauty; formal Brutalism a nice idea for architects with minimalist spectacles. There are six decks of concrete and glass, like a ship dry-docked among waves of flats and low rises lapping at its perimeter. For months it has lain foundered, virtually empty, some question about whether or not these kinds of vessels could ever be safe again. But here they are, slowly firing up the boilers, trying to get her moving again. From down in the hold comes the banging of the Technology department and the crashing of the kitchens, steaming galleys where dinner ladies who once tended vats of custard now rack pre-grilled burgers into microwaves. High above, up the spiral staircase, there are geography classrooms and, in between, the great hull of the liner strains as storms of English, Mathematics, and Languages blow through. This was the comprehensive promise of 'all aboard,' local children invited to sail together, the vision Victor had handed on to Jo, part of the fire that's kept her going.

Some who've now disembarked haven't got far. She sees them sometimes, old students she's taught approaching with a nod and a skulk, mid-twenties but still calling her 'Miss,' catching her up on what they've been doing — *just this and that innit* — asking if she's still there at Cromwell, her always a little embarrassed as she reports that she's not got further herself.

'Perhaps it's because, deep down, you love them more,' Dad had told her when she'd finally confessed to her split with Ben. She'd told Dad about the strain that had built up with her workload, the arguments over her late nights of marking, the constant attention to planning. And she's been thinking about this over the summer, this question of love over time, and how much more she still has to give. 'You're too like me,' he'd added. She still can't work out whether he meant her to enter this in the ledger as good or bad, just knows that there's damage she needs keeping out of sight for now, under the waterline, bulkhead doors shut deep inside. Sometimes you have to leave things trapped so you can stay afloat.

A man marches past, a phone clasped to his ear saying, '10 minutes away mate,' aiming a half-finished takeaway from *Mr Chips* at the scarred opening of a bin, missing, cussing but not stopping to pick it up. He climbs into a BMW and pulls away, revving, the chip carton going under the wheels, fries squelched in a pool of cheap sauce. A pigeon lands, begins pecking, throwing chip flesh around, then — alert to movement — takes flight. Jo sits up, spies someone skulking around the corner of the base of the Tower. A boy peers, pulls his gaunt face quickly back behind a pillar.

Too late. It is Darren.

If she wants to call out to him she cannot immediately requisition the air. Muscles tighten, deny the request, ready themselves for flight. A puff of smoke and he reappears, hooded now, face half-hidden, and he trots off with a hold-all, hopping a low wall and heading away, thin limbs hardly holding up a billowing tracksuit with gold lettering.

'Darren,' Jo begins weakly, but then finds herself emboldened and stands up. 'Darren!'

He turns, sees her and makes his assessment, doesn't pull closer, stays a safe distance but not for that reason.

They are examining one another, scanning for threats, for hints of movement. The gaze runs between them over twenty-five metres of concrete and back again, crackling with the tension of those last few lessons where everything had ramped up. Jo sees herself handing him back that comprehension paper the week before it had all exploded, his face crumpling briefly at the grade before hardening back into shape as she'd told him he was going to have to do a lot better.

'Boy proper bombed!' Jordan had laughed, catching sight of the hopeless score marked in large red scratches on his script.

'Hole it, fam,' Darren had said.

'Fuck you. Scraping with "fam."'

Family, that basic need to feel belonging. Jo had turned in anger to slap Jordan down, then back to Darren. 'This is getting real now. Exams next year, actual qualifications. This is about your future.' He'd said nothing.

He had already become an infrequent visitor to her lessons, his attendance degenerating, her grip on him dissolving. Enough of her father's pastoral heart, she'd thought. Because he was so tough to love some of her mother's tough love might do the trick. 'Darren, you need to knuckle down, commit to work, not be mucking about outside school.'

'Miss,' Jordan interjects, 'he *likes* working OT, the countryside, the great outdoors.' The class all laugh and Darren blushes. 'How you think he's paid to upgrade that brock-up phone?'

OT. Out There. Code for journeys out along county lines.

She takes a stab at a knowing joke. 'Enjoying the grass eh?'

She wants to recall the words even before they land. A few chuckles in the class, but uneasy, ducking as this grenade arcs.

Darren had blinked, had looked like his eyes might be tearing up, but then suddenly he'd torn the paper up and pushed the pieces to the floor. 'You used to be safe Miss,' he'd said quietly, shaking his head before continuing more loudly. 'Not all getting up in man's face stressing about "rest of your life", breaking man's balls about grades when you're just vexing because it makes you look bad.'

She'd bristled. 'That's not true Darren. I want you to do well because you could...'

But he'd cut her up. 'You don't know *shit* about me, about my life, innit,' jumping along the line of desks, taking Jordan's essay, ripping that, grabbing Charlie's, scrunching and throwing it, people beginning to grab and protect their work, so he'd pushed tables and kicked chairs instead. 'Nothing. None of you know *nothing*.'

'Go ahead Darren!' she'd told him, staying firm. 'Walk out! See if that helps anything. Screw things up and tear things down!'

A week later, he'd returned and she'd helped him do exactly that.

Now all these words burn and stupefy as she inhales them again. Her mum had offered a withering assessment — "you should have *told* someone Jo. Always the same, trying to carry everything yourself" — and Jo had immediately understood the story her mum had been thinking of: her piling everything onto a tray when she'd been asked to lay the table, trying to impress but sending crockery and glasses slipping and smashing, mum turning from the stove and shouting, Jo tongue-tied, head-down ashamed, Dad running from his study, saying it was all alright, starting to pick things up, telling her, 'say sorry to your mum.'

Your mum. Piling everything up. Anger, exhaustion. *You used to be safe.* Words worm in through her ears and gnaw at her insides, stewing on them after he'd stormed off, bitterness heating and simmering. Then she slips and it all bursts out.

Just FUCK OFF.

She tries to hold thoughts steady, to push the past back and focus on the present in front of her. His gaze is locked on; no mask, but face obscured by the shrouds of smoke he produces in regular metre. He takes a long slow drag, a tiny point of burning fire glowing between the V of his fingers, fingers that fluidly flick the smouldering butt away and halve themselves into an erect and quivering bird. Whatever he has been up to has rewarded him with brand new clothes and the confidence to hold himself with a swagger.

'I'm sorry,' she calls over, 'sorry they off-rolled you.' And he lets this land and roll to a stop, looking down to examine her confession before brushing down his top and booting it back.

'You will be,' he laughs, raising his hand in a cliched pistol gesture taken straight from a rap video. 'All your bullshit, I swear down,' he begins, but then there is the clang of the school security gate. It's out of her eye-line, but he sees something, flits his head, pulls a hood up and turns. By the time she has glanced across and back, he's gone.

He has gone, but it's now that she starts shaking. If she'd hoped that he has put what happened behind him it seems that she is wrong. Raising it on his turf feels like it's less a school matter than a street debt now. No forgiveness. No forgetting. Payment will have to be made.

She sits back down on the bench, tries to calm herself, closes her eyes and wants to rub them with the tips of her fingers but knows that she mustn't touch her face. When she opens them she sees Sami Karim.

He has a beaten rucksack slung over his shoulders. He doesn't see her at first, but when she sits up this movement alerts him, both caught now, unable to ignore the other. Some might have run but he stops, waiting for Jo to move. She does so slowly, raising her back until it rests flat against the bench, doing what she can to hold him there with her eyes.

He is a creature she doesn't yet know.

'You should be in a lesson,' she calls over gently, a smile to attempt to disarm her prey. It's only then that she notices the bruise on his face, his head cap-less. 'Are you OK?' — this said more urgently. But he isn't OK and as he twists to look over his shoulder at the school she sees him wince in pain. She glances over too, is reminded that she should be following Jackson's stiff procedures — masks, distancing, bubbles, a show of authority, march him back into lessons — but something else in her stirs and stretches. Fuck him, she thinks. He has dispensed of Darren, but there is always another child to fight for.

Sami doesn't speak, but he doesn't flee either, just holds the situation in balance, rocking slightly in his shoes, weighing things one way, then another.

'Was it them?' she asks. 'Those boys from earlier? After my lesson?' She has run back the tapes, realised what has happened.

There is a slight movement of his head, embarrassment perhaps, trained to be wary of calling attention to himself, and he reaches a hand to touch the bruise, inspecting his finger afterwards as if assessing tender flesh against a register of other entries.

She wants to tell him not to touch it. 'I could take you to the medical room?' she offers, but is glad to see him shake his head more firmly. A gentle breeze rolls the flattened chip box across the floor in front of them and lays it down again, slightly closer. She looks around but Darren seems to have gone. She smooths down her skirt and moves along the bench a little. A simple kindness, but she knows that this breaks a whole host of rules.

'Sit,' she says nonetheless, and after a moment he does. The bruise is going to be a nasty one.

'I'm so sorry,' she tells him. There's no school counsellor to send him to anymore. 'I should have picked up on what was going on. I was... It was...' Nothing seems clear enough to form itself into a word, but she mustn't let him go. 'Do you know their names? We can find out their names and get it dealt with, get it sorted out so it won't happen again.'

He says 'no,' whispers it suddenly, the sound coming out of him so quickly and quietly that she's not sure if he's just made a noise or actually offered a response until he says it again, 'no,' still barely audible but said more slowly, him placing the word on the bench between them, his considered adjudication.

'You live here?' she asks, signalling with a hand the Tower and the flats lined up as if ready to march on the school.

His head is down, but she thinks that she sees a nod, is straining ears in case she misses something.

'Any they live here too? The boys who attacked you?' The same response.

She takes a breath, knows that this is the drug, the high, the core of her addiction, this joy of thinking that a child can be helped, that their life can be changed. 'Sami, you can trust me. You can tell me their names. I've worked here for a long time. I promise you, if you don't speak up now, it'll just go on and on.' She watches her words hit his head, hoping that his English is good enough, wonders if they have bounced and fallen or eased their way through the untidy mop of hair. 'The school can put a stop to this. Find them, put them in detention.'

Sami snorts quietly, and Jo winces. Stupid, she thinks. Far worse detention threats on his mind perhaps. Home Office vans. Spit hoods. Dawn flights.

His forearms are on his knees, his feet bouncing. 'No,' he announces finally, the ground in front of him hearing better than she can. 'Maybe that stops it in school, but I think that just makes it worse out here.' He's not stupid, that's for sure. His words arrive thickly covered, but they're the right ones, in the exact right order. 'I just wait,' he continues, brightening a little. 'Then it stops.'

The sky is all summer light but the air surprisingly cool. Jo pulls her jacket closer round, tucking legs under the bench to shelter them.

Language seems to have deserted her, all apart from curses. A child acting like this in class and she'd be offering strategies, examples of opening phrases to get the words flowing, filling any silence with questions and hints. But she's hardly allowed to come alongside them now, is meant to stay a safe distance inside her taped-off area. Sterility. Distancing. No kneeling by their desk, heads almost touching, pointing with her pen, the words she breathed out, breathed in by them, this intimate act of shared space the way she's always provided help. What this boy needs the very thing she is not allowed to give.

She sees the bruise weeping quietly under his skin, thinks of the wounds she herself has hidden, well-versed in the ways of secreting pain away. She has to try to do something for him.

'It can be cold here in winter,' she says, finally.

'Yes, at home too,' he replies informatively, gentle with her ignorance.

'Sorry,' she says again, aware of the length of the list of things for which she could be asking forgiveness, taking the little grunt he makes not as a complete pardon, but as a sign that what's already happened needn't be dwelt on further. So she asks if he is staying with family and he confirms what Jordan had mooted in class earlier: an uncle.

'But I am glad to be here, really,' he says cheerfully, looking up at last, all juvenile moustache and spotted face. 'London. In school.' His words are suddenly more confident. 'Big chance for me, I know.'

And something stirs, something clears. A spark only, but she knows that she must capture it. She gestures to his bag, asks if it's ok to take something out, the copy of *Great Expectations* she can see poking through a gap in the zip.

'This book,' she says, 'this book I gave you in class. You know it?'

He shrugs inconclusively and stumbles over something about his brother.

'Not an easy book,' she explains excitedly. She shouldn't even be touching it, should have left it for seventy-two hours or pulled on surgical gloves, but she cannot resist, is leaning into him, pushing through the musk that comes with closeness. Learning isn't a sterile art. Her classroom is a theatre, but not like that. A lesson isn't an operation. Remove the messiness and something deeper is lost. No, she thinks, this fucking virus has taken too much already; she will not let it take this. And she feels the whole tale of the book loading itself back up through her hand — the smell of the forge, the fire and metal, the infant tongue of Pip's wounded beginnings, stolen food and the threat of violence, a sudden change in fortunes, a heart that grows in expectation. 'Not easy, but it's perfect,' she says. 'A boy given a big chance, coming to London to transform his life.'

He happily takes it back from her and turns it over. 'A challenge,' he says, as if examining a puzzle and deciding whether or not to begin trying to work on it. 'But good. Maths OK, almost the same; science too. So English good to work on.' He flicks through the first pages, looking for the beginning of the story proper.

She feels some valve opening, some chamber beginning to refill. 'Sami, I think you can do this. I can help you.' That would really be something. Her own Pirrip. Six weeks until half term. Work hard with this boy, do something incredible. Something to put on a plate and serve to Jackson.

He nods slowly, as if weighing up her offer, focusing on the paving stone under his feet as he does so, toeing at a crack there.

She expands her pitch, tells him that if he works hard on his English the big change he wants will become easier. 'Good results are the best way to leave bullies behind.'

He takes the book, puts it over his heart and pretends to stab himself. 'Like this? This book can save my life?' he says, laughing.

She gasps at this, but then steers it into a laugh. 'Yes, maybe, books will save your life.'

A slanging match is kicking off in one of the flats above and she can see hurried movement over in the classrooms. She makes it clear that they should go. A heavy voice shouts from over a nearby wall but it doesn't sound like Darren.

'Come on,' she says, 'let's get you back to school.' She stands up but he looks unsure about this. 'You can't just run off and hide,' she says. She holds up her lanyard. 'I'll swipe you back in and write a note on the register, say that you were with me. Trust me, Sami, no one will know.'

Show love by speaking half-truths, she thinks. Like Dickens' Magwitch, goodness wrapped in transgression.

He consents, gets up, begins to walk as she opens the pages in her head and starts telling him about Pip. A young boy in a graveyard, a fearful, hat-less man seizing him, threatening him, demanding metal tools to give him his freedom, Pip unaware that his own liberty was closer than he thought.

Sami trots along beside, thumbs tucked into rucksack straps.

In rushed précis, she ignores Mr Wopsle's aunt and her dreadful teaching, the huge and terrifying things that would later tear through little Pip's life. No, she decides, don't mention this. Keep to the surface. She pulls a distance ahead of him and presses her lanyard to the sensor, a nervous look around, holding the gate open as she steers him through ahead of her.

5

In normal times voices would bubble and flow as Friday afternoon oozed into early evening, Jo and her colleagues gathering for drinks somewhere away from Cromwell, beyond the estate and into the grand brick terraces that lap nervously against its edge. Teachers would visibly brighten as they approached, the light feeling different, the week done, some time to decompress a little before re-entering the adult world again.

Jackson has made it clear that close gatherings of staff are not allowed, though — in a mirror of the bemused confusion across the country — no one is quite sure if that means a drink after work is OK or not.

'The new normal,' Cara had sighed as she'd packed things off her desk into a bag to take home for the weekend, just in case they were teaching from home again by Monday.

'Except it doesn't feel new,' Jo had replied, before adding a beat later, 'or normal.'

They'd exchanged glances. They were in the English department bubble. Fuck it, why don't they just go get a beer together? The new arrivals deserved that at least. The Rule of Six...ish. Not like they're maths teachers.

The Fox and Hounds is the closest pub but is just an abandoned shell now, skulking low to the ground, prefab walls and flat roof. In a similar style to the rest of the Tower development, the windows are all boxed out in steel panels pocked by air gun pellets. An optimistic sign — Under New Management! — has long been tagged over and over by those who seem now to have the run of the site. Just behind is the youth centre in similar disrepair, an abandoned parish hall next door. Don't let Dad see that, Jo thinks. He'd be out of retirement in godly disgust in no time.

They choose the Green Man, tell the others where to find it. In the kind of costume change London manages between one road and the next, it's only a minute or two further on from the Fox yet sits among beautiful mansions and a well-kept park, all solid oak tables and reclaimed pews.

Jo sips her lager. Cara tells her that it's good to see her smiling. Both Sally and Maria have been in touch. One with a new husband and the other with a new baby, but both would love to do something soon. The embrace of relationships, the warmth of a circle of support.

The afternoon had zipped by, the noise and quake of the school singing with tremulous energy. Arriving after lunch, Year 7s fresh from their primary schools had inched in in nervous packs. The local young gathered to learn the values of the community. Coming through her door as children, they would leave in a few years as young adults; between now and then it was up to her to feed them, mould them, grow them. What greater privilege was there than this?

Jamiliah had got upset because she had mislaid her ruler. 'Kelsey,' Jo had asked, reading the name from a list, 'would you lend her yours please?' Stationery was precious, would have been assembled over many trips to the shops, wasn't technically meant to be lent to others, not without spraying and wiping down. A frown, a pause, and then assent. Words of thanks offered.

Keaton had nearly wet himself. A scuffle near the boys' toilets apparently, so he hadn't gone at lunch. Six weeks ago they had ruled their playgrounds as princes. Now they were in a different kingdom, little currency or influence, biting their lips and wondering where to sit. Anxious, excited, frightened, swapping names and latching desperately into friendships, Jo had let them start the lesson sharing what they'd gleaned about the best lunch options and the cleanest toilets. Teaching as mothering, them suckling hungrily, quiet as they are fed, some still yearning for a hook, their name in calligraphy and a picture underneath.

'Write a few paragraphs explaining what you did over the summer,' she'd told the class, their bodies so small, their mass so delicate, shoes still clean, hopes undented. They'd poked tongues in concentration, sharpened pencils and fussed over margins while Jo had scribbled notes for her final year A-level class and thoughts about a plan for Sami, all of which still glows in her in the pub.

'Bloody hell,' Cara says discussing the changes to the staff, 'so many new faces.'

'So many *young* faces,' Jo adds. New colleagues not dissimilar to her new students, discussing food options and clean toilets, swapping names and sticking with those they know. 'We should steal their lunch money,' she adds.

Cara nods as she places her wine back on the table. 'Definitely. Then shake them down for red biros and staplers.'

Twenty or more new to the school, and Cara seems to know the names of nearly all of them. Jo can recall about three at most.

There was Dan. He had introduced himself on the corridor, gone in for a handshake, and then remained rather too close. New in Science. They'd swapped names, then he'd asked the inevitable follow-up. 'Good lockdown?'

She'd tried not to flinch, had lied and told him it had been great, glad for the small mercy that apparently he didn't know that it really hadn't been.

The doors of the pub swing open and it turns out that the Science Department have had a similar idea. When they troop in Jo points Dan out to Cara.

'He seems keen,' she says.

'On me? God Cara, don't.'

'I meant keen on the job,' she cuts in, with a roll of eyes, and Jo laughs, apologises.

'One of those fast-track schemes for top graduates, so he can't be stupid.'

'Or more stupid than you think.' She looks him over. They have bought drinks and taken a group of tables a good distance away, just in case Jackson had spies. 'My money is on a crash and burn.'

'Three years?'

'Oh, God, three years *max*,' Cara says, as if she had far more than that under her own belt. She's young but Jo knows that she's a rare find, a really good teacher, a survivor. Cara watches him and rolls the stem of her glass between her fingers. 'He'll be Head of Science next year...'

'Yep, Chris won't hack another after this one. Not with Victor gone.'

'From what I'm hearing, if their results don't shift he won't have a choice,' Cara adds, 'so Einstein here will take that on for a year...'

'Then burn out.'

'Toast.'

'End up doing something in marketing.'

'Promote the next one.'

'Repeat.'

Jo sighs and takes a drink. Horrible when new staff struggled: the growing anxiety, quiet tears in the staffroom, the question someone has to finally pose, 'are you sure this is really for you?' How the hell any kind of proper support was going to be given in this new environment was beyond her. She'd once described the place to Ben as a blast furnace: get young staff in cheap and burn them. But she has got Cara: apply heat and pressure and some miraculously turn to fine glass.

'Who knows,' Cara says. 'Maybe he's really good,' still looking at Dan talking on the phone. He catches her and she looks away.

If he isn't they will hear the evidence even if no one sees it. Thumping, crashing, shouting on the corridor above English. Then silence. Talk of support but the sound of management knives sharpening.

'Come on, you're empty. Let's get another.'

A barmaid in mask, visor, and gloves comes to take their order.

'Good to actually see you,' Cara says when the drinks arrive. She clinks Jo's glass.

A flicker of a pause before Jo looks back to say, 'you too.' It's gone in an instant, flushed down with another long draft. Before Cara can say any more Jo sees Geoff from Music has also arrived and is sat alone on a table behind them with his bitter. Not a man who finds things easy. She turns to say hello, asks him how his summer was.

'Here we bloody are again,' he says. The same words in a major key could sound funny, jolly even. But there's a flatness, a downbeat tone like a collapsed piano.

'Chin up Geoff,' she says. 'There might be karaoke later.' She turns and winks at Cara, who gives her a glare and shakes her head. Geoff says nothing. Jo takes a sip. 'How do you think things will go this year with GCSEs?'

He winces, makes no sound, just shakes his head slightly and lifts his glass, hand in faint tremolo.

'Me too,' she tells him, trying to sound comradely. 'Jackson is going to be all over me like a rash this year about my results.' He says nothing back and from his silence tendrils seem to weave around, choking the brightness.

He looks over at Cara, who smiles and turns in discomfort, which seems to decide something in him. 'Good to see you, Jo,' he says, replacing his mask, and holds onto his lanyard as he turns himself back to his table. There are more staff arriving now, but none stop to say hello.

Jo sits back down. 'God, he can be such a downer.'

'Doesn't look good, does he?' Cara says. 'But mind your language.' Jo looks at her quizzically. 'They're not "your results," isn't that what you told me? Wasn't you who'd mucked about, didn't concentrate, didn't do enough work.'

'Alright, fuck off,' Jo laughs. 'I was only trying to be helpful.'

Cara throws back. 'With Victor gone, you're pretty much the old guard now, so I defer to your greater wisdom.'

'*You*,' Jo shoots back, eyes wide, wiping her mouth. 'Third September in this department makes you something of a veteran!'

'God no! I'd hate to think of myself still washed up here in ten years.' She pauses and the laughter stops, hastily adds, 'no offence.'

Jo pretends that none is taken. She turns to check on Geoff, but he's gone.

'Perhaps I'll be doing something in arts management,' Cara says drifting off into a story about a BBQ over the summer, a group of people she'd been introduced to.

Jo lets her talk on, allowing herself to be carried. Her dad always claimed that his work was ordained by the above; she'd told him that teaching was the opposite: most of her colleagues fell into it from some higher thing that hadn't worked out. Everyone had their 'other job' spiel. Cara and her festivals, Victor and his screenwriting. Dad had taken this in, mulled for a while but not said anything in reply. Then when the thing with Darren had kicked off he'd finally shot back, come out with it and asked Jo what she would do instead if the worst came to the worst. She'd grasped for words — something, anything — but had fumbled her answer and plunged. 'I don't know, I just don't know.'

We're "key workers" now, Cara is saying sarcastically, teachers are. Jo can't quite work out how the arts spiel she was on has ended up here, but whatever. 'Jobs that people are glad get done, but *very* glad that they get done by someone else.' She knocks her glass into the tabletop for emphasis. 'Anyway,' she says finally, 'we've got to get through this year first. How's your day been?'

She lays a hand softly on Jo's arm which makes Jo quiver inside, like Cara's touch is hypodermic. She has to move and break contact, presses a stocky heel down hard onto her toes.

'It's been fine,' she says brightly but Cara isn't done, is asking how her father is. Jo doesn't want to be thinking about him, doesn't want any attention in that direction, so though she's not even spoken to him for a few days she hits straight back, insisting that he's absolutely fine too.

Now the geographers have turned up too — so many bubbles connected that the pub is becoming a foam. The bar staff look around nervously, but there's an eagerness too as they reach out card machines. A dripping tray of drinks is handed noisily over Jo's head. She mimes cheers at them and then blinks hard as Cara carries on, pressing, asking if Ben has been in touch, Jo wondering why she doesn't get that this isn't the place, not seeing that she needs to face forward now, needs to focus on what is good, the conjunction of 'Ben' and 'touch' knocking her the other way, where she really doesn't want to go, back down into her thoughts. She knows that her mum had thought her grief was all out of proportion, too generous for the loss of a silly boy, her sadness too absolute. *Dig deeper*, Jo had wanted to plead, but it was as much as her mum could do to squeeze her fingers and stroke her palm, before twisting to ride a searing jolt of pain. Only a day or two more and they'd be told they would have to leave. No visitors. Locking the whole hospital down.

'Forget. That. Bastard,' Jo says to Cara in staccato, knocking her glass against Cara's with each word, then draining it.

Cara tilts her lager back at her in concord and elevates Ben to '*fucking* bastard.'

But she'd not been able to obey her mother, had struggled to forget any of it really, and when mum had turned away Jo had carried on talking, firing words at her back like an X-ray. 'He says he'd been thinking about it long before you got ill,' all this between sobs, the square box of tissues the nurses had put out for her mum almost used up. 'And what with everything, he thinks a clean break now is best.' The chimera of a deft surgical cut. As if things could be that *clinical*, she'd complained, as if lives didn't begin to graft into each other, start to share a physiology.

There's a kerfuffle as a drink is knocked and sploshes on Jo's skirt. Masked apologies are made and napkins and fresh drinks brought.

'Anyway, no, no contact, thank God,' she announces to Cara with finality, then launches an offensive before she can ask any more. 'All good with you and Jules?'

Cara waits. 'It is good,' she says after a moment and smiles a little, as if she might elucidate. But she doesn't, just repeats, 'no, it is good,' before adding some balance. 'Though freelance graphic design isn't exactly a goldmine right now. His work has almost totally dried up and I'm pretty much covering the rent myself. I mean, what am I even doing thinking about other jobs, or...' and she fades out again.

Too many reports for it to be funny. Food banks and homeless shelters. Whispers around the staff room about someone apparently living out of their car.

'You know I *actually* have dreams about getting a mortgage?' Jo tells Cara to shush, but to no effect. 'I do! I'm serious. I have these amazing dreams where Jules and I have an offer accepted and we have the letter from the bank saying yes, and I'm so happy it feels like my chest will pop. And then I wake up, and it's like the most depressing thing. You are so bloody lucky.'

Not exactly a Victorian terrace on some quiet street in Clapham, but even ownership of her single-bed flat in a block in Brixton is something to hold on to right now. *Always be grateful*, her Dad's words still echo in her head. *Say thank you every day*. Not in the boom of his preaching, but the voice of the quiet man in their living room, skilful with a poker, fine adjustments to a reluctant fire.

'You're lucky too,' Jo says with a prod to Cara's arm before arranging a more serious face, 'compared to some of these kids. I mean, look at my Year 11, this kid Sami...'

Cara splutters into her drink. 'I thought you were going to say Darren.' She throws her head back. 'Just FUCK OFF,' she half-bellows, half rising from her chair. A few people turn and there's a cheer from a couple of tables close by, a raising of glasses in salute. Cara ebbs back quickly down to her seat and Jo hunches her shoulders in. If they want to repaint her as renegade staffroom hero she's desperate to dodge the brush. Cara apologises but is still laughing. 'He was a little shit Jo,' she says. 'Tough for him I know, but the fucker made his own bed.'

Bed, Jo repeats in her head, *crib*. Still a child, without agency enough to change where he slept. Though surely he is old enough not to soil the sheets, to choose whether to keep his linen laundered. She has spent whole days over the summer worrying about how these Tower children have fared. When the youth leaders and counsellors and shop owners and publicans have all quit the estate and the web of next-door grandmas and aunts is weakened, when your mum basically gives up on you, what is left? Only the local school remains and everything is hauled and dumped at its gates. Go on, society says, we're a bit fucked right now but open your doors back up, take this lot and teach them respect, love, tolerance, obedience, justice, ambition, a healthy diet. All at two metres distance. Or less, actually. Make bubbles, but squash them into the same space. Impossible, she thinks, just an impossible ask to manage all this. *But you have to keep trying*, Dad whispers. *Never give up looking for the good.*

She shakes her head as if scrubbing a thought, asks Cara if she wants another but she says no, says she's good. There's actually a crowd of noisy drinkers now and the two of them look a little nervously at one another.

Cara turns her glass thoughtfully. After a while she says, 'seriously Jo, how are you? How's things been?'

She has to look a couple of times to assess how much she means this, how much she actually wants to know. She tries to slough the question off with a snorted laugh but Cara's eyes are a fond embrace that won't just let her go.

'Look,' she says eventually. 'Look. It's.' She is stumbling again, trying to find a sentence that will go in a fixed direction as all around it swirls. 'It's been horrible. Hard. Weird.' She pushes the drink into the middle of the table and circles it with two thumbs and two fingers. Cara reaches across and takes an index finger, clenches it softly. 'Honestly? I'm not sure if I actually *feel* it yet. I know she's gone, is absent, but...'

'Were you close?'

The question crashes and draws like a sudden larger wave, and Jo braces against it. If only I knew, she thinks, if only I could measure out how close, and how much further they'd still had to go... She can't look at Cara and speaks instead to the table. 'I mean, we were *becoming* that. I think? Towards the end.' She feels as if she's pushing fogged thoughts into the air that only solidify into words when they're past her mouth. Anger still at this theft at the last. 'But nothing prepares you for that Car. To be told you can no longer visit your own mother. Aren't even allowed to go to her funeral.'

Cara doesn't say anything, just keeps stroking this one finger with her thumb, and it's almost impossibly painful how tender and welcome this touch is, and how unbearably visceral too, memories gushing through this tiny point of contact like heavy rain through a flysheet. She suddenly wants to tell Cara everything, starting at the very beginning with her own difficult birth and how that had meant her mum could have no more, the way that that seemed to have driven something between them from the start.

But then the four new English staff arrive to sit with them, all ordering the same drink. Cara looks like she's about to ask them to give you a moment but Jo says no, welcomes them in, looks along the line and repeats their names, narrowing her eyes in a play of struggling to make sure she gets them right. Martha, Matt, Sandra and Rose. They all smile as she succeeds and Jo raises her glass to each in celebration.

Cara sits back, a little worried. Dan then leans over her, addresses her and the new quartet. 'A few of us are going out after, heading into town to find a bar. Fancy joining us? Make a six?'

Cara looks across at Jo but Dan's gaze is held, his focus singular. 'Maybe,' she says politely, tipping her chair back to try to regain some distance. The others nod together, clutching their glasses. Alex then pushes by, joins them as Dan retreats.

'All good?' he asks, smiling round at his team.

'All fine,' Cara says, raising an empty glass.

'Another drink?' he offers, seeing this. 'What will you have? You coming out after?' They are seven at the table now, but only Jo seems to be counting.

'These guys might,' she says sardonically. 'Think I'll just go and finish my crocheting.'

Cara tells her to shut up and signals to Alex. 'Nothing more for me. Getting a bit busy in here for my liking to be honest.'

He now does a count and looks uncomfortable, as if not used to the fact that he is now a manager, that he'll never quite be included anymore, will feel rooms change when he walks into them, jocular conversations hurriedly dying down.

He stays anyway though, shifts his beer on the table and breaks the awkward silence. 'About the thing with Jackson earlier.' He leans in, rolls his shoulders forward conspiratorially. 'Jesus, he's nothing if not demanding. I believe you Jo, if that's any help, about the ridiculous target grades. But he's not going to budge. Says he can't, because of people above him. So... I mean, we're just going to have to push hard and try to hit our numbers.'

Cara's set will all sail through, as will the next two groups down, so in effect the target falls squarely on Jo's middle set, on getting most of Jordan's class over the line. She bends her foot, turns and presses her heel. She wants to tell him that she doesn't care, that she knows what she needs to do and isn't doing it for him or for Jackson or for any other goddamn reason other than it's the right thing. But she knows better than to announce this. Better to just nod, to work in secret with Sami and deliver a surprise.

No one says a thing, so Alex pushes on, explaining his plan to test and test and test them until they could write exam-style essays backwards.

'I apologise,' Jo says drunkenly, turning to the new teachers, 'if you thought you were coming into education. It turns out you've actually signed up to an industrial canning business.'

Alex laughs uneasily, tilts his pint towards her. 'Algorithms are hungry creatures. If it does turn out to be calculated grades again we've got to have the evidence.' Cara is about to interject but he cuts her off. 'And that's just the GCSEs. Jackson's not giving us an easy ride with the A-Level either.'

Femi, Mo, Anya, Rasheed, and the others. Jo's first lesson with them is next week, the last year of their A-Level and it should be pure joy. Even they still don't officially know what had happened with her mum. Cara had urged her to tell them, said that they deserved the truth, but Jo had insisted. They'd been sent off in lockdown with copies of *Howards End* and a bunch of essay titles. Work posted online each week, but a decree from on high that no video lessons were allowed, just in case some couldn't access it, didn't have internet at home. She wondered if these people had actually seen a child in the last five years. Most of their day was spent on YouTube. It was a long shot to expect them to have done enough of the work. Femi will have, surely. Arrived in Jo's class from a failing Primary, silent reading pretty much the only kind she'd known, hiding in corners, feeding her hungry head, desperate to gorge on the richer food a Secondary school library had to offer. Jo can't wait to see her, her little prize, her final year, Oxbridge not out of the question. But who knows how far behind they'll all be. A few notes made perhaps? She feels nervous when she thinks about it, the prospect of them having failed to keep up somehow less their responsibility and more her fault.

'Anyway,' Alex concludes wryly, 'no pressure everyone.' He strokes a hand around his baby-smooth chin, lifting his glass to take a drink before putting it carefully down, bang centre on craft beer mat. 'Except the pressure of my nuts in the vice that Mr Jackson will be slowly closing.'

'Gross,' Jo says, frowning.

'Though his nuts are doubtless in the Academy chain's vice,' Cara adds.

'Which is probably why he got rid of that dickhead Darren that you burned,' Alex jokes. Cara stares coldly at him and he realises that he should apologise.

Jo shakes her head and pushes back from the circle as Cara tries to change tack, asking the new lot how Year 11 had been earlier today.

'Mine were fine,' Sandra says. Martha swallows and inspects a mark on the table. She looks pale. 'Some proper characters in Martha's group,' Sandra adds.

Don't, Jo thinks, don't descend now. She can feel shadows yawning, a dark mood slipping quietly behind her. The rest of the department are leaning in, Cara speaking assurances to them already. Jo sighs. They'll surely all have heard by now what she'd done to Darren, perhaps too that she had lost her mother and not been allowed to be at the funeral.

She wants to stand up, turn with a lit torch, wave flames to ward off the dark. There are too many spirits here, she thinks. Unsettled souls. She needs her whole body alight to get through this, a whole store of energy to combust over these next weeks, a heat and light to press these thoughts back. Sami can be that spark, she knows. This boy who actually wants to make the most of his chances could be a flame cupped in her hand. Great Expectations.

There's a loud guffaw behind her and Jo reflexively turns to drink it in, the young camaraderie, the joy of working with teenagers. But Cara is frowning in disgust.

'Common or garden chav,' Dan is saying in summary of his story, standing right behind them in a large group with a whole crowd of teachers, no masks, laughing in each other's faces, deflecting the blame for a lesson gone wrong, pushing the heavy blows onto the heads of children.

'Absolutely 30 watt,' another throws in and it becomes clear that they're talking about Charlie. Charlie now, but then moving on to Nishaan, though none quite get his name right, just mimic him crashing into a chair. Then they're trampling on Hayley, impersonating her accent, 'Hay-leeeeeee-ya,' mocking her nails and selfie duck-face, hair brushed back so tight it looks like it hurts, the venom coming now as they sink their teeth in, bitching and bantering, the drinks acidifying and sharpening their tongues, all of this spreading freely between them tightly packed together.

Idiots. Selfish fuckers. Jo pulls her mask on, slips a bottle from her handbag and wrings hands clean. They don't know these children. How dare they line them up and shoot them down? 'Hey, come on, that's out of order,' she says, though she knows too what it's like. During the course of the day they'll all have been laughed at, shouted at, cursed and ignored, maybe even threatened. They will have soaked it up in their classrooms and now, as they squeeze into this bar, they'll want it all to come out. She knows that. They'll have had to stand there and take it, take it and take it and take it, never once allowed to give it, and now, full of Friday drink they want all of that bile out before they leave, all of that poison gone.

But it is inexcusable, being cruel about children they don't know, haven't had time to even begin to care for. She frowns over at them. 'Seriously guys, stop it. And get some distance.'

Alex is still banging on about the importance of targets for each child, but all Jo can see is Charlie and Hayley and Ade and Nishaan and Radha, each with a target stuck to their heads, crosshairs at which these barbs are being aimed.

'Enough!' she says more loudly. And this time they turn. Dan takes her in. Cracks a laugh, lets out a cheer, raises his glass as he turns back to the group and shouts, 'JUST FUCK OFF DARREN!' There's a roar and a thick clink of pints.

'Legend!' someone shouts, but Jo doesn't know who they are.

Cara is on her feet too now, watching Jo shake her head in disbelief. 'I'm going to go,' Jo says suddenly. 'This is out of control.' She gathers her things, wobbling from the beer, pilot light unsteady inside her, all she has against the mushrooming darkness.

'Stay!' Alex calls, but Cara tells him to shut it and she pushes around the table to Jo.

She grabs her bag, pushing through the waves of them, shoving harder and harder through the mass of them, finally out of the pub and onto the street, voices finally quietening behind her as the double doors swing shut. Cara follows and throws a hug into her, holds her, really holds her before Jo pulls back.

Standing for a moment before moving on, grateful for cool new air, for space around and above, nothing standing between her and the heavens, she looks up to take in the Tower. It is silent in the distance, a tall shadow in the falling light, its mass bending the dusk and swallowing it.

'Really didn't like that,' she says to Cara.

'I know,' she says in reply, trying to load all she can into these two words. 'Come on, let's go.'

Jo turns and walks, knowing that the Tower still stands behind her, still watching, hundreds of eyes lit against the sky — Jordan, Michael, Sami, Hayley, Darren somewhere — all of them needing her to go into battle for them, to do something extraordinary in these extraordinary times. And she grasps Cara's arm and picks up her steps and pulls away.

6

She emerges from the underground in the dark. Some incident, an announcement that the tube was going to go no further than Vauxhall. The crack of a dropped suitcase as they'd all stumbled to the surface and one person started rushing, fear and adrenaline like mist through sprinklers, everyone breaking into a mildly panicking trot.

Nothing. It turned out to be nothing, of course, but still the relief of pulling her face free, the welcome roar of traffic, angry and hooting once she'd escape the hallways. This the real national lottery now: an invisible bug, a bomb-wired terrorist, some careering van, the chances slim but it *could* be you. Yet in the face of it all London's traffic still engorges, still the scooters weave and whine, still the deliveries shuttle like crazy bastards and all of it Jo loves.

With the tube down she has to take a 345. Through tight black nylon teenagers curse each other in terse couplets and a nasty fight nearly breaks out, but passengers bury themselves in fast-food boxes as the bus rocks gently down the South Lambeth Road.

The gang of boys swing down from the back seat, one of them knocking into a man sat by the doors as they got out. 'Idiots!' he bellows, his outrage held back until the doors have passed the point of no return. But one boy bursts back, slapping a hand hard against the window, the other banging it with his fist, seething under a baseball cap, and Jo grips her bag and quietly urges the bus to leave. She has clocked off; any powers she has in Cromwell are nothing out here.

It seems to take ages taken for the lights to turn and the traffic to shift, enough time for the boys to muster, the three of them now thumping on the front doors, trying to persuade the driver to stop again, let them back on. A moment of confusion as he looks in his near-side mirrors as if to do so, the whole bottom deck tensing, the man by the door half out of his seat, mask down and ready to shout for him not to. Jo scans the top of each face, paranoid that one might be Darren, or Jordan or Michael or Ade. But then the bus lurches out and her heart slowly settles again.

When she finally reaches home she puts her handbag down, hangs up her coat and leans back unsteadily on the door before turning and putting on the chain. Months of longing for normal life, to be out and about among people, but something has shifted in her and now there's an odd comfort in solitude, a sense of security from dangers she didn't know she feared. Some syndrome or another, she expects. The days upon days she'd spent inside these walls going from one room to the next, looping round and longing for novelty. Tidying up for the Zooms, affecting an acceptable background, arranging books and fruit. But the place had begun to become indistinguishable from the cavities of her own thoughts. She'd move room to try to tunnel away from brooding on one thing — Mum, Ben, the kids in her classes — but find herself too quickly back again with the same thoughts. Then just when things had started to ease a little she had ventured out to Brockwell Park, come down with symptoms and had to go back in for a fortnight. By that time she felt insane enough to hardly mind. Inside alone was simple. There was an attraction in having no choice.

She washes her hands and face.

In the height of it all, silence had fallen like muffling snow. So few cars. No planes. The streets empty. But these things going mute allowed the quiet to speak. Actual birds in Brixton. The sound of a church clock striking, though she knew not from where. Silly, she'd thought, that she found all this so profound when she spends her life trying to convince children that all things whisper, if only people will quiet their minds and listen. Every poem the ineffable transposed into human range, yet this beauty she now found was matched by an opposite horror: the chorus that rose to sing her loneliness as soon as her door was shut.

Her job: to find a melody, to press the tune into major, resist the collapse the other way. Hard to do with the drag of the drink and it's only a moment before the three old ornaments once beloved of her mum begin to chip and malign. Put in a box and handed down by Dad, a girl with balloons sits on the dresser in her bedroom, an old fruit-seller hunches in her shawls in the lounge and on the shelf in the hall a work-weary donkey, clay head hung low, braying again about Ben being gone. Still the half-hoping look each time she comes through the door, him having changed his mind, using an old key, here waiting for her, sorry.

"Still gone," the chorus swells to remind her. His coat is still gone, his spare umbrella still gone, the scent of him, gone. Sometimes she looks at the space on the hall floor, regretting binning his slippers and unlaundered shirts, the bag slung angrily into the rubbish chute. The fruit-seller in the sitting room picks up the refrain: the flat is all Jo's now, hers alone, again. The hall she had tried to brighten with lamps and white paint. The bookcase pocked with narrow slits of him, finger-wide cracks where a couple of his sports biographies had ended up, these gaps untouched, unfilled. The kitchen straight ahead, with the Ikea plates that are hers and the Tate mugs that are all now hers. The lounge is all hers. Both ends of the sofa are hers and both chairs at the dining table are hers. At the end of the hall, the bedroom. The playful arguments all done, the midnight trades settled: the duvet, all of it now, all hers. Once cherished, the girl on the dresser offers no comfort. Once loved by her mum, gathered together and tended, all three ornaments sit undusted. They are now hers.

The light blinks on the answerphone she still keeps just for Mum and Dad. She walks over, presses the button and listens for her father's voice. 'Hello love,' he says. 'Just me.' This, the wound still: that it is just him, him alone.

But she mustn't call him yet though, can't speak to him while she feels like this. She needs to climb back up, find a positive place from which to speak. She picks up last night's wine glass, stacks it onto last night's plate with Wednesday's glass too, then walks back to the kitchen and lays it all in the sink, wiping the toast crumbs from the sideboard, running the tap hot and leaving it all to soak.

Peppermint tea, and a square of chocolate. Her mother's daughter in so many little ways. Three squares. She will find a way through somehow. The past few months have been hard, but she has lots to be thankful for, plenty to look forward to. These the lines she tells herself, sometimes believing them, sometimes not.

A while later she sits forward on the sofa, puts the handset on speaker and closes her eyes.

Dad picks up with a slightly startled *Hello?* Still this expression of surprise whenever he answers, odd for a man who believes in water turned into wine that wires and lights are something of a miracle.

'Hi, it's me.'

He will be in the cubby under the stairs, the desk he made and the lamp and telephone on it. A notepad and a pot of pens. A church notice sheet painstakingly printed out, waiting to be filed.

He asks her to wait a moment while he nips to the lounge to turn off the television, the same cumbersome box sat on the same low table, the video player underneath. Six years or more since they — he — moved back south to the Bedfordshire borders, finally retreating from Doncaster, no mention this time of burning bushes or voices heard. Chastised, one might say, though he's never spoken of it that way.

She knows that nothing in that room will change quickly, worries that it will be the kitchen that will have felt things most, the fridge thinning and untended, cupboards quickly losing weight. She has battled to arrange online grocery deliveries, tried to help him understand that he doesn't need to pay the driver, that he can't hand a list of things to the man to get for next time, but still she worries about what he's eating and how it's getting to the plate. She can't remember ever seeing him cook.

Fingers crossed, she thinks, that he'll have had a good day. Will have gone outside, perhaps had a chat over the fence. No one would blame him if he retreated. This is about as Job as life can get: a biblical pandemic, your wife taken from you, you the sole mourner allowed. He knows his hermits too well and she worries that this will be his model: reclusion into his cave, the sanctification of loneliness.

When he comes back he sounds a bit dour. She asks if he's alright, and he says, 'oh I'm OK,' then sends the question back. She mustn't return the same way, cannot just add another layer of sadness and sling it back.

'I've been out for a drink with a few people,' she tells him, says nothing about the nonsense on the bus, nor about seeing Darren earlier. He can't quite remember if it's a new Head she has, or a new head of department, and she tells him about Alex and reminds him about Mr Jackson, and he tells her that they both sound like muppets.

They laugh, and this is good.

Then she sighs and pauses a moment and admits that's it's going to be a very busy year.

'Oh love, I don't know how you do it.'

'Right now,' she jokes, 'the question is more "why" than "how."'

There's no reply, but she can hear him shuffling with something, wiping his nose perhaps. Eventually, he comes back. 'Lots of "why" these days here too. Looking back, you know. Wondering about things. Choices.'

He's like a misaligned car. She takes her hands off the wheel and he just drifts into the blue, her having to keep steering him the other way. 'I thought when God called there wasn't any choice?' She launches this with levity, but it seems to land hard and he makes a sound like he is a bit hurt. 'I'm sorry Dad, I...'

'No, don't be silly Jo. You're right.' He stops for a moment, seems to be pondering.

Good enough, she thinks, that he's processing stuff at all.

If she has become proficient at piecing together narrative fragments it's maybe because all her life she's had to try to work out from sporadic eruptions what the hell was eating at her mother. She knows that Mum started her own teacher training but fell pregnant with Jo just as The Lord pronounced on her new husband's future. She knows that there was a "difficult birth," over time this coming to mean an octopus of obstetricians trying to stem the blood flow and save Mum's life. Weak then for months, a major blue, Dad's passion consuming so much that she'd struggled to get anything much of her own life back. She knows that the cost of all this still cannot be accurately calculated, knows only that she and Mum had been left messily detached.

There's a little ladder starting in her tights and she stretches her toes out, watching it lengthen and narrow as Dad goes round it all again, wondering what could have been done, if they shouldn't have spotted the signs earlier, should have been more willing to go to get things checked out sooner. She squeezes her temples with her free hand and scrunches up her eyes, throws a hand into a gesture like an upturned spider. They both know now that it was Mum who had kept things hidden for weeks. 'Dad I just don't think there's anything more you could have done.'

'I suppose you're right,' he says, attempting to brighten. 'Do you think we'll be allowed to see each other at half term?' he says, filling in Jo's silence. 'Don't worry if it'd be too much.'

Jo rolls her eyes. He can be exasperating, graciousness presenting as weakness, his constant desire to accommodate too close to spinelessness. But underneath a steely core that she respects, a bloody-minded commitment he's had to selfless work, decade after decade of giving himself. There must have been an attraction in this for a young woman.

'I hope so Dad. You know I need that very much.' To take the ashes somewhere Mum would have liked. To have something of a ceremony to say goodbye. Robbed of her funeral... that wound still so raw she can't even look at it, knows she's likely doing herself damage burying it, but what can she do? She's lost one parent, has had symptoms over the summer and self-isolated, can't get a test for love nor money. How can she risk going to see him, a seventy-five-year-old asthmatic?

'First priority is making sure you're looking after yourself,' he adds before she can say anything more, and she knows what he means but cannot just turn off being an English teacher, can't help but unpack the language. She doesn't *want* to be looking after herself, is tired of looking after every meal, tired of having to load every wash, unload it and hang it up, knickers and blouses and jeans sometimes sitting there for minutes on the floor, pulled out of the machine in damp, sinuous strings while she stares numbly at them, willing there to be some other way for them to be carried to the lounge, untangled and smoothed and arranged over the ribs of the sagging clothes horse. She is tired of having to do all this herself, then moving to the kitchen to get stuck into a stack of dishes, knowing that no one, literally, no one was going to help.

But this is his life too, this is what life has been for so many this year, shut away from loved ones for so long.

'We'll just have to hope that things look better,' she tells him as if addressing a child. It seems an impossibly long time away, six weeks of brutal work to endure first. One-way systems, anti-viral sprays, work under quarantine, trying to enforce bubbles, to keep masks being worn... all before tight surveillance from Alex and Jackson, a sixth form class to reinvigorate and all that she now wants to do for Sami.

'Perhaps we could go to a spa,' he suggests out of nowhere. 'I have to say, it's been a while since I had a full wax and pedicure.'

She laughs. 'Where the hell do you pick this stuff up from?'

'You'd be surprised,' he replies with a giggle. 'But let's just pray that we can see one another. That would be amazing.' Then one of those silences comes that is immediately recognisable. He breaks it with a short sob. 'I think *you're* amazing,' he says, struggling to compose himself. 'Doing what you do, with all this going on. I worry so much about you, being sent back into all of this, with no proper protection.' He falters again. 'She was so proud of you.'

But Jo cannot face these words head-on, tilts her cheek into her shoulder as if to dodge them. She shuts her eyes even tighter, curls toes and pulls her knees up, then digs a nail into her scalp. If only I could have felt it one more time, she thinks, have had Mum's pride verified by touch.

'Thank you, Dad.'

There's a pause, and neither quite seem to know how to fill it. Jo looks over at the seated porcelain woman who pierces her with a stare in return then pipes up to remind her that she had been malleable once, had been moulded, borne scorching heat to become solid, able to support herself.

'She was,' Dad repeats, and the donkey haws out in the hallway, the workhorse that broke its back to carry the saviour, highlighting for Jo the tense that Dad uses: *was*.

She shuffles herself on the sofa, adjusts a cushion and pushes her hair back behind her ear. 'Most of the time it feels like I must have been a disappointment.'

Used to be just a humdrum teacher, only now is she a "key-worker," some kind of national hero for getting kids back into school, allowing parents to resume their lives too, get the nation back on its feet. Not quite the standing of delivery drivers yet, but half the country think they've had a six-month holiday anyway.

Yes, she thinks, this work as an act of atonement. Deliver this miracle for Mum. Children relying on her, their life-chances on the line. *All we lack at birth is the gift of education* — Rousseau's words coming back to her from her own training. What a sense of achievement that would be, get to scatter Mum's ashes knowing that Sami's life had begun to be transformed, that she had somehow put things right with Darren.

She rubs her stomach, her basket of slowly-turning fruit. On the way to the Green Man Cara always pointed out the grand houses in the avenues, big cars outside, double buggies no doubt inside. Ben was meant to have been the man who would lift her away from the grind of the classroom. A Bugaboo and a slightly unmanageable Volvo. But this isn't where she is now. For now, all she has are these orchards of children to tend.

Dad is still falling. 'More me than you, if we're talking disappointment. I can't think that I achieved anything at all really,' he says, his tone sinking. She wants to catch him but isn't quite sure how. All she can think of is him standing alone in the crematorium, left to suffer his wife's funeral alone. *Municipal,* this the word that keeps coming back to her. No rite or ritual. A quick disposal. No measure of a life, no proper marking of a death. Some council jobsworth making sure regulations were being followed, even as Dad broke down with no one to comfort him, even as she sat obediently in this flat on this very sofa while her mother was... processed. Twenty minutes and done. Next.

She wants to feel the weight of a body, the heat of tears, things beyond language that a telephone has no power to transmit. But it's all just air, and she tips backwards herself, back to when she'd call and both would be gathered around the handset, these brief conversations an exercise in the dramatic tension of their marriage. Books vs The Book, and her now a complex alloy of both. Liturgy her first literature, Common Prayer her first poems, weaned on the idea that words could save. Then Mum working to lean things the other way, quietly placing *Of Mice and Men* by her bed. The moment of conversion is clear even now, her own private reformation through *Jude the Obscure.* She must have been thirteen years old, spread on the old sofa in the sitting room, Dad out at another meeting, bored enough with whatever rubbish her teacher had set to pick up the Hardy Mum had happened to leave lying around.

No more church, she'd announced to Dad over breakfast the night after she'd finished it, no more being the awkward vicar's daughter at Girl Guides. Mum's influence grew, the beginning of a different crusade, English at university, to London for teacher training, determining to join a tough school where lives could be changed.

She fingers the hole in her tights again, then sits up more straight. 'Don't say that Dad,' she tells him in an attempt at comfort. 'You did wonderful things.' She pictures him hunched over the phone, identical to the man she'd grown up with, but with so much of the air sucked out.

'You are the one doing wonderful things,' he says quietly. 'You make us both very proud.'

Yes, she thinks, more of this man in her DNA than she'd like to admit. His bloody-minded commitment to working for other people, breaking his back for small change, a slave to hopes so rarely delivered on. A poem hangs in his study: *here once on an evening like this, a preacher caught fire and burned steadily before them.* 'Sometimes you just keep labouring faithfully and the air moves and something happens.' Words she recalls from one of his better sermons. Sometimes the curtain tears and the air crackles. Just occasionally, after years of nothing, after so much hard graft, something pierces the everyday. The bush bursts into flame. The near-broken mule finds itself carrying a girl, the girl carrying a child, a child who will change things. Far from home, a humble donkey does its part, labours on and does not give up, finds itself embroiled in a miracle.

She closes her eyes and renews her vows. Yes, she thinks, even in the face of all this, I must keep serving.

He thanks her again for calling, then says he should go; she says she's tired, doesn't mention that she's also a little drunk. They send each other love.

She gets up and goes to the kitchen, pauses to think if she should but takes out a fresh glass anyway, opens the fridge and pours what wine is left, taking it back into the lounge, the chill of it, the warmth it spreading. She passes the glazed beast on her return, hooves stood flat to the earth, head bowed.

With porcelain steadfastness, through all this isolation the balloon girl in her bedroom has watched her wake before dawn, rising to refill her glass, checking her phone, that sole picture of her and Mum and Ben together, taken by Dad at Christmas, a walk together up to the beacon. She has watched Jo break again and again, break and pull herself back together, hardening a little each time.

She takes a gulp of wine. So much to do before half term, things she wants to have achieved for these children before her goodbye to Mum. So much that is harder now: covered faces, distances kept. She must find a way to keep her flesh soft, to hold all of them even if it must be from afar.

Not all though. Sometimes a child *is* lost. Pain grabs at her face and she draws her knees up as if to push back a thought, scrunches at her hair to stop it taking its form, insists on another in its place: redemption. Darren is gone and there's nothing she can do about that. But now she has Sami.

The wine rushes from an empty stomach through empty veins, inflating earnest claims about great expectations fulfilled and life chances transformed. She still has not eaten, is running on fumes, has a weekend ahead to do planning but wants to begin now. She pulls out her copy of Dickens, tucks the book under her arm and takes it with her to her bed, sitting atop it like a carpet that will bear her up, propping up all her pillows and pulling the whole mass of the duvet around her, enjoying the warmth of her body as she takes a red pen from the bedside table and begins rifling through the pages, drawing new blood under newly resonant lines, sketching out lesson plans in her head, drunkenly declaring to her mother's *Girl with Balloons* that she will carry these children and deliver. The girl looks back at her, watching, and says nothing.

7

Year 13 ease their way to Jo's room. They ride through the swinging bags on the corridor, the dashing kids making a mockery of bubbles, the brawls and catcalls, rolling with relaxed gait. 'Calm,' Mo and Rasheed reply when they come through her door and are asked how they're doing, *caaaaaalm*. They are now in the final year of Sixth Form, and although this means huge pressure after a whole term virtually wiped out and complete uncertainty about how they are going to acquire grades come summer, it still means constant attention given to remaining coolly above the churning waters of the rest of Cromwell below them. They pull out heavily decorated folders and lay them on their desks, pens and notepads following.

A part of Jo wishes she were in this class rather than teaching it, youth's elixir, still potent. She tries to mirror their relaxed attitude, but this morning's tube had been feeling particularly pandemic-hit, and made everything more of a struggle since. The ageing carriage had stood motionless, couplings creaking, no one speaking, everyone straining their collective minds, trying to push this bloody train on with the power of thought alone, thumbs flicking angrily at screens, sighs and curses muttered under breath. No time to print everything she's prepped for Sami's group later, but she has a free period after her Sixth Form so can do it then.

For now, she tries — as Year 13 would say — to 'style it out.' She takes a moment, pretends she needs something from by the window and looks for the bench out beyond the perimeter. Reminding. Drawing fuel. 'Morning,' she says brightly as she hears the door and sees Femi walk in.

'Hey,' Femi says, looking pleased. 'Good weekend?'

Truth was she'd woken on Saturday with no plans at all. She'd taken time making a proper coffee but each thing in the flat had ached with quiet, no more so than the phone which followed her around, a small black rectangle of longing. But nobody had been in touch. No body. No touch. So she'd sat and tried to make better sense of her energetic scrawls about Dickens from the night before. Alex wanted fast-food quotes that they could slide easily into plastic essays, stock arguments that were vague enough to add a little bulk to pretty much any question. She wanted to give them something more, go for actual understanding, genuine passion for the themes, but she wasn't sure that she had the energy to prep full gourmet from scratch. Her own scant cupboards didn't help the situation, and she'd been about to relent and get a pizza biked over when her phone had jumped into life. Sally. Going out to meet Maria and the new baby. Did she want to come? She'd tried not to sound too desperate, to scream YES too loudly.

She tells Femi it was great.

Anya sweeps through the door, plonks her leather bag down and apologises for being late. Despite living in a different world, a large townhouse not far beyond the Green Man, her parents had sent her here, fervently believing in supporting the most local school. Champagne socialists, or whatever the term is now that everybody drinks prosecco. With her settled, they are ready to begin.

Jo takes a deep breath because she knows that there is now a moment, one she'd turned over in her head as she'd waited for the train to move, reminding herself that audience is everything, that these kids more than anyone understood different share settings for different groups, telling herself that they will be adults soon and deserve to be treated as such.

They are fussing with stationery and swapping stories of the holidays, Anya holding back a little, her deep, lithe tan noted but not discussed.

Trust. She has to trust them, so she stands up, waits for Mo to quieten. They shuffle a little, then lend her their ears.

'I want to apologise for not being very present during lockdown.' A ripple of movement, arranging themselves to get comfortable. Anya clears her throat. 'Perhaps you heard, but if you hadn't, just before it started...'

She so nearly stumbles here, has to breathe in sharply, wonders how so few words can take so much air to speak.

'...just before it started my mum fell ill, and...'

She doesn't quite make it, has to pause a moment, and they look down respectfully, carefully inspect the tops of their desks and the stickers on their folders. This was the beauty of Sixth Form teaching, she had always thought, this possibility of slightly blurring the boundaries, them seeing their teacher as someone who could be included in their world, and her reciprocating and treating them like adults able to bear the weight of heavy words, of the truth told plain, not lightened by allusion.

'and sadly she...'

Talk of "battles" had been banned. Even as she had worsened Mum had insisted on being exacting with language, that metaphors of fighting were stupid.

In a rush of words, she now lets them have it.

'...sadly she was found to have an incurable cancer, and passed away at the beginning of April.'

They are in the last year of A-Level English. Students of language, but there are no words for this. Jo looks down at the floor, turns a pen over in her clutched hands. She has spun the bottle; the truth always a dare, honesty always a risk, but she wanted them to know, knew it would be impossible — even though they must already know — to carry on without them knowing, disingenuous, a fiction of entirely the wrong sort.

In the short silence she can't help wonder, having rejected talk of "battling," whether her use of "passed away" should go unchallenged, whether it adequately captured seeing your mother worsen by the hour, curling up in gut-tearing agony but then being ushered away, told that you were not allowed to be with her, would not be there to hold her hand as she died or even to be at her funeral. When she'd first gone into hospital Jo had read to her from *Jude* and *Precious Bane*, thinking that, in some reverse osmosis, she might build her strength with power from the same pages that her mum had once fed her. But they seemed to offer nothing in this world, and as the tides of pain had surged and swelled, more and more she'd wanted only widening passages of quiet.

But this cannot be said. This baggage cannot be unloaded here. She wants the class to see the heavy load that she has carried, but they are children and she must hide the true hideous weight of it.

'I'm so sorry,' Femi says, and there is a murmur that builds in support.

That is enough now. No, she is not one of them. She is their teacher. 'Thank you,' she says, gathering herself.

'You're alright Miss,' Rasheed says, raising a paw in acknowledgement, and something about this casual signal cracks them all into laughter.

'Oh my god Rash,' Femi says.

'What?' he laughs. 'What? She is! She's alright man, what's so funny?'

The moment is beautifully broken, a sign that no more need be said, that words can now return.

'So, *Howards End*,' she says, settling them down. 'I trust that all the reading has been done?' She turns to Femi first. She knows she will have. She confirms that she has, and the rest of the group roll their eyes and put their rather less-thumbed copies of *Howards End* on top of their stuff.

'Miss man,' Mo says, 'seriously, why did you even ask?'

'Yeah,' Rasheed chips in, looking up from his phone, 'it's Mo you should be asking.' And Mo protests and says no, he swears down, he did actually read it.

'Most of it.' He pauses, smiles bashfully. 'Some of it.'

Jo winks at him and turns it back round. 'Rasheed, perhaps when you've pulled your attention away from your phone you could enlighten us with the book's major themes and motifs?'

'His corporeal patronus is a smartphone,' Femi says witheringly, a full Potter super-fan, for which Jo likes to take some credit.

Rasheed rises in protest as he slips the screen into his pocket. 'Sorry Miss, but I swear it's your fault! Your generation gave us this brain crack!'

All of them are nodding in agreement. '*My* generation?' she asks in mock offence. 'You're saying I'm old enough to have a kid your age?'

'Round the Tower you are,' Mo quips. 'Could be a granny already, no word of a lie.'

Laughter from everyone as she drags them back to Forster. 'So Rasheed, in the depths of your six-month digital lockdown bender, did you rouse yourself at all to read the book?'

'Yes Miss, I did. I did. Now see this.' And he opens his folder and turns to a page of biro-scribbled notes, produced at God knows what speed.

'SPARK NOTES,' Mo coughs, and Femi looks over Rasheed's broad shoulder and says she recognises it more as Wikipedia's work.

He pulls it away from their view, theatrically clears his throat. 'Leonard Bast,' he announces, poking his finger into the page. 'That dude. Social mobility.'

'Poor sod,' Anya says, and Jo jumps on this, suggesting that she wouldn't get much credit in an exam for arguing that he was a sod, but that yes, yes, Forster had made him poor. Poor, but not destitute, and Jo wants to know why.

'That would mean no drama?' Femi asks, intonation rising. Jo urges her on. 'If he was already destitute he wouldn't have anywhere to go? No place for him to fall to?' And she continues, edging forward, sentence by sentence, beautiful and captivating, this girl from the Tower explaining how Forster stands Bast right on the edge, not already fallen, but in danger of doing so.

'Excellent, excellent,' Jo tells her. There are university applications coming up fast, thoughts of warm lawns in Oxford, questions about whether it would be right for her.

Jo switches focus. 'Mo, what date are we looking at here?' And he scrabbles around in his folder before pinning down 1910. 'Meaning?'

'Just before World War 1?'

She prods them to assemble ideas, to pull them from their other subjects, establishing that this was pre-Welfare State — pre Spanish flu, Rasheed throws in — the risk of tumbling into the abyss very real, London swallowing so many, nothing needing to be added about the food bank that Jo knows has taken root on the estate over the summer. Marching back to the interactive board she writes BAST in large pixelated letters, dragging a cloud shape around it and beginning a spider diagram, 'poor' as the first leg.

'So you are half right,' she says. 'Bast was poor. But he wasn't a sod. Why?' A scope round and she sees them beginning to copy the diagram, proud of the feast of ideas she has prepared, and hungry mouths in front of her keen to devour them. 'Because he has *aspirations*,' she answers for them, the next spoonful ready, adding it to the board. 'Forster creates him, unlikely as it might seem, as a poor man who is desperate to be cultured.'

A pause for them to process, swapping coloured pens, uncapping highlighters. In the lull she touches her copy of Great Expectations, just straightens it slightly on her desk, thinks of her own narrative of elevation that she is working on. To have him in here, his desk embedded in a group of positive role models... that would be something. But this is the task: to create that ethos in *his* class, to find a way to cast that spell on Jordan and Hayley and Chanel.

Seeing that they've caught up Jo asks Anya to push further. She does this succinctly, smoothly noting how Leonard Bast's lack of cash meant he couldn't go to a concert whenever he liked, or even buy a programme when he was there, Forster contrasting this with the Schlegel sisters' easy access to everything. The rest say nothing, perhaps don't even think about it. She's part of the furniture but her confident tone is clear, the composed cadence something nurtured in a large, warm bedroom, her name probably spelt out in wooden serifed letters on her door, one of the countless tiny angels that have lifted her since birth. 'Good,' Jo says, Anya's comments not given quite as much credit as if they'd been cashed in by another.

Jo can't deny some taproot of envy at this girl. Up in Doncaster she'd been the only middle-class child in her classes too, but Anya has the looks, has the parental wealth expected to match her status. That was the clerical paradox: Jo had lived in the largest house but Dad had earned the tiniest wage. Hand-me-down clothes, heating on only as a luxury. Another jumper if you're cold, or go and chop some wood. A far cry from Notting Hill.

She asks who else wants to elaborate and moves to one side of the board, not wanting to shadow the image, stepping away from the light of the projector. Waiting for them to think, she reaches out casually to lean on the wall, but as her arm extends she realises that she's about to land her palm on the light switch, and she flinches, pulls to one side to avoid it and nearly slides into a fall. Mo sniggers, but it seems the others don't notice.

'Anyone?' Jo asks. Femi has her head down deep into her notes, and Anya doesn't look as if she wants to help. But she waits, skilfully she waits, knowing that she can't do it all for them.

Femi's pen slows and she looks up, readying an answer. But Rasheed is the one who speaks.

'You see that cat lip-synching to Kanye?'

'OH MY DAYS,' Mo hollers, his focus resilient as a candle in a hurricane.

'I mean,' Anya adds, leaning back for emphasis, throwing her pen down on her pad, 'that is literally *the* best meme I've ever seen.'

'Literally?' Jo queries in exasperation.

'*Literally.*'

'You know they changed the definition Miss?' Femi throws in. 'So...'

'I'm fairly sure I saw that, yes.' Jo rolls her eyes.

'*Man I can understand how it might be.*' Rasheed is bouncing his torso, rapping into his pen, Mo joining him in duet, '*Kinda hard to love a pussy like me.*'

Impossible to know where these distractions came from, what neural processes led to them being given priority over the *actual bloody work* they were going to be examined on.

'I was crying all night man,' Mo says. 'I swear down.'

All night? Of course he wasn't, but that's not a fight Jo could hope to win. Hyperbole the norm, exaggeration the rule. 'Focus guys, please,' she sighs, 'and try not to sing into each other's actual faces.' But Femi has stepped down, the moment gone, and before Jo can retrieve it the door has opened and Mr Henderson has come in.

'Sorry to interrupt. I just wanted to introduce myself.' A millpond of blank looks. 'The new Head of English,' he adds.

Rasheed throws Jo a face like, *who is this weirdo?*

'Really go for it this year,' he says, pumping his fist. 'I know you guys had a tough deal last year, but if we can all apply ourselves we can do something amazing. So let's get Cromwell those great grades.'

Jo masks a smile with her hand, then reaches for the sanitiser as Mo ties his face up into a quizzical expression straight out of a Jim Carrey film.

'Can I just remind you,' Alex whispers loudly to Jo as he leaves, 'about that data-grab? The monitoring for this lot?' A flick of a thumbs up to the class, pulling the door behind him.

'What the actual...?' Rasheed begins, and Jo raises eyebrows to stop him.

'Monitoring? Sounds painful,' Mo says, miming putting on a rubber glove.

'Nothing for you to worry about,' she assures them, wanting to move on, to push past this.

But Anya looks anxious. She's pushing her pen into her pad, sliding her fingers down and turning it over and pushing it in again, thud, thud, thud. 'If it's about the calculations for our grades, it sounds like we should be worrying about it.'

'God, Anya stop it, that's so annoying,' Rasheed says, grabbing the pen.

She snatches it back, but stops tapping, starts twisting it in her fingers instead.

'Mr Henderson just wants some more regular monitoring.'

'How regular? And could each result go into our calculation?'

She doesn't want to tell them, but doesn't want to lie. 'Listen. Hopefully, there won't *be* a calculation. Hopefully, you'll sit the papers as normal and it'll all be fine.'

Mo and Rasheed start another seated dance. 'F- the algorithm, f- the algorithm,' raising their fists in sync then rolling the shoulder and turning their forearms round like a mixer. A pang goes off inside her and she wants to tell them that she misses dancing, the sense of bodies close by, the rhythm and heat even though the truth is it was years back. Mo then actually says 'fuck,' and she glares at him.

'Look,' she tells them, 'It's an extraordinary situation, and a bit of a new regime with this guy on top of all that.' She hesitates, knows that they're not going to like the prescription, can't even say that she agrees with the treatment plan. 'He wants exam-style data gathered every two weeks.'

'A tracking assessment every *two weeks*?' Anya's face has fallen in horror.

Femi's rises with ire. 'As if having mocks at Christmas wasn't enough!'

'I agree,' Jo says. 'I'm with you.' She sits herself on the edge of her desk, watching as the class deflates. 'Look, personally, I'd prefer to keep off that kind of pressure for now. Who knows what this virus is going to do.' She is talking conspiratorially, setting herself on their side in blind hope of pulling the lesson back. 'I mean, if you genuinely fall in love with a book, you'll do the work anyway.' Rasheed is turning over his copy of *Howards End*, not looking as enamoured as one might hope. 'So let's try to find a way to get some data while not letting that take over.'

'Screw them,' Anya says, still looking distressed. 'Miss, you've been here longer than all of them. Why don't you just tell them we're not doing it?'

Not the time for full disclosure. She can't exactly explain that she is under caution, that a blade is hanging six inches above her neck. 'I'm afraid the pressure is coming from far higher up,' she tells them. 'Mr Henderson is set targets by Mr Jackson, who in turn has the Academy chain bosses to please, and it goes up and up and up.' Ministers crossing swords with the qualifications body. It didn't get higher than that. Anya's leg now is juddering up and down, her mind miles away, fretting, and Jo can't help wonder if any of these "bosses" were near enough to the ground to see actual children anymore, to see what they were doing to them.

'Prodded us like lab rats,' Mo adds.

'Truss,' Rasheed adds blackly. 'I do biology mate. Can't examine nothing without killing it.'

Rats, or factory-farmed geese, Jo thinks. A few months to force facts down fast, cram in knowledge regardless of what might reasonably be consumed. Any positive cases among them and the whole year will be home again for two weeks at least. So it's exam foie gras for now. Each child measured and remeasured, as if you could better fatten a goose by constantly weighing it. A few Grade A turkeys might stomach that sort of lesson, but most passed it undigested or threw the whole lot back up.

'Look, it's not how I want to do this,' she tells them. 'And I'm going to make sure that Mr Henderson is made aware of what you've said.' But they are shaking their heads, the coals of the lesson kicked over, the heat gone. She can't help but drift a little too. She looks over at Dickens, has the raw ingredients from the weekend but just an hour after this lesson to cook up something really good.

'Come on, let's get back to Forster.' Wanting to salvage something. 'Let's continue with Bast.'

'But Bast is hard,' Mo fires at Rasheed.

'Bast-hard,' he fires back in mock Indian accent.

'Hard Bast-hard,' they say together.

'Oh my goodness you two!' Jo cries.

'No time for jokes!' Anya quips sarcastically.

'No marks for humour,' Femi says drily, and this hurts the most, the possibility of losing her. Not now. Not this far along. She cannot let that happen. If she couldn't keep her on side, what hope did she have with Sami?

'Guys please, I'm serious. I'm as against this as you are.' And she sees a spark and grabs it. 'Look. With Bast, Forster is asking whether social mobility was even *possible*, whether going to all these plays and immersing himself in high London culture would lift him away from this abyss...'

But Femi stops her. 'Bast must have gone to school and sat exams?'

Jo isn't precisely sure, desperately tries to flick through her meagre Rolodex of history — The Education Act of 1944... too late... but what the hell had happened before that? — she has no idea, so she lies and confidently tells Femi that yes, Bast would have done. But Femi leaps right back at her.

'And those hadn't worked for him? Helped him up in life?'

Her brain is trying to keep up but feels like butter, soft and fat, and she can only splutter a reply, admitting that she couldn't be certain but exams probably meant more now and class had meant more then.

She remains unsatisfied, returns for more. 'Well, he can't have done that well. And no matter how much theatre he goes to now, he's still stuck, still hates his job.'

'Yeah then look at those sisters,' Mo interjects, prodding at his copy of the book. 'More cash than education, and they're alright, innit?' The timbre of the street becoming more prominent with each syllable. 'My point being, why bother Femi, why bother? You can't school this system.'

'Estate stays estate,' Rasheed says, 'Tower stays Tower,' and Jo wants to protest but knows damn well that study after study backs him up.

'People need to get out and *vote* for change, that's the basic right that we all share,' Anya announces with articulate conviction, as if beginning a town hall speech. But it's as if she's playing a local comedy club, Rasheed and Mo falling about laughing.

'Politicians... help us?!' Rasheed roars.

'OK boomer,' Mo adds, sending the rest into fits.

'Anya, your brain got furloughed or something,' Rasheed continues. 'I ain't being rude...'

But Jo jumps in, won't have it. Can't have it said. 'OK, OK, enough Rasheed. This is all good stuff, but let's keep the focus on the text.' Anya's eyes are reddening, focusing straight ahead at the board.

Jo is about to continue when the door opens and Mr Jackson pokes his head around it. Jesus, what is this? An inquisition. She flusters, doesn't know whether to push on or stop, whether he's come to see her lesson or wants something else.

'Sorry Mss Barker,' he says, blurring and stumbling somewhere between Ms and Miss, unsure of her status. He apologises for the late notice, didn't want to leave it to email, but he needs her to cover Mr Hand next lesson. Year 11 music. Geoff.

Fuck. Her prep time for Sami's lesson, stolen. But she has no option but to be obedient, to show compliance. He smiles as if knowing that this is a test. She thanks him and having given the class another tub thump about hard work and making the school proud, he leaves.

She shuts down. Visibly, physically, verbally. She brings up the slide with their essay title, tells them to get on with it and sits.

A sharp wire of anxiety tightens down her throat and through her chest, each new thought plucking it inside her. There is no time. Never enough time. She tries to rally. She stands again and says, 'OK guys, if you can get these essays done for this time next week,' but it comes out flat and she sinks to her seat.

'His back gone again?' Rasheed asks.

'His back,' Mo repeats, scare quotes with fingers.

'Less spine than a paperback, that man.'

She ought to be leaping to a colleague's defence but before she can gather the energy Anya has stepped in, saying 'that's cruel, Rasheed. Don't.'

'Yeah well you didn't do music GCSE did you?' he hits back, with venom.

No, though she did manage Grade 8 piano. One-to-one lessons and fine instruments at home. Rasheed and Anya continue to snipe at each other, but she hasn't the strength to stop them now, too many battles blowing up in her own head, this ground she was going to spend an hour landscaping, beginning to build something on it, something solid and good.

She curses under her breath. The crude notes she's scribbled at the weekend now feel like scaffolding only, the outline of a structure but no substance underneath. Onto the computer on her desk she calls up the scheme of work for inspiration, but it's all bones and no flesh. *Students should understand how Dickens uses memoir as a device at the opening of the novel to establish the main characters*. A destination, but no map, no thought given to the ruggedness of the terrain, no advice on how to help Nishaan, what to do to engage Charlie, how to persuade Hayley that this will have any bearing on her life, and certainly no recommendations for applying Dickens to a boy who might have just arrived from an active war zone.

She bites her eyes shut. Teaching as a black art, the spells more complex and nuanced than people could imagine. She needs time for typing and photocopying, yes, but it's time in her head that she craves even more, space to do the quiet contemplation, the required mental prep.

Femi fishes a ruler from her Gryffindor pencil case. Changing one person's behaviour, controlling a single person's actions: this counted as high magic at Hogwarts but, Jo thinks, she has *thirty* to tend with at once, a roomful of sluggish bodies, a different potion needed for each and every child, different incantations to bewitch, spell-bind and transfigure.

She curses again and pulls a hand violently through her hair. The class see this, say nothing but do so loudly, sniggering as they write. Mo coughs and the rest recoil, tell him he's dirty, that they'll all be home for two weeks if he doesn't cover his mouth.

A chasm opens, them on one side, her far away on the other.

'Find a way to believe in *something*, love,' her father had said to her at breakfast, the morning after she'd finished *Jude the Obscure*. She'd been deftly sweeping Marmite to the corners of her toast, telling him that she no longer shared his faith. 'That's all I ask,' his lack of anger at her heresy had surprised her. The kitchen window looked out over a small piece of scrub. Someone had dumped an oven in the far corner, the hob plates scorched black. 'The Bible or your books,' he'd laughed softly, 'it's not for me to tell you which to follow.' He'd forked some egg into his mouth then pointed the tines affectionately towards her. 'But if you're going to do some good in this world you have to believe in *something*, put your faith somewhere then be prepared to fight for it with your life.'

Yes. Whatever battle she now finds herself mired in, she had raised that standard and ridden out under it. Mum had stood quietly at the kitchen sink that morning, her back to Jo, saying nothing. A twinge of hurt at this, she realises.

Rasheed and Mo are silently miming the rap again and Jo snaps at them to belt it.

'Calm, miss. Calm.' Rasheed says, with a concerned look, and she apologises, asks him to just get on with his work.

She bites the inside of her cheek hard. Believe in something then fight with all one has. Forwards only, no retreat. And she stirs herself to pick up her weapons again — mask, pen, planner — and head to the next battle. Music. 20 synths in 12 different keys and no working headphones. *Fuck.*

8

She slips off her shoes to let her toes breathe out, front door finally shut again behind her. A large bag of exercise books relaxes and folds, looks thankful to have made it, handles stretched until the plastic has begun to whiten. A little more weight, a little further on and it would have narrowed, stiffened and snapped. Out of her heels — low and sensible enough as they are — she feels as if her feet were about to go the same way.

She washes her hands then pads to the bedroom, takes off her tights and returns in checked pyjama bottoms. Ready for bed but a long watch to go until then.

'Easy street isn't it?' Ben had ribbed on an early date. Weeks into term, months after the split, still she finds herself trying to pick over these bones, identify the place where things had gone wrong. '3:15 finish every day?'

It hadn't taken him long to grasp the truth. Another eight-hour day began once that last bell had gone. Meetings first, then marking. So before their journey here, after three days lying in quarantine, the pile of books had sat mute and untouched by her ankles while she and Cara and the newbies had laboured through Alex's agenda. Dirty tea and a packet of bourbons. Coats on, hands clasping mugs. Orders to keep windows open for ventilation. Give it a few weeks and they'd be dying of hypothermia, not the bug.

'Evidence,' he'd kept repeating, 'but where's the *evidence*?'

Cara had started laughing, shaking her head. 'So let me get this straight, you're saying that unless we can provide you with evidence for the learning we've delivered, then that learning will be considered to have not been delivered?'

He'd struggled to stay on the right side of exasperation, wanting to appear strong to his masters above him. 'But without evidence Cara, how can those above us be confident that kids are learning?'

'Trust, perhaps?' Jo had said, snapping a biscuit and brushing the crumbs from her skirt.

'Yes, OK. But at some point that trust has to be backed up. Some progress figures Jackson can show the MAT.'

'The who?' Cara asked, whip-smart.

'The Multi Academy...' he began, before realising he'd walked into it. 'yeah, OK fine, *Trust*.'

She'd let this land before ramming the point home. 'All due respect Alex, but we teach English. Behind every one of those scores you're after there's a kid with a story, one that a single number can't tell.'

'Except that everyone has just come out of an algorithm horror and we're going to need more and better data in case next summer...' He'd then stopped, decided to get to the nub. 'Look, what I'm coming to is that — in line with our sister Academies — I'm going to need everyone's lesson plans submitted two weeks in advance, and evaluations completed within a week of it being taught.' He'd turned to look at Cara. 'With evidence of progression.'

Matt and Sandra frowning, Rose wide-eyed in panic, so new they couldn't speak. Martha had looked nauseous.

Jo hadn't wanted to do anything to wind Alex up, but this was ridiculous. 'How can I write a plan for two weeks from now when there's five lessons of Jordan and Michael and Charlie kicking off before then, and who knows how many kids off isolating? It's not an industrial process. Lessons evolve and adapt.'

'Easy there Alex,' Cara had warned. 'None of us mind working hard, but you want to at least feel you're doing stuff that actually helps the kids. And this... this...'

'Bottom line,' he says, 'we *have* to raise standards.'

Jo sees battle flags, mounted and lifted by columns of riders, declarations of allegiance. *Put your faith somewhere then be prepared to fight for it.* A crusade, Jackson had called it at the beginning of term, "a crusade to raise standards." Ask the Syrians, she thinks, ask Sami's family how that turned out.

Cara's opposition had faded, and Alex had pushed exemplar lesson plans and evaluation forms around, his silence only affirming that this was immutable, a word from on high. Jackson had found a young officer who wouldn't answer back.

Jo had bitten into her lip doing grim calculations in her head looking for efficiencies in her day to be able to fit this in. Whichever way she totted it, sleep was where the savings had to be made.

But Cara had rallied again once she'd started reading, saying it was an f-ing joke, prodding pages of the documents, asking how anyone could need a health and safety assessment for every single English lesson. 'Oh wait, and before you get to any actual planning, first you'll need to explain how you're sterilising each surface, cleaning each resource, respecting social distancing and ensuring adequate ventilation — oh, that's before you get to the boxes on promoting fundamental British values, being vigilant to extremism, watching out for safeguarding concerns, flagging potential careers links, not forgetting the list of keywords, the split-screen objectives and all the different questioning strategies you're going to use, differentiated for each ability range. Jesus, Alex. It'll take two weeks just to produce *one* of these.'

But he'd sucked it up and, everyone aware of the time ticking away, she had eventually surrendered. The meeting had broken up, Jo saying quietly to Cara, 'I feel sick, I literally have no idea where to start,' Cara too angry, too shell-shocked to respond, both knowing already that the only answer would be earlier mornings, shorter lunch breaks, later evenings. So rather than move towards home with the bag of books, Jo had sat shivering as she'd hammered on her computer for an hour, doing as she was told, listening to the cleaners finishing up around her, wiping the door handles and light switches, running cloths over window openers that'd been broken for years.

Now the Year 11 books wait quietly while she heats up a bit of pasta and throws in a half-jar of sauce. Munch something quickly then pour a small glass of wine. Insist it'll just be one. Find an excuse to add another drop. That won't be hard. After a full day of lessons, after a meeting to inform her that she's *still* not doing enough, after all of this she has brought twenty-five children back to her flat because... because, she keeps telling herself, they have been through a terrible time and she must to do her best for them. Try to catch them up on time lost. And marking is the nappy change of teaching: a shit job but if you care about the kids... well it's got to be done. She hears her Dad's voice. *Your Father, who sees what is done in secret, will reward you.* Education too much like religion: always somebody bloody watching. Constant observation, higher powers making impossible demands. Demands like the Cromwell marking code. Green pen for positive comments. Switch to red for critique. Underlining errors, annotate with the correct acronym. Guidance for improvement. Back to the student to write a reflective response, in purple. Back to her. Blue pen to mark their marking. Record the grades and effort scores in a spreadsheet. Rank them. Format them. Share them. She has a contract somewhere, but it won't mention that the only way to even attempt to fulfil her role will be to work every evening and most of the weekend, and all that before every time things are given back and forth they're meant to sit for seventy-two hours. It can't be done. It'll fall apart.

She pours a second glass, closes her eyes for a second, wanting silence, nothing more than silence. She thinks back to the rare evenings when her own homework was done and Dad was back early from a meeting, the three of them might play canasta or mah-jong. Shuffling, dealing, trying to re-establish order, a world contained on a card table where chaos could be pushed for an hour before bed, her father so keen and attentive, as if the fight genuinely had meaning, his minor victories some parallel in life's labours.

But she can't daydream. Can't put it off, not without having to pay double another evening. She's got to mark the stuff handed in by Sami's class after their lesson last week. In truth she is intrigued because it had been a bit odd. The music cover preceding it had been a disaster, them refusing to follow instructions, talking, talking, talking, her struggling to find anything to hook them with and grab their attention. And as for the Year 11 lesson coming afterwards, well Jackson had robbed her of her prep time so if it had gone a bit wrong then Jo just needed to forget about it. But rushing up to meet them she'd unlocked her door, asked Year 11 to sit and be quiet and for some reason, for no reason she could divine, they'd pretty much done that. Perhaps each had just had their own reasons to be a little subdued, to not be in the mood to mess about, minds may be on something else, some girl, some guy, some message. Perhaps Jordan and Michael and some of the others were just stoned. Bug-eyed. A quick joint between lessons. She knows that it happens, that people have reasons for not clamping down. There's a global pandemic. Didn't everyone need something?

'Right,' she'd said as they'd waited quietly for her instructions, 'we're going to do some reading aloud,' and when she'd asked Charlie to start, the class had opened their books and he'd begun.

My father's family name being Pirrip, and my Christian name Philip, my infant tongue could make of both names nothing longer or more explicit than Pip.

Each taking a couple of sentences, the pace so slow they'd be in their graves before they finished it, but this determined look on Jo's face: no matter how many mumbles and stumbles, they were London kids and were going to read a bit of this London story to each other.

I give Pirrip as my father's family name, on the authority of his tombstone. As I never saw my father or my mother...

And it had been beautiful, Nourin's Pakistani lilt bumping into Michael's Caribbean, Nishaan straining and squinting at each word, but the class giving him time because they knew, they'd grown up with him. Jakob's Polish then taking over from him and taking it somewhere else, Jo's heart soaring as the symphony grew, Danny's proper East End coming in and everyone taking a moment to work out what country he'd come from before realising, tongues tumbling around happily in the same drum but all the colours still their own.

'Sami,' she'd said, his turn come round. 'Sami, can you carry on?' But he wouldn't, a tiny shake of the head.

He'd been in the music cover lesson too. It was a room full of kids Jo didn't know, and he'd got lost on the way, or so he'd said. Geoff's computer hadn't seemed to work so she'd paid out the network cable until she'd found the end crushed and broken. No connection, and not a cubic inch of quiet headspace to do any planning. Giving up, she'd sat with Sami and tried to help him with the introduction to Dickens.

A surge in volume from the squabbling rest. 'We're trying to have a conversation here, and I can't hear a word.' Sami had looked out nervously, one kid shouting back that it was a music lesson, not a library. Jo had told Sami to ignore them, but he'd wriggled uncomfortably. Someone had hit the demo button on their keyboard, and Sami had smiled, become lost for a moment. 'Chopin,' he'd said quietly to Jo. 'First nocturne. Mum used to play it.' An electronic beat had taken over, then a ball of paper had arced into view and hit him on the head. He'd pulled his head into his shoulders and withdrawn for the rest of the lesson.

So it was a bit of a gamble then asking him to read in her lesson, but she'd been disappointed nonetheless. If it had been Jordan she'd have pushed it, told him not to worry about slipping up. But Jordan seemed robust in a way that even Darren hadn't been, and Sami seemed less so. So she'd let it go, asking Chanel to take over, Ade muttering 'k's sake man, even Nish did it,' Jo shaking her head and glaring at him, catching others staring into Sami's back, Jo wondering if she should have forced him. Chanel had then got to the bit about

Pip begging for his throat not to be cut, which drew eyes down again, fingers following the lines.

'Once more,' said the man, staring at me. 'Give it mouth!'

And at this Danny had begun to screech. 'Oh my DAYS,' he'd shouted, 'I didn't know this was going to be so sick,' Nelson poking Chanel in the back asking her to give it mouth, her telling him to f-off, get his dutty hands off her, get two metres, Jo flushing, trying to stamp out the twenty different fires that had spontaneously combusted, shouting 'quiet!' but knowing that they were fifteen and could find innuendo on the back of a crisp packet.

'Miss man, I thought you said we'd be watching a film,' Charlie had moaned as she'd fought to settle them. A chorus of agreement rose.

'*Excerpts* of the film Charlie. And no, not this lesson. Soon. Perhaps. It depends on how you get on with the written work first,' She'd typed the homework onto the board. 'Dickens writes Great Expectations like a memoir,' her reading it aloud as she wrote, just so they had no excuses. 'Imagine you are much older, looking back at your beginnings.'

A descriptive piece, like Dickens, exploring their origins. Talk about homes and families, she'd told them, the raw materials of what had made them *them*. A none-too-subtle gift for Sami. 'Finish for homework,' she'd announced.

So this is what she has to wade through this evening. She pulls out her rainbow pack of pens, takes down a heavy slug and brings the first child up onto her lap.

If she has brought them home, they have brought their homes to her too. Here is Chanel's book, a heady hit of coconut hair products, a single grain of coloured rice hiding in the page fold, a piece of glitter that won't shift. In tiny writing, angled on a curled corner, someone has scribbled the word FANNY. Elsewhere, multiple hearts flutter around a name that has been crossed out. Among this, the bare bones of what Jo had asked for, Chanel looking back from the future, writing of pride in her father and her older sister, all she has learned from sharing care for her mother. She is a lawyer now, big cases and a big car. Fresh air, windows she can open wide. She ends with an emoji, a visual shortcut. A tiny picture worth — well, Jo estimates, her pen hanging over the page — perhaps somewhat less than a thousand words.

Charlie's turn next, whose home must be doing sixty a day. His book opens with an acrid bloom, pages crisp white but their edges already ashen. She finds a few lines only, broken sentences, the plump bulk of paragraphs ditched for lean points made in bullets. He has become a professional footballer, playing for Chelsea. A deep sigh at this, another draft of wine, his dream so ubiquitous it hardly took imagination to have it, so fantastical it made Pip's tale seem mundane. She doesn't want to put a tick, doesn't want to affirm this nonsense, opts for a violent double question mark instead, suggesting 'more detail and explanation needed,' saying something stronger under her breath as she writes. None of them any idea what it really took, the years of graft, the endless journeys to far-flung matches. No concept that it wasn't like winning the Lottery, some mysterious bloke turning up one week and offering them a contract.

"Looking back," he has as a subtitle, writing underneath it "I would thank the youth club." The youth club that no longer exists. The youth club that the council shut last year, the council that's now going to be so crippled with debt for years to come they'll be lucky to get streetlights and emptied bins. WWW Jo scribbles in green below this — *What Went Well* — and congratulates him on getting the basic idea. EBI, she added, switching to red — *Even Better If* — and has to pause, irritable, needled at the fag smoke and the bare ash of the tiny fire he's made of the task, wondering when he might lift his gaze long enough and high enough to see that you don't simply walk out of the Tower and into a footballer's penthouse, that life was a continuous line of one thing leading to another, desired effects having to be caused, causes always needing more work than choosing 6 numbers or rolling up to an audition on X-Factor. But Jo bottles this up, swallows it down, pours another glass and writes YOU WOULD GET MORE OUT OF THIS IF YOU PUT A LOT MORE WORK IN, closing the book and tossing it to the floor.

She wants Sami now, feels ready, so digs through until she finds him, pulls him onto her knees. She flicks through, past the first fill-in worksheet hanging loosely at the front, past the context sheet she'd given them, past the few lines produced in the music lesson — lines that peter out into nothing — Jo feeling for a heavier page further on, dense with ink, a detailed carving in biro.

She'd asked him to stay back after the lesson when he'd refused to read aloud, Jordan and Michael giving him a stare as they had left. He'd been narrow-eyed, Jo telling him not to worry, that it was fine if he didn't feel confident reading in class yet, apologising for putting him on the spot. 'Focus on getting something into your book,' she'd said. Not public, just between the two of them. There had been a loud burst of laughter from outside the door, him spying it anxiously, and Jo had tried to ask him how things were, how he was, if there'd been more trouble, looking him over for signs. He'd inspected the floor, said he had another lesson to get to. 'But look,' she'd told him, 'look, let's find another time,' and he'd begun to move. 'Remember Pip,' she'd called after him. He'd actually stopped and looked at her then. 'Remember Pip when you do the homework.' He'd turned, nervously looked both ways before pushing into the corridor.

Courage, she thinks now, it will take courage to start writing about his past. She gets past the opening pages and turns to find a half-page doodle, more than that to be fair, an intricate drawing of a peach, a sketch looking out from under laden vines, out over thick orchards, what could be olive groves, a far-off house with a hill beyond, land and space. Underneath, in the same faint pencil, letters curving in crude script.

In the future, I would like this.

Lines left, as if he might come back and expand on it. But he hasn't. Just empty space, then:

Go back.

Next to it a fleshy stain, a map of an island formed from a dried spill of juice.

She looks over his drawing, this longing for land and fruit. Green pen, she adds a smiley face.

The other books wait, patiently at first then more restless as she scans the drawing and his brief lines over again, thinking back to the bench, re-running the commitment she has made.

She acknowledges her disappointment, tells herself that she shouldn't expect too much so soon. She works up a positive comment, nothing too heavy, writes, *well done Sami, an encouraging start, but SEE ME.*

Yes, they should meet again. It can be hard to express things on paper or read aloud in class. Hopefully, she can coax his voice out of him. She snaps his book shut, casts him aside and moves on.

Pungent, a roach-sized rectangle ripped out of the back cover, a scorch mark on the front, Nelson is up next. He's written about the same amount, but what excuse could he have? Perhaps she hadn't explained the task clearly enough, given enough of a steer or set appropriate expectations? In the crease of the open page, there are green flecks of weed and she doesn't know whether to brush them away and pretend she hasn't noticed, or confront him about the fact that she's found a controlled substance in his book and ask what's going on. Her pen hovers, wine coursing, all the different inks pressing, knowing that it isn't her place to judge him, not in the current climate, only to mark his work. When Ofsted said a teacher was "good" they didn't mean like Jesus. But perhaps I should comment, she thinks, care less about the work and more about the poor choices he might be making. She breathes out, pulls back, stands up. This was the abyss: a single book opens and you could dive eternally down into a child's life, never reach the end of the corrections.

She stretches, reaches under her top and takes off her bra, scratches under her breasts then goes to the bedroom to change into her pyjama top and dressing gown. Back in the living room, she scrolls through her feed for a quick change of air. More baby photos from Maria. Sally wishing her darling husband a happy birthday. She hovers over the search box then stops herself, flicks instead through her messages, pausing on Sally as if trying to find a reason to call her. No. She mustn't. Not on his birthday. Work quicker. Stay in the shallows.

An hour later and her brain is smoked, hardly able to tell one child from the next as the tired parade of futures moves slowly past. Actresses. Singers. Sports stars. Successful in things they've barely shown competence at yet, and all in a climate where everything was fucked. But she had given them Dickens, set them this homework. These are their expectations, and if they are great and hopelessly improbable then they only reflect the original tale: a criminal deciding that a barely-educated child should be plucked from obscurity, removed from his impoverished existence and be turned into an aristocrat. Maybe it's not that their dreams that are too grand, but that hers are too small.

She is in bed with the last of them, Jordan. Like her, he's a minister's kid, but if Jo is the dutiful elder, he has chosen the path of the prodigal, his undoubted talents mostly buried under rebellious bravado.

'That is peng,' he'd said last year, getting the same test back that had started Darren's descent.

'I'd be more minded to congratulate you if you'd not sabotaged other people's chances,' Jo had told him. Wisecracks, interruptions, petty fights, occasional flares of aggression — and then sparks of incredible work. This was why she'd rather focus on Sami rather than him. Jordan already had all he needed.

'Don't lie Miss. You love it,' he'd told her with his cheeky look.

She didn't, but the rest of the class did. The kind of charisma you couldn't pray into a child. If he ever did convert he'd fill his father's mantle easily.

She expects little, a few gruff words perhaps, another rapper on the cusp of a breakthrough. Instead, she finds a dense page, the script all cursive tags and mostly caps, but the style belying considerable substance. London has collapsed, apocalyptic fires burn, the banks upped and gone, yet Jordan has learned to survive and now looks back, remembering the night he first had to hunt for food, leading a group around the Tower, cornering their prey.

So typical of him, he sets this up then, at the bottom of the page he stops mid-paragraph and takes it no further. Jo turns over, searches through, but there's nothing more. She pushes the book off the bed in irritation and closes her eyes. So many things she could write, this infuriating younger brother, but she knows better than to express it now, not with the wine as diminished as it is, not with the time as late as it is.

She is tired. Exhaustion has got in through the skin, is pushing through muscle and pressing at bone. Now she needs to sleep but worries it won't come because her mind is sparking. She looks jealously at the books, teenagers able to crash anywhere, anytime, falling deeply into that other world then able to wake and not worry about having to get somewhere. She'll likely end up worrying about their grades more than some of them will.

Her body slides down the last few inches to horizontal, her head onto the stack of pillows. Eyes shut. Eyes open. All these expectations still swimming. If they are allowed absurd hopes then why isn't she? But if she's serious about better things then she should cleanse, should brush, should do everything just in case she still has dreams to come. She doesn't want to move but the girl with her balloons fixes her with a hard china stare that says she must. So she kicks off the duvet, alert to the danger of becoming a still life, her evenings like paintings, her whole flat these last months a tragic diorama and her stuck in it, wondering if this could still be *called* a life.

She drags herself to the bathroom and takes out her wipes and remover and washes and scrubs and rubs-in serums and creams. No, she tells herself, I am not done yet. Still a chance out there for her if she'll put in the effort and take it. She inspects her cheeks and holds her behind as if weighing, measuring, calculating her odds and the time she still might have, kicking the books to one side as she climbs back into bed, rubbing her stomach before wrapping herself in linen, praying for the night to take her down entirely.

9

It is World Book Day, and everyone is allowed to come to school dressed as their favourite characters. If there were literary versions of *Scary Movie* or *Frozen* Jo must have missed them, but she lets it go, thankful for what enthusiasm there is. A few have come in full hazmat suits and are pretending to clean up a chemical spillage out the back of the DT labs, though each time she thinks about it she's less sure. Every day is a kind of Halloween. Washed so often, her own hands are turning Voldemort again.

Cara has dressed as the young woman from The Hunger Games. Jo had got up early, vacillated between Bridget Jones and Miss Trunchbull but — worried that the references might get lost — plumped for Alice in Wonderland instead. Alex suggests that she could have made more of an effort to get the hair right and asks her for another sample of her marking, switching her into a very modern adaptation, sweary Alice with bloody hands.

She sees a Wimpy Kid being chased down the corridor by Darth Vader, then Femi dressed as Hermione. 'You look great,' Jo tells her. Always that pang of worry for the father. A simple dentist, a man with a solid profession, his magical daughter lost to another world, one he cannot see or ever hope to understand.

Vader has tripped the kid, and they are brawling on the floor, laughing. If the helmet does its job they'll be safe from infection. A few real predators, yes, but most are sheep in wolves' clothing, modern crustaceans, their hardness on the outside, protecting soft innards. Here is Nishaan in full Storm Trooper outfit, scuttling between lessons, people laughing and banging on his helmet as he passes. Then there is Sami. As Femi heads off to lessons Jo glimpses him far off across the ground floor foyer, uncostumed. She hurries along to catch him.

'Hello Sami.' He stops, stands by a wall.

'Hello Miss.' He smiles then bows his head.

'What have you come as today?' No reply to this. 'A closed book?' Her joke falls flat, so she steps over it. 'I wanted to talk to you about your Dickens homework.' She's looked through it again, the scribbled sketch, searching for some long-form written work that she might have missed.

Her teenage schoolbooks had always been pristine of course, nothing in them or her report cards that could be cause for worry. Handled with such manners even her rejection of religion hadn't really given her father any cause for complaint. Plus, she seemed to have heeded his advice, throwing herself into an evangelical faith in literature. He'd run his fingers down the new spines that Mum brought home for her. 'Good for you,' he'd say each time Jo burned through another classic, his silly hit of praise the high she yearned for, her nose already in the next, snorting up line after line. Even now she finds it hard to understand why everyone isn't equally addicted, why the whole class hadn't written pages and pages.

'Mmm?' Sami is already edging to go.

'Were the instructions for the homework clear enough?' From two metres the words slow and lose power, bounce harmlessly back, no visible effect. She wants to break through and shake him, tell him that if she's going to help him get this GCSE pass she needs him to play his part too. 'Come on Sami!' she says, attempting to inject some energy and he mumbles an apology.

'Listen, I'm sorry too,' she tells him with a sigh, opening up space for confession. She wonders if he knows who she's come as, whether a Disney-blue dress and white apron mean anything. Perhaps it isn't important. 'Have you had any more trouble from those boys?'

A shrug, and the slightest shake of the head, a furtive glance around at who may be watching.

'You can't just let it carry on. You need to speak up.' White stockings, black shoes. Oh God, she thinks, maybe he doesn't realise that I've dressed up. 'I'm Alice, by the way,' she explains, wanting to clarify and to lift the mood. 'From Alice in Wonderland. It's...' But she's not really sure *what* it is, only that it's not the rabbit hole to be disappearing down now. 'Anyway,' she continues, 'let's talk about this next lesson. I just wanted a little more in that homework.' He still says nothing, so she decides to leave it, to let him go. 'But it would be good to hear you speak up,' she says, finishing. 'Read something aloud, offer some opinions? There are marks for that that I can give you. It all helps.'

'OK,' he says impatiently, twists his head, turns and dives into the crowd.

That night she sits curled on her sofa, the black plastic of a microwaved curry hollowed out on the low table in front of her. Half a dozen future lessons have been divined and submitted, but the books she needs to keep on top of are only half done. Book day had felt like one of those zombie re-writes. Ashen faces, protective gear. The Hate U Give, but without the warmth. Ruby Redfort with all the colour drained. Cara joked that all the antiviral spray was slowly killing them, but it basically was. Bleached. Blitzed. The grind of all this on top of everything else. The anxious wiping down. The constant fear of contamination. The support of colleagues pushed out of reach, while children continued to jump on one another, kick and hug and sing, throw arms around and fists in, masks casually around their chins, zero fucks given that this meant she was too scared to visit her Dad.

She gives up, holds a cushion against herself, closes her eyes and holds her breath. No. She can't stop yet. Change tack. See how Dad is, see if she can cheer him up on the phone, even if a visit is still out of the question.

But when she calls him any cheer she gives appears to leave her overdrawn. Phone tucked into her shoulder he is happily saying something about his day while she makes dutiful encouraging noises, eyes meandering along her bookshelves. Thousands of characters between all these covers. Another job to do at half term, winnow out the chaff. There's plenty here she could get rid of. Her eye stops on *Touching the Void*. How has she not seen that before? She pulls it off the shelf and opens it. No sign that it is actually Ben's, though it certainly isn't hers. She goes to put it back then stops, places it on the table, reaches forward again and turns it over, dog-eared cover face down. The others around it breathe out and fill the narrow slit on the shelf.

Too tired to stop her thoughts running downhill, before she can pull up she has Ben discarding her like a book he was done with. A professional hazard: always a new metaphor ready to pounce.

The woman with the balloons whispers. *The story had taken a difficult turn. The mother starts dying, and he is no longer into it.* The End. His hands probably running down other jackets by now, she thinks. Some lean thriller. Bookseller's descriptions pile in to mock. Clean. Tight. No tears. Not too old. No crumple or droop.

Sensing distance her father probes and she reins her mind back in and apologises. 'Sorry, Dad. I'm just a bit worn out.' She's not even sure what he was saying and is embarrassed now to ask.

'You still missing Ben?'

God, she thinks, how does he do it? 'A bit I suppose,' she tells him, then apologises again. 'Yes. I don't know. Sometimes.'

'In the evenings,' he says gently, and her heart breaks a little more, reminded that he's the one they should be focusing on. But before she can move to comfort him, he's trying to do the same for her. 'You'll find someone else.'

Love in the Time of Covid. Fat chance.

Of course she misses Ben, a bit. But what she really misses most is the idea of him. He was a badge, an epaulette: with a man on her arm she felt her mother react differently. Not that she would have said that she loved her daughter less when she wasn't in a relationship — quite the opposite, she would have argued, she loved her so much that she wanted the fullness of life for her. But try as she might, Jo never experienced it that way. The loss of Ben coinciding with the mess with Darren just meant two black marks against her, two disappointments, two slips she would have to recover to regain her mother's approval. It is bollocks, she knows it is all bollocks, but it's bollocks that she doesn't know how to resolve. She never got to hold mum's hand, hear her tell her not to be so silly, never got that moment of acceptance, unconditional, never even got to stand by a cheap coffin in a council crematorium and make peace with all that hadn't yet been said.

But the world is huge and so many are still suffering. She has so much more than so many others. A bleak mid-winter coming, the radio keeps reminding them all. *If I were a shepherd, I would bring a lamb.* But she is a teacher and what she owes now, what she does have to give is her unrelenting hard work. She bites hard into the skin above her thumb.

'I'm OK, Dad,' she assures him and digs up from somewhere a cheery tone. 'It's just going to take time. Plus, it's you I'm worried about, not me.'

She reaches to the side, takes another book off her shelf — *Precious Bane* — and flicks through the pages.

'Oh goodness,' he scoffs. 'Don't do that.' More comfortable being the minister, with the focus on him he starts flapping, pushing words out to fend off the attention. 'At the end of the day,' he tells her, 'the best thing we can both do,' stopping, unsure, like a man suddenly asked to give a vote of thanks, 'well, all one can do is try to keep being loving.' Jo realises that he's trying to reference St Paul but his voice is more the clanging cymbal, rambling, snatching at what he can remember. 'When I was a child,' he says, then fades, struggling with the rest. But she knows how it goes: when you were a child, you were a child, but now that you are a woman childish fantasies should be put behind you. Like the privilege of being loved, having someone who will see the true you, face to face.

This is why people create gods, she thinks, to have a perfect being who will love them, always, even when they are ugly, harelipped and broken. She slams *Precious Bane* back into the case.

'You're right Dad,' she tells him. 'At least, I hope you are.'

He doesn't respond straight away then, as if plucking up courage to ask, says 'what do you think of our chances for half term?'

The chances of her ending up killing him by going to visit? The chances that she'd be allowed to leave London and travel to another part of the country? It doesn't seem real, sometimes it just doesn't compute. A few weeks to go, but there could be thousands more dead by then, hospitals overrun, students locked up, another run on Andrex. Whoever had written sci-fi about pandemics got the horror but missed the banality, the comic absurdity of excitement at finding a shop that still has eggs.

'Got to keep hoping,' she tells him. But her eyes are on the pages and pages of books yet to be marked. Lessons to be honed for tomorrow, each one producing another load of marking, another plan to write, another set of assessments to deliver. Each year-group passing through, only to be replaced by another batch arriving. Sisyphean work, heaving children's bodies upwards, straining to push them over the line, the briefest flicker of joy at this achievement before realising another has appeared at the bottom of the hill.

'One day we'll be through this,' he says, trying to be comforting.

One day, but right now, mid-term, it feels as if her labours will never be done. Her turn to scoff. 'Feels like something isn't quite right if I'm 30 years from retirement and already looking forward to it.' He offers no immediate reply which pulls her up and she breathes out. 'I'm sorry. Here's me moping and moaning about things, when it's you who's really been through it. I should be there for you, not the other way round.'

He brightens at this. 'Well, if it happens it will be lovely to see you.'

It will be, but at the moment she just wishes he was OK. There are parts of her strewn along her commute, around the school, parts she can't seem to find space to regather, reassemble. She needs time to pull herself together, to pick up the pieces, if she can even find them.

'It'll be great, Dad. Can't wait.' It will be, but she can't fully muffle an undertone of impatience.

'I do worry about you,' he says, words offered as an opening, an invitation to step beyond pleasantries. Many faults, but he has always been a pastor, has somehow sustained a genuine sensitivity even after all these years. Jo closes her eyes again, disarmed, aware that she is talking with someone whom she could actually wound, a man who has nurtured vulnerability as professional practice. His hands were still so gentle you could crucify him with cocktail sticks, but to live like that, she thinks, to survive all these years and still retain that softness, to do that has taken an iron skeleton. Could put him on a cross with dressmaker's pins, yes, but you'd struggle to break his legs. Not like Mum. She was the opposite. An impenetrable exterior, any softness she kept well shielded, hidden beneath. Her whole life, she thinks, seemingly spent trying to find that tender place, to be accepted there.

'You're too lovely Dad,' she tells him. 'Please don't worry.' She rolls her shoulders, imprints teeth into a knuckle, watches the indentation slowly fade. 'I'm tougher than you think. You have to be in this job.' She pushes out a stoic chuckle.

He absorbs this and doesn't return it, just waits a while. 'I know you are, love. But...' A well-practised pause, space for words to be poured slowly into, well experienced in these things, knowing that grief and loss can build callouses as well as expose wounds. 'Maybe you can be a bit too tough. On yourself. Not let anyone offer a hand.' Placing this, then retreating. An offering for Jo to edge towards and take.

But she leaves it there, in between them. Not rejected, still available to be opened at a later date, perhaps, but she cannot deal with it now, is pulling limbs back, curling up again to protect her underbelly, starting to remove herself.

'Thanks Dad. I...'

He knows that it is over, and they perform their chivalries, polite goodbyes and the usual promises, the bout ending honourably. But in the silence that then falls the dark embrace smothers her once more and she hears the characters in her books calling out to chide, to list her failings. Uncaring. Ungrieving. Impenetrable.

She pulls her phone back into her claws and calls Sally, then Maria, needing proof that she was still loving flesh, wanting to share warm stories of the children in her care, to hear that they miss her, that they have heard that Ben is miserable, that there's someone she just *has* to meet...

Both are busy. Birthdays, babies, she can't blame them. She leaves no messages, write no texts.

No matter. She tells herself firmly, as if speaking to a child, that she must turn over a new leaf. But she knows that before this new page can come she has some tough chapters that she must finish first. Perhaps things will be better by half term. Or Christmas. Spring, surely? Then she will be able to relax, to think of other things. For now, she needs to knuckle down, needs that armour of her mother's, a hard shell to wrap around and protect her. She pulls up an exercise book and opens it, praying to God that they've done something vaguely close to what she'd asked.

10

She does not knuckle down.

After marking one homework she goes and lies on her bed, flicks through some spa hotels, promising that it will be just a moment and then she'll raise herself again. The unmarked books are left piled mute around her, the required quota of plans remains unfiled, the ream of emails that have arrived since she left work are not dealt with.

Exhaustion does not equate to sleep. The night acts as therapist, drawing out what the day has tried to bury. She makes fevered lists of all that needs to be caught up on, knows that part of her must still be sleeping, that Jackson cannot possibly expect her to build a scale model of Victorian London out of egg boxes and produce a film about Pip's mother. A wave of panic yanks her fully from these dreams, head crammed with the actual things that she really does have to get finished. It is half four in the morning, the day hardly born but still she should seize it. Strong coffee, two heaped spoons and sugar on top, and she returns to the sofa to steal a march.

Muscle memory: as she finishes the last of the marking tiredness floods over, but it's actually time to be up now and so she pulls herself to the shower, shuts her eyes as the warm water folds into her, knowing that she can't dally because she needs to get out and get on. A little hard work now, she repeats like a mantra, and she can then regroup.

Quickly dressing, going to collect the books she finds them now slumped in dozing piles, making themselves at home, taking over the furniture, sniping at her as she picks them up and packs them into her bag: *do you spend time marking because you're lonely, or are you lonely because you spend so much time marking?* Summer is long gone; term is accelerating. She jams them in, leaves for work hoping to shut them up, knowing that there will be a fresh chorus of thirty voices tonight. *Have Sally or Maria called you back?* More lesson plans to write and file with Alex this evening. *You can't see anyone with your hair in this state.* No, but a cut will have to wait. *Don't forget the assessment for Year 9.* If she is going to work harder she ought to eat more healthily. On the tube, an advertisement for mouthwash. *When did you last get to the dentist?* Are dentists even open? She should go to the gym, if they haven't all shut. That would help. But when? Perhaps she has tooth decay. Only an examination will tell, but the time to make an appointment, let alone the time to go to one. She should get to the shops. What if she met someone today? The actual state of the fridge. She ought to be counting calories. *Man cannot live on bread alone.* Well, pasta. And condiments. She eats yes, but when did she last have an actual meal?

They keep on pressing, keep on talking. She mutters and berates in reply as she walks, tells them to shut up as she gets off the tube, tries to empty her mind but it's so full it's nearly bursting open anyway. Up towards the school, children are already circling, helpless hungry beaks that need feeding. *Don't you want us to fly?* Jackson and Alex now join in the chorus, Jo rehearsing answers to imagined interrogations as she mounts the stairs, them asking her if she is genuinely committed to this, observing and inspecting as she makes herself another coffee. *If you did that a little more quickly you would have more time.* Nothing more important than a child, so drink up quickly now and wake up early again tomorrow and work a little later because haircuts and dentists and holidays and exercise can all wait 'til half term. Then she'll feel like she's properly earned it, done her very best.

'Hey, slow down,' Cara calls as Jo rushes past, piles of copying still to get done. 'Slow down,' she repeats, following Jo, stopping her, waiting until she actually looks at her, not down at the floor. 'You OK?'

Jo runs her spare hand through her hair, grabs it and pushes it back. 'Sorry, Car. Running to stand still.'

She smiles, her gaze almost maternal. 'Well, not so fast you trip up, yeah?'

Jo laughs, points her papers towards the copying room, thanks Cara and speeds away. But it won't ever ease up, she thinks, because even when all this is over the kids around here won't have changed. A chorus of them rushes up behind her, saying *that's cynical, that's too harsh,* outlining for her the systemic and complex reasons why some children don't pay attention and don't apply themselves to homework and can't shut up in lessons. Ritalin. ADHD. Impoverished parents. *We are only children. It cannot be our fault.* So it is your responsibility, Miss Barker. All yours.

She tries to throw up a defence, says that she's too tired, that it's been a tough few months. *Really? Worse than Sami's?* Voices harangue from every side, calling from toilets and out of marked books, from scribbles on the board and graffiti on the desks. *But don't focus too much on him. Remember Femi has to get her grades too.* Oxbridge a very real possibility, if Jo can give her all the help that she will need. But would it be the right place? Perhaps it would all be online, and what would be the point? Perhaps it would crush her? Only if Jo didn't prepare her expertly. Only if she didn't do her job properly.

She feeds paper into the hungry mouth of the copier and it licks and swallows and multiplies. She nods to herself as if to confirm her commitment to do better. She is lucky, she tells herself, lucky to have a secure income when so many don't. Lucky not to have a boyfriend right now so she can focus on catching these children up after all they've missed. She wipes down her classroom tables, talks to herself as she prepares for Sami's class, rushes a break-time coffee, pinches her arm until it hurts, reminding herself that the holidays are long and are an incredible perk, that she should always be grateful for the chance to impact young lives.

Her father's voice joins in, whispering that *it's all about sacrifice in the end,* though this does nothing to settle her nerves as the class pogo down the corridor to her room soaring on their sugary breakfasts and fast-glugged energy drinks, bodies barging, iced buns and Coco Pops, tongues lashing curses, eyes agog at a photo, popping a pack of cheesy puffs, screeching, trampling underfoot, everything building to a climax in the chorus that screams in her head, the song she had blasted out of her room over and over during her A-Levels, a tortured star howling, *here we are now, entertain us.*

11

Calm down, she tells herself. You need to calm down. Sometimes it's easier when they're actually in the room. Actual bodies, actual voices.

'Sorry Miss, didn't see you,' Charlie says cheerily as he bumps through the door, head returning to level from slugging a Red Bull, nearly walking into her.

'Allow me some of your drink,' Danny asks as he swings his bag into Charlie and clouts him round the back of the knees.

Before Jo can stop him he's given a little shake of the wrist, assessing how much is left. 'Sky it though,' he says and hands it to Danny, who tips his head back ninety degrees like an old sweet dispenser, lifts his arm above it and deftly pours some drink into his mouth without the can touching his lips.

Charlie then finishes the last and arcs the can towards the bin, but it clatters around the square rim and falls out. He turns to walk away.

'Pick that up please,' Jo asks sternly. There's almost a relief having an actual thing to focus on, an unmistakeable misdemeanour. Charlie gives a short stare, trying it but he's not that kind of kid really, then goes to the bin. But he doesn't pick it up, tries instead to flick the can up into the bin with his feet. Tries, and fails. Tries, and fails as the rest of the class arrive so he can't back down. 'Come on,' Jo tells him, trying to make light. 'Just pick it up.'

'Nah Miss, that's dutty.' Dirty. Clean enough to drink from just seconds ago, but it has now left his hand, become so filthy his fingers cannot countenance contamination. Flicking, failing, flicking, failing. Once upon a time the terror of thermonuclear war; that fear now compressed to the invisible, shrunk and crushed into dread of the viral.

To everyone's surprise, the can finally makes it into the bin. Charlie dabs, wipes the drips from his shoes onto the backs of his trousers and heads to his seat.

Jo checks her lesson plan, looks at the detailed timings, asks for quiet as she gets the objectives on the board, ticks that off, masks up and starts to give them back their books. There are ten or more conversations going on. Laughing, arguing, complaining, sympathising… doing all this but not listening to her. As she circles the room she asks them to read what she's written, telling them to get their purple pens out to respond to her comments, spend a moment reflecting, then write some critical thoughts themselves.

'Miss, what?' Ade asks.

'You've done your homework, I've commented on it, and now you're going to write your reflection…'

'Last time he saw his reflection the mirror broke,' Jakob says.

'That's not what your sister said.'

'You wish.'

'No mate, *you* wish, that's the problem you fu…' And tables are thrust forward and chairs are knocked back, this the ritual percussion of young male aggression, both of them standing, neither wanting an actual fight but needing to prove something to the rest of the pack.

Jo cuts them both down, talks about being disgusted then has to ask for Lauren and Chanel to be quiet, unsure if the girls even registered what just happened or if they'd heard it all so often that they just deflected it. She worries that they get steamrollered by the boys, flattened under this constant cockfighting.

Another minute smothering the flames, trying not to raise her voice, trying not to single any one person out, kicking over the coals of each chattering group, deflecting the teeth kissed and the stink-eyes.

'Miss you need to chill down man,' Jordan says, purple pen turning in his fingers. 'Not being rude or nothing, but you're way too stressy about every little thing.'

'Init,' Michael agrees. 'Relax Miss man. Can't you do enjoyment for a change?'

'Trust me,' she beams sarcastically, wide-eyed and simmering, keeping a lid on the steam. 'I'll be all smiles when you all get fantastic grades.'

'Truss?' Michael sniggers into his palm. 'Ain't happening.'

But she absorbs this blow, barks to quieten them again. 'I would love nothing more than to come into this room and know I didn't have to stress about you lot.'

'Allow that Miss,' Danny pipes up. 'Saying we dumb.'

'Speak for yo' own dumb self,' Jordan laughs, and they all roar and hoot and Jo knows that Danny won't dare step to him so she pushes past the whole thing, runs through the register to change the subject.

'Where are Sami and Hayley?' she asks, and just as she does Sami is delivered through the door, sent sprawling into a desk. Jo dashes to the corridor but is too late, the backs of various heads already running, dispersing.

More precious seconds, but she can't just let Sami carry on being treated this way. Back in the room, there is an odd silence, as though much seems to have just been said.

'We *cannot* tolerate —' she starts to tell them.

'Leave it Miss,' Sami snaps back, drawing an 'ooooo' from Ade and Michael. He sits down, slumps into himself, picks up his book and opens it.

Everyone waits and watches, assessing what she'll do, if she'll just take this from him.

'Cap off, Sami.' Win a lesser victory, just to make a point. Plus, she doesn't want him thinking he has to hide under that thing. 'And I'll see you after the lesson,' she adds, words that land unwelcome on all ears. Ade turns to Jakob and gestures crudely with his wrist. Jo pretends not to see but mouths 'wanker' behind her mask for her own satisfaction.

'OK!' she announces, desperate to steer back to the lesson plan, determined to railroad them through it if that's what it takes.

'Done it, Miss,' Nishaan says.

'Good. Well done Nish—'

'Reflection. I've done it.'

'Thank you Nishaan,' she says, wanting to introduce the next task, glancing up at the clock again.

'It's here Miss.'

'Thank you Nishaan – please, just let me finish for a minute.'

'Exactly!' says Charlie. 'Let her finish you twat!'

'Charlie – that is quite *enough*!' Hints of anger in her voice.

'Sorry Miss. Blimey.'

'RIGHT,' she shouts, picking up the plan again, demanding that no one says anything before she has finished explaining. She opens her mouth but the door speaks first, banging loudly into the desk that stands behind it. Hayley walks in and goes to sit without a single look at Jo. The sudden noise had drop-kicked her heart into her mouth, but it eases back down and she asks Hayley where she's been.

'Toilet.'

Which isn't unreasonable. Children do need to go to the toilet. All this she must weigh in an instant. Hayley isn't a bad kid but school rules are school rules. She hears Jackson berating her for not following them to the letter, pictures him naming and shaming her on the next staff briefing email. Boundaries are good for children, she reminds herself.

'Hayley you know you are not meant to go to the toilet between lessons.'

'Yeah well, I was desperate Miss.'

'Desperate,' Nelson echoes, and Hayley raises her middle finger, a gesture he mirrors, then slides the finger into his mouth.

No, she can't have this again, won't tolerate the girls being constantly demeaned like this. 'Hayley,' she begins.

But Hayley is defensive, thinking she's going to be told off. 'Miss man, please. I beg you...'

Nelson mimics her voice. 'I'm down on my knees.'

'Snaps, or it never happened,' Ade throws in, and there's an instant animal stench, the drip of hormones under shirts and trousers as the boys hoot and stomp, Jo apparently invisible, standing, demanding quiet but getting nowhere, the flash flood of testosterone rendering them temporarily deaf, blind and dumb.

'Outside,' she bellows at Nelson.

Probably little she can tell them about geography. By this age, they surely all know the moisture cycle, have seen every valley and crevasse. Chemistry comes and goes, and history is impossible: half claiming heroic pasts, half denying any past at all. But she won't stand for this constant drip of comments.

'Come on Miss, allow it. We're just having jokes.'

A forest of incident logs sprouts in front of her, emails she'd need to send, forms she'd have to fill in, statements she'd have to take, safeguarding considerations she'd have to be interviewed about and the time, the bloody *time* it would all take. But more than that, the backdraft of blame Jackson would doubtless direct her way — *why wasn't the class under control?*

She backs down. Knows that she shouldn't, but she does. She knows that she ought to treat this with the utmost seriousness, but she needs to keep it in the room, can feel the minutes running away, her lesson objectives disappearing through her fingers. So she retreats, insists that Nelson apologises to Hayley, which he sort of does.

She gets the class to open their anthologies and read over a poem for a couple of minutes, just to let the waves lull and the surge drain away. 'Page fifty-five,' she tells them. 'Song for Autumn.'

'Miss mine's at home.' Four or five of them without their copies, but no matter, she'd predicted as much and has made photocopies. They haven't been quarantined but she can't do everything, she just can't. Perhaps the heat of the copier, she thinks. The powerful light.

They are good kids, she reminds herself. Basically, they are good kids. But they are teenagers, excited by their bodies. It doesn't make them bad but she just wishes that they would show one another respect.

They open the anthology, some knowing where to look, some flicking through laboriously, some coughing in overly pronounced ways, some sniffing more loudly than they need to, these constant noises just signals of continued existence, as if silence might render them invisible. She can empathise with that.

She stands at the front of her taped-off area, smiles at Sami following a line of text slowly along with his finger.

'Autumn,' she says with a flourish once they've all had a chance to read. 'Mary Oliver is a poet very connected to nature.'

'That's what season we're in Miss,' Ade says.

'Well done Ade.' Frowning, a little sarcastic.

'Found out on Instagram last night, innit. "The best images of hashtag Autumn."' Jo looks dumbfounded, and he lets her hang, then cracks up. 'I'm only rinsing you, Miss. Don't take everything so serious.'

'Lord have mercy Ade, what am I going to do with you?'

'I don't know Miss, but I'm Muslim so... you know.'

And they all laugh at this, and she has to let them. She apologises and he tips his fingers to his head in mini salute, letting her know it was all good.

Needing to hear girls' voices Jo asks Kelly to begin reading.

In the deep fall
don't you imagine how comfortable it will be to touch
the earth instead of the nothingness of air.

Jo then nods for Chanel to continue, Sami's eyes gently shutting as she speaks of the golden summer flowers whispering goodbye, the fox running through shadows.

At this Jordan calls to Michael and makes a whelp.

The piled firewood shifts a little

Something has disturbed them. Jo waves for Chanel to stop.

129

'Jordan, you have something to share?'

He shakes his head. 'No Miss.' But she's pinning him with a stare and he gives it up. 'Just this fox thing the other night,' gesturing to his book.

'Something that you latterly alluded to in your homework?'

He doesn't flinch at the vocabulary, just nods shyly. They are quiet, waiting for him to act.

She squirts some sanitiser, quickly rubs her hands and dons her mask again, then walks down, picks up his book and tells him that she'd been intrigued. He doesn't blush exactly, but looks pleased with himself, pleased enough for Michael to turn round.

'Oh my days, you put that in your homework?!'

'Just sprung off it a bit,' he says, immediately diminishing his labours, not wanting anyone to think that actual effort had been made.

But Michael is laughing, telling her, 'Miss you got to hear this, this was some sickness.'

She looks at the clock, then at Jordan, as if sizing up permission for him to go ahead, knowing that she had planned for this anyway but wanting the class to think that they have agency. Jakob and Ade close their books like it's carpet time. She tells Jordan to go to the front but stay out of the teacher's area, saying something about 'good practice for your... speaking,' hoping no one notices the tiny pause, swerving to avoid the word "oral."

He lumbers to the board; Jo perches on his desk at the back, the curved plastic bumper nestling into her thighs, watching them, the class quietening at his presence. He pops his hands together, softly but purposefully, thumb caught in opposite palm, separating, coming together, leaning his generous frame back slightly, bouncing a little on his knees.

'Like...' he begins, and Jo sighs, everything hedged as metaphor, nothing allowed to *actually be*, speech all peppered with caveat, refusing to land solidly on meaning. 'Like, those of you from the Tower know there's been noise all hours,

130

round the bins, out on the hard, everywhere. And though it sounded like babies getting strangled and shit,' — a profuse apology thrown quickly at Jo, a genuine vernacular mistake — 'turned out it was like, foxes.'

'Hold on,' she says. 'Before you start that, roll back a bit.' He shrugs, has no idea, so she prompts him, asks for this to be placed in context. 'The homework was about framing a memoir, like Dickens does for Pip at the opening of the book. So...'

But he shakes his head, laughs. 'Miss man, I'm baffed.'

Baffled, lost, unwilling to do the necessary mental work, waiting for her to do it for him.

She picks up his exercise book, turns to the page and reads his own words back to him. '"London has collapsed..." This was a really good start Jordan. I want to know more.'

Danny and Charlie give each other looks, which Jordan feels the need to slap down. 'What you looking at? Think I'm dumb and shit?' Another apology, ungratefully accepted. The boys look down into their desks, and he begins again.

'That homework... I was just thinking,' he says, choosing his words carefully, 'like, what if it all kicked off? Properly kicked off. People say enough of lockdown, enough cooped up and fines for parties. All that energy and anger from BLM, you know, like next time the police cap a ni... a guy, people say "enough."' He surveys his congregation, looks unsure whether to push them further, but decides he might as well. He picks up Nishaan's copy of *Great Expectations*, Nishaan slapping a hand down to try to stop him, but missing. 'Not gonna lie, low-key I read some of this you know.' Michael laughs, and Jordan does too. 'Don't laugh man, don't laugh. But I swear down, nothing has changed. *Nut-ting*. Couple of rich people keeping a lid on a whole lot of poor people. Like, how do they do that man? *How*,' he says, voice raised for the first time. 'Because even before all this they've been locking us down for *time*.'

No answers given. No fists raised, no shouts offered in solidarity. Blank faces mostly. Not so much that the revolution would not be televised, but that a million tiny screens had deflated it, prevented it, left everyone a bit too distracted.

'Just get to the fox, blood,' Michael shouts.

'I am, fool,' launching a scowl that silences Michael in an instant. 'So I wrote this story about what it might be like, after some big collapse, having to hunt for food. Because who knows? Times are cra-cray. But, like I said, the *inciting incident* Miss' — emphasising each syllable — 'was that there's been these foxes around the Tower. Making bare noise in the night.'

And he begins unfolding the story, a bunch of them gathered one evening, nothing much to do since the youth club shut so just talking, swapping rhymes, moaning about the noise, foxes keeping people up with their shrieking.

'They're not even meant to live round here, scavengers come from far.' He swears down that they'd been known to drag babies out of pushchairs, wipe diseases over benches. 'But on the OT, out there in the countryside people don't be taking that, aren't having that. For real they get gangs of dogs and horses to hunt foxes down, a proper traditional thing too, all in green Barbours like you see down Portobello. So we thought, why not? Vermin keeping us up all night, why not go country on their vulpine asses?'

Dare vulpine asssesss. Just the briefest flick of attention to Jo, making sure she had clocked his technical vocabulary. The good, the bad, the ugly, all present in just three words. Jesus, she thinks, let me at this kid for A-Level next year.

A couple of dogs had been gathered. No horses, but minor horsepower: two of them had had scooters, lean petrol steeds, faster, more agile. Others had fetched bikes.

'We all go tool up, blaze up, everyone revving, some kid tooting a vuvuzela, dogs barking, rest of us howling like a pack, all hyped and we set off. Young ones running in front, b-ball bats, lengths of wood, whatever, in and out of the bin store, kicking, shaking, proper jokes, not really serious or nothing. But then this fox makes a run for it. Not thinking we'd actually find one, but now everyone's blood is up and it turned into proper madness, some low-key focused dudes, the dogs straining for it now, no laughing anymore, everyone tearing after this thing like, "we'll teach you to keep us up, to go for our babies, spread viruses." Not gonna lie that fox was a bit lame, I mean like hobbling, all thin. *E-may-see-ated.*' Another glance at Jo. 'Dodges under a car so we think we've got it, then scarpers out but we follow it, this thing bare terrorised, dogs yanking at leads, scooters whining, wheel-spinning round and cutting it off, cornering it. Tries to jump a wall but doesn't make it.'

A bead of sweat down Jo's back, hands moist, clutching Jordan's desk. She can Sami's knee bobbing furiously, the class silent as they hear described a howling mob, sounds of the chase echoing off brick walls and down concrete channels.

'Nowhere for it to go now, dogs off the lead, the fox snapping at them, little thing trembling for its life, then some dude's pit bull leaps in and gets it by the neck, proper blood, throat ripped and it's rasping, this horrible high pitched bark before it gives up and goes quiet, still moving its legs in little jerks, like it might still get away, but there's no chance. So caught up in it low-key we don't notice the van roll up, coppers piling out, like "what the f is happening here," jumping in all heavy, calling us animals, monsters, breaking this rule and that. And true dat: not going to lie, with all the blood and flesh there was a bit of shock, like holy s what have we done.'

A touch of pride at his self-censorship, Jo wondering if the exam board would consider his context-appropriate ironing over of expletives mark-worthy.

'Then Nate — this older brother who knows bare about everything — fronts up, telling them like if it was Chipping whatever with all them Lords on horses la-di-da on big estates the police would be doffing their hats. And he starts preaching it, "watch, soon as black people start hunting foxes on *their* estates, everyone be in a mad panic." And the police had to back off because someone searched it up and if it's a hunt it's like lockdown exempt or something and you can have many people as you like. Plus apparently, two dogs isn't a pack so they couldn't do nothing anyway.'

He stops. No one moves and he holds them cupped in his hands, then nonchalantly lands the story. 'So like when I went indoors to do homework all that was on my mind. Then the form all went a bit end-times, a bit *dystopian* Miss. Apocalyptic, like. Book of Revelation, you know.'

He stops again and looks at her, signalling he's done. She ungrips the edge of the table, trying to process, running through the assessment criteria, the flashes of mature vocabulary, horror and joyous pride in equal measure, knowing he has held a narrative, captivated a room, shown an understanding of drama.

'That was bare lit,' Michael clucks in approval. High praise in local tongue. Pure naked flame, powerful enough to set something alight.

Jo lifts herself up, beaming at him, wondering what best to say and how to frame it without actually validating the violence. But the first person to break the silence is Sami.

'Disgusting,' he says, almost to himself, head down, addressing his desk. 'Torturing an animal, killing it like that.' Jo's face flushes with pride. He has taken her advice, is speaking up, for the first time becoming a solid object in the room.

But in perfect mirror Jordan's face changes again, muscles switching it in an instant, pride to animus. 'Who the *fuck* do you— '

She doesn't even think about it, just does it, rushes between them, palms held out, telling Jordan no, she will not have it, will not have that language, people have different views, there must be respect.

'Nah miss,' he continues, all furrows and bulging eyeballs. 'Nah miss, I don't care. He does not get to come to this school, cotch at Darren's desk and start chatting at me.'

'Yes, I do,' Sami says, stamping his words out, Jordan's vicious gaze nailing him. As if to resist this pinning down he raises his voice. 'Yes I *do* get to speak,' he howls above the rising chorus of abuse.

He looks so vulnerable, so alone there with everyone gathered around him and before she knows it a surge of emotion has cascaded up her throat. 'Sami,' she says gently, a little Yorkshire in her lilt, lifting an arm towards his shoulder, feeling like she's teaching Primary. 'Please don't shout.'

But now they're all shouting, braying. 'Ooooooooo! Sami!'

'Stop that!' she orders, her face reddening but Sami's properly burning.

Jordan doesn't care, is playing the angry kingpin. 'Nelson, you got to sort this boy out.'

'What, just because I live opposite!?' Nelson argues, a scowl and a dismissive wave of a paw.

'Same corridor, same problem.' Jordan tells him, rejecting his complaint. Some stupid Tower code he's demanding is respected. He takes in his audience before ramping up the menace. 'What? Too busy gripsing up your dick you butters sack of shit?'

Nelson stands, the boys arrayed around Jordan, Hayley with one hand on the top of her blouse pointing and laughing, all the other girls around her. He looks like he's boiling in his own skin, the pressure to obey Jordan rising in him as his face contorts and finally rips, spilling its bile over Sami. 'Shut the fuck up you dirty, sponging, teacher-licking FUGEE.'

The words hit Sami, take out his knees and he drops to his chair. Jo is calling for them all to stop but they've formed a ring around Sami and are completely ignoring her.

'Watch it,' Ade laughs, 'he might pull his blade on you,' and makes a tiny, worm-like gesture with his finger.

Sami tries to hide his face, but Nelson is more in his stride now, wants to make sure he's fulfilled his obligation to Jordan. 'What, you going to cry?' Sami's head twists for a moment, desperately wondering why anyone would be so cruel, Jordan looking on fiercely, but Nelson thinking he might as well go for the kill. 'That's it. Miss is here. Go blub on her cos you can't go to your mum.'

Your mum.

Jo is trembling, her voice box warning that it will shake if called upon. She looks at Sami, his face pure sorrow, no doubt in her mind now: his mother is dead.

She must not cry. She absolutely must not cry.

Jordan is stood, breathing like a bull, wrestling something inside himself. He looks back at Sami, utterly defeated, and holds his hand up to Nelson.

'Stop,' he says finally, and everyone pulls back. 'Safe, Miss,' as if returning control to her. She pushes through the ring of boys and stands at the front of the classroom again. Jordan walks to his desk, sits down before rising briefly again, a warning in case anyone thought he had gone soft. 'Best watch it,' he snarls, poking a finger towards Sami.

But Sami is done, has been punctured, whatever air he had gathered to speak out now gone.

No surprise that Golding had taught before writing *Lord of the Flies*. Violent blood in young veins. Struggle. Privilege. Power. But it is over, and her first thought is to cast a glance at the door, making sure that Jackson wasn't outside of it, secretly observing.

'SILENCE,' she shouts at them, mask on and hot against her face, and though there is quiet she knows that it is not her orders they are following. She stands with her arms folded, digging a nail hard into her armpit. 'We *cannot* —' she begins to say, but Michael cuts across, breaking ranks, a scowl of irritation.

'What can't we have Miss? Different views being expressed? Robust debate?' He is angry, properly aggrieved.

'You know *damned* well what I mean Michael. We cannot —'

136

'Have bad language? Got to speak to one another with respect? Alright Miss man.' Face bitter, 'lemme just go check that one with Darren.'

A more brutal silence now in the room. Jordan moves a hand over to Michael's arm, gives him a subtle shake of the head, stands him down.

'Michael, Nelson, Jordan I will deal with you later.' They shake their heads in disbelief. 'Let's move on, not waste any more time,' forcing her eyes wide so that they will not well up, dealing with it but not dealing with it.

Sami is wrapped tight up in his arms, face buried. Jo knows that she isn't getting in, and he isn't coming out. Not for now. With a stern, emotionless voice, she tells him that she will need to see him after school.

'Open your books and start the analysis of the Autumn poem. There's bullet-points coming up on the board.'

She turns the projector on and it grumbles as it warms, gradually gathers what light it can and weakly throws it forward.

'Read the text carefully before you try any answers,' she says, and stays stood in the middle at the front, scared to retreat, breaking down these words and forging a shield from them. *Your mum.* Repeating them to herself, piercing herself with them again and again.

'Quiet!' she snaps again as Lauren and Chanel begin chatting. They eye one another and snigger. Nelson has tunnelled down deep into his desk. Michael and Jordan have legs stretched out in front of them, are leant back in their chairs, pens moving in sporadic bursts. Blades truly pulled in the middle of your lesson, she thinks. Tongues displaying a brutal sharpness and control at least as good as she'd demanded.

She releases her grip on her upper arm, enjoys the blood running back. She bites into her lip and returns to her desk, takes up a red pen and steels herself.

Soft flesh over iron skeleton. Yes, the only way to get this done was to keep the hardness on the inside. *Suffer the little children.* If you commit to carrying them, you do so knowing that they can wound you. Education as redemption. Teaching as dogged vulnerability. *No sacrifice without bloodshed,* her father's voice whispers. *Wounded for their transgressions.*

She just wishes she could get closer. Could walk out among them, kneel and speak to each one in turn. That simple thing, lost. The little slashes of red into their books, the affirming words, "good, well done", before moving on to the next. A touch of an elbow on forearm. All of it gone for now. Lecturing and pointing all she seems to have left. But she has to find a way, she thinks. There must be a way.

12

When the final bell cracks through the air the fabric of the day is torn asunder. It's October still and there is just about light enough in the late afternoons for those who want to use it. Outdoor mixing, plenty of air. Inhaling deep before winter shuts them in again.

In the seconds before the day's end, the clock shuffling slowly round, a hush falls over her class of Year 7's, their breath held. They are in uniform, told when they can visit the canteen, with whom they can sit, where they should be and when. They eat their lunches apart, still comply with most of the rules, pull masks from old takeaway boxes, help spray down the tables, march in and out in single file, steer hard on corridors to try to preserve distances. Hands. Face. Space. The mantra of anxiety etched into brave expressions. Each step they take is checked against the regulations they try to swallow and internalise. All of this beats metronomically through their day, like Sergeant Pepper marching to its conclusion, building, building, a quaver-rest of silence then hanging, the air removed as the whole class inhales, the day hanging suspended between two states of being until the building clangs in unison, announcing the transition. In an instant school becomes after-school, moves to shouting, running where they will and with whom they like. A daily moment of joy. Fuck the bubbles, give me a hug, allow me some of your drink.

Still that daily high, she thinks, though now it is not as potent. Though the building quickly empties and quietens, different demands flood in. Pens, computer, board, desk... everything must be sterilised. Her little theatre now more operating theatre. She is glad Victor left when he did. They are all young enough now in the department not to have too many worries. Not about themselves, at least.

Once the battlefield has cleared she needs to tend to her wounds, to the parlays and back-channel negotiations that will construct real progress. She arranges her desk, arranges herself, scrubs her hands, and waits. Two minutes, three minutes; time enough to replay the lesson with Year 11 over and over — the horrible power of Jordan's speech, the irresistible forces he could lever on the others, Nelson and Michael's words still orbiting her like a meteor, burning on each approach but hardly losing mass.

Much as she might have wanted them to, they have not forgotten about Darren, nor forgiven. He might not be in lessons but he is out there, his presence still a gravity strong enough to reach through fences and walls and turn the tide in her room. Expelled from school, he's not been expelled from their gatherings around the Tower, nor from their thoughts either. At least when he was here she could face him down and offer counter-narratives. Now he speaks what she cannot hear, feeds them thoughts that she cannot know, cannot easily be erased or wiped away. This is why, she has concluded, this is why it's more important than ever to expose Sami's bullies. She is sure she'll find Darren at the centre of them.

A gust of wind grasps the building a moment, moans and lets go, rushing on to split and race itself through the concrete courses of the estate, knocking over cans, getting up into the faces of old and young alike.

Still no Sami. Arguments, fights, simple forgetfulness: countless other things could have delayed him. As the minutes pass, the odds of him turning up lengthen, but then her door darkens and he skulks in. He poises on a desk, chooses one that can't be seen from the door.

'Thank you for coming Sami,' Jo says. He keeps his head down but turns his eyes up. 'So, about the lesson today.'

'You wanted me to speak, so I spoke.' This said into his broken collar. No mask, but he's doing his best to cover his mouth.

'Yes,' she affirms, readying herself to deliver her points. But he cuts her off.

'But then when I speak, you tell me to be quiet innit, so.' His English is improving quickly, though not always blooming in the colours she might have hoped.

'I asked you not to shout Sami.' A pause, Jo hesitant, unsure whether to say more.

'I grew up around animals,' he says eventually. 'It was cruel.' He is turning things over in his mind, his breathing heavy, sounding as if it is igniting angry embers in himself. He lifts his head, says into clear air, 'you said stand up for an argument.'

'You did, and Jordan's response was unacceptable. Nelson too. It will be dealt with.'

He lets out a short laugh, shakes his head while keeping his eyes at the floor. A new gust comes and he steals a look at the window, at the Tower, unmoved by the wind.

'If you could just give me their names...'

He pulls his gaze back from outside, back to the floor as if building courage, then dares a look directly at her. 'Not just Jordan. I read more of your book too.' Less a statement of fact that an opening to his case. 'Does Pip speak up? No. With the prisoner, he says nothing. So.' He stops, thinks, then launches again. 'The book *starts* with this. The man gives this money *because* Pip stays quiet, does *not* speak. But...' He pauses before pronouncing judgement. 'But you want me to speak.'

'It is not as simple as that.'

'It is simple. If Pip speaks, then...' He makes a slashing gesture across his throat. 'So he does not.'

Jo thinks: he's too scared to give up Darren. She needs to try another tack.

'I get that. And I understand it took courage to speak up. All I did was ask you not to shout.'

At this he laughs openly, shaking his head incredulously. 'Not shout? When they shout all the time? When the whole lesson people are shouting, using words and you don't say anything?!'

She bristles, straightens her back. 'This is not an easy class Sami.'

He lets her have it. 'For me or you?'

Jo fires a wounded glance, but he offers no sympathy. 'I want to help you,' she tells him, but it comes out weakly, emphasis the wrong way round — like she *wants* to help him but can't — and he snorts again and lowers his head.

Soft flesh, and a tough core. Be vulnerable, she thinks, trust him with her own secret, do her own homework. *Looking back at your life now, at your beginnings...* show him the forge that has formed her, the great expectations, the convictions, the losses she's endured. 'Sami,' she says finally, 'I'm sorry for what Nelson said about your mother. That must have been very hurtful.' No response. 'I know I found it hurtful myself.' Just the smallest tremor across his face.

She is going to have to tell him, take the risk and trust him.

'This pandemic has caused a lot of hurt, some of it harder to see. Buried in different ways in different people.' He moves his head from side to side as if accepting this. 'I'd like you to prepare something for next lesson,' she says. 'Write a proper, careful response to Jordan.' She moves to stand in front of him, arms folded, cardigan crumpled, a mark on the sleeve that will need dry cleaning. 'What happened was cruel, but I want you to explain your argument to the class and offer them some background, some context. That's always going to get more marks in the exam.'

He sighs as only a teenager can. 'So now this about a better grade.'

She closes her eyes, concedes the truth. 'Yes, of course. But it's about you too, about helping us to understand who you are.'

Imperceptible changes. Tiny movements above his cheeks. Silent signs that he is listening now, is calm enough to receive. A rare jet rumbles over, lining up to fall into Heathrow.

'I know it won't be easy. But my turn first. To show you that I'm serious, like that homework I set, I want to tell you something about my experience these past months.'

Alex's head pops round the door. 'Hi Miss. Hello…' he waves a hand generally at Sami and returns his attention to Jo. 'Sorry to disturb. We're meant to be meeting?' A tap of his watch.

She rolls her eyes, can't help show her frustration. 'Right now?'

He tightens at this. Looks at Jo, and then at Sami, at the blank board, no paper, no screen on show, no work being discussed. 'Sorry Miss, but I have another meeting with Mr Jackson shortly, so if this could be rearranged?'

She watches Sami's shields rising, hatches being battened one by one, his chin and mouth disappearing back inside his jumper.

'I go,' he says.

'Sorry Sami,' she replies with a sigh of resignation, and tells Alex that she's on her way. She moves to her desk and grabs her planner, a pen she hopes works, the tide of things still to do sluicing back and rising around her. 'Prepare that presentation,' she tells him, 'and we will find another time I promise,' though she's no idea when that might be, and when she turns back to apologise to him again he has slipped away and gone.

13

Alex soon finds his own priorities interrupted, his own protests ignored and over-ruled as he's called down even earlier than expected to an urgent management meeting with Jackson. A small, unexpected window of time left open, Jo's four new colleagues immediately begin grinding their way through marking books they took in days ago, writing plans for lessons they'll deliver in a fortnight. Jo makes as if to go to her room, to collect her stuff to head home and do the same, but Cara stops her.

'Stay, Jo. Stay and have a cup of tea, would you? Talk to me.' She looks tired, pleading.

If she does stay she'll have to recalculate her evening, but she relents and puts the kettle on.

The room is cramped, each small desk covered in papers, the top of each filing cabinet an experimental literary ziggurat, comedy piled up with tragedy, Roddy Doyle leaning into Emily Brontë, Shakespeare trapped underneath Zephaniah, Angelou currently perched atop both. There's a sign on the door indicating that the maximum capacity is four people but from the first day back they've ignored it. Kept the windows open, tried to steer clear of one another. Packing the shelves around the walls are straining folders of syllabi, each one a new angle on how things should be done. Less Shakespeare. More Shakespeare. More grammar. Less Shakespeare. Tougher spellings. Whims of successive ministers thinking they know best. Much of it is untouched for years, should be confined to the bin especially now Victor is gone, but it's a huge amount of work that no one wants to take on. Not without gloves and a good quality mask. Heavy lifting. Old stuff. Dust. Jo doesn't want to tackle it.

Martha, Matt, Sandra and Rose listen intently as Jo confides in Cara what had happened with Jordan's speech and Sami's reaction, Jo then having to find a way to put the lid back on it all before someone got hurt.

'Please don't tell Alex though,' she mouths quietly. 'I just don't need him or Jackson...'

Cara insists she never would, 'cross my heart,' she whispers, makes sure that the others don't hear her, raises her teaspoon like a scalpel and makes a slashing motion across her chest.

Jo has to remind herself sometimes that if she and Sally had done medicine together at university, only now — all this time later and after a decade of close tutelage and hand-holding — might they be considered skilled. Three years of study before being let loose on actual bodies.

She looks at the four new staff, exhausted, gaunt, given so much to carry so soon, trying to dredge up sympathy for them. A few months of lectures, a couple of dead classes to practice on and they are already considered expert enough, sent to work alone with children presenting such a myriad array of conditions that some are like a different species altogether. They look a bit sick already.

She and Cara are sat at their prime places nearest the window, cold drafts in winter compensated by the warm light in the summer, the windowsill a prized extension to desk space. Cara is hardly able to get a word in edgeways now that Jo has begun talking about how much work there is to do with Sami, a look of patience on Cara's face as if she has something to share too but is willing to wait.

Their voices quieten again and in response the others work more gently, move their heads to better hear Jo whisper speculation about apartment blocks bombed out, the strafing of gunfire, fathers taken away, sisters married off. Rapes and murders, wounds that they will never see, and who knew how he'd got to Calais, then across the Channel?

'You think he's seen this kind of stuff himself?' Cara asks.

'Hard to know,' she replies with a shake of her head, voice turning more anxious. 'But I've promised him a chance to reply next lesson, give more context.'

What if he started into huge trauma? What if it all got political?

'A chance to emphasise democracy and the rule of law — go you,' Cara says in mock cheer, talking more loudly now. 'Hope you'd already noted that in your lesson plan two weeks ago, the entirely unpredictable in-lesson event that you now have to respond to.'

Both snicker caustically and Cara calls over to the four others, 'you guys all got that?' They lift their heads, glad to be included. A little audience and she's off on a roll. 'Leave the poetry and prose for a minute. How's the instruction in biosecurity, mental health, drugs awareness, getting enough sleep, the rudiments of cookery, sex-ed, managing screen-time, first aid, riding a bike and self-defence going? Did I miss anything Jo?' She shakes her head and Cara continues. 'There's kids turn up here who can hardly count to three and wipe their own arse, let alone spot the early signs of grooming or what to do if their stepdad pulls a knife.'

Their turn to laugh, the four of them pretending to find this funny when in truth they've got a right to be terrified.

'My first term —' Jo says, taking the conch from Cara.

'In about 1897,' she throws in.

'Fuck off, but yeah it sometimes feels like it — God I had The Fear so badly.'

No one is laughing anymore. Cara slowly pours more hot water into her mug then owns up about her own first term not even two years ago, coming into work and regularly being sick in the toilets.

Martha blinks, stares into her pile of papers, puts her pen down and takes a short sip of her drink.

Fear. The kind of afraid that sits in the stomach, knocks at the heart and screams in the head as you lie awake in the dark moments of the night. You put on the bravest face you can find, work all day to try to keep it there, but Martha and the others don't look like they are winning that battle: pale cheeks, clammy collars, bitten nails. Their insides are probably squirming, asking why they get up each day in the midst of a global pandemic to slog for children who defy their every instruction, seem hostile to their every word. What kind of job is it where you feel so much dread so often? Most likely they'd been kids from nice homes walking on nice roads to nice schools. Children — like Jo — who'd sat at the front, doing what they were told. School was fun, teaching looks nice, thinking they've applied to be village bobby when in reality it's the riot squad. Now they just want to know just how much this is actually going to cost. Sworn at, kicked in the nuts, scratched and laughed at — is this the price they must pay?

But Cromwell children are still children, landed in this world naked as anyone else, and what they are trying to do here is level them up. Education as liberty. School as a fucked-up *Fortnite* and knowledge as actual power. Get smart before they get shot, before those who know the game better grab all the good stuff. And here in this room was a group of people who believed that getting schools back was the right thing to do, who genuinely wanted to empower them, who had the means to do that. At least, she has to keep believing that they could, if only for her own sanity. Has to believe that it's possible to make an actual difference in a child's life, in *Sami's* life, in spite of the battles he's already lost.

Matt is picking out the copies of *An Inspector Calls* that still have their covers intact.

'He's being bullied,' Jo says eventually, breathing out loudly. 'On top of everything else, Sami is being bullied. But I can't get him to talk about it. Probably as much out of school as in, but I can never put faces on the kids involved.' She doesn't mention Darren.

Cara frowns. She hadn't realised it was that serious but yes, she's seen some kids having a go and knows at least some of them. The office suddenly feels energised, like they can all work together and perhaps get a win. Jo looks up the names Cara gives, says that she's sure that that's them. She begins writing an incident report, clattering excitedly at a keyboard.

Alex then slips into the room, back from his meeting. He seems reticent, guarded. Cara tells him to spill the beans.

'There are no beans,' he shoots back, slumping into his plastic chair.

A collective look of confusion.

'The bean counters have done their work, and report that there are no more beans.' He sits, looks defeated already, exhausted. 'The school is broke.' All these extra costs, academy sponsors struggling, no more money to give. Debts already rolled over as far as they can go even before this damned bug kicked off, so Jackson has been told that's it. No more.

'No more?'

He shakes his head. The department's annual budget gone before October is done. No more books, no more stationery. He looks down at the floor before sounding the death knell. 'So, no more photocopying.'

They all erupt. Lesson plans, worksheets, extracts printed from books, model essays, assessments.

Cara stands up, looks over at Martha, Matt, Sandra and Rose, white as sheets, her tongue still loose and muscular. 'For god's sake Alex,' she says, 'how are these guys meant to cope with that?' A smile from Sandra, like she's been noticed for the first time. Martha has her hand to her mouth, eyes open in shock but the lamps in them are dead. 'Do you have any idea how impossible that makes everything?'

'Jesus Cara, this isn't my fault!' Anger flares but he then deflates in resignation. 'Hopefully, it will be just for a few weeks. Jackson is going to write to parents, ask each to "make a contribution."'

'Ask parents on the estate for money? With all they're going through anyway? God, I *hate* this job sometimes,' Jo says bitterly, seeing Cara looking wounded. 'Plus, that's a lot of paper being used to ask for money to buy more paper.'

'Very droll Jo, thank you.' She bristles at his sarcasm, watches him tap something into his notebook.

'That should add a nice frisson to parents evening,' Cara adds. 'Will we each be issued with a card machine?'

'Contactless?' Jo asks.

'Of course,' Cara throws back. 'No touching allowed, you know that.'

Jo throws a laugh over to the four at their desks, but they don't take it, don't join in. They are already wondering how to deliver lessons without worksheets. Martha is telling the others that she has a fairly reliable laser printer at home, Matt offering to add a couple of reams of A4 to his Amazon order of "Well Done" stickers, spare highlighters and cheap biros.

Alex has his eyes closed, is breathing in, looks like he is biting into his tongue. 'I'm sorry,' he says. 'All of you, I'm really sorry.' The way he is sitting it looks as if he no longer fills the suit. 'This isn't how I'd wanted things to be.'

With only a year more under his belt than Cara, he was always going to have to inflate to fill this role, but he now looks as if the effort has left his skin thin and frail, liable to split.

'We will make do,' he says, recovering a little. 'It's going to be hard, but come on team, we'll make do with the resources we have, get a quarantine rota going, make them stretch until the end of the year.' Jo rolls her eyes, breathes out heavily and he turns and snaps impatiently at her. 'For fuck's sake Jo, please try to be positive.'

'Well school's going to have to find some dough pretty sharpish,' Cara says before Jo can reply. She is stood stiffly, as if needing to get her words out quickly before some other part of her decides against.

'Because?' Alex asks, turning wearily towards her.

'Because they're going to have to pay for maternity cover,' she says, now uncapping a beaming smile and a stream of tears, the uncertain silence in the room forcing her to make sure that people understand. 'Because I'm having a baby.'

14

She hugs Cara of course, straight away in the office, effusive in congratulation. Cara tells her that it wasn't planned, that it had been a total shock, promises that she hadn't known when they'd sat in the pub that first Friday.

'Good for you,' she says over and over, 'good for you Car,' as if needing to repeat this to herself to make sure that it is true. She waits while Cara gathers her things, the two of them leaving Alex to try to manage the fallout as they walk out of school together. But when they're out of earshot Cara turns in different tone.

'We can't do it, Jo,' she says. Less joy in her voice now, more worry, the two of them descending the stairs to reception. A shot of confusion across Jo's face. She wasn't planning on keeping it?

She stops, then steps after Cara again. A wave to the cleaner as she moves through the foyer. 'Hi Mary,' Jo calls, and Mary jiggles a mop back at her.

'We can't do it,' Cara repeats. 'No way we can stay in London with a baby. Not in the middle of all this.'

'Wait, so you're going to leave?'

Stopping by the steps down to the main doors Cara turns, looking miserable. 'What choice do we have? The figures just don't add up. I mean, *really* don't add up. Jules' work has completely tanked and he's self-employed so doesn't seem to qualify for support... I don't know.' She lifts her bag of marking. 'It's pathetic. This should be the happiest moment, but look at me, worrying if we can afford a baby.' Jackson walks by, a perfunctory nod at them both as he strides towards the bursar's office. 'We'll need another bedroom,' she continues, beginning a ledger of her own. 'A child-minder, nappies, bottles, clothes, a cot,'

'But your reduced alcohol spend will cover most of that, right? And I'm *pretty sure* I could persuade Jackson to add something to the letter to parents, ask them for a whip-round.'

Cara laughs and then doesn't laugh, slumps her shoulders, puts her bag down as Jo gathers her in.

She can't help it, knows that they shouldn't, feels the breaking of some membrane between them as she reaches round and pulls Cara's body close. She doesn't care who sees them, who might censure or complain. She needs to touch and be touched, to say something with her hands that cannot be crammed down into words and sent across the two-metre abyss. When she releases her embrace Cara brushes herself down and wipes her eyes and they both laugh and apologise.

She opens her mouth as if to speak but Cara's focus is far off and she holds the words back.

'You're so lucky Jo,' Cara says eventually, still looking out of the windows into the car park, and she is so surprised by this that she says nothing in return. 'You have your flat, and you have so much experience here.' Then she bursts into tears. Jo guides her gently to one of the soft chairs outside the reception hatch, now shuttered for the evening. She fishes out one of the crumpled packs of tissues from her bag. Cara takes one, wipes her eyes then blows her nose. 'Seeing those four up there just brought it all back. The last couple of years have been so hard. Just *so* much harder than I'd ever expected.'

'Oh Car, I'm so sorry. I...'

'It's not your fault. You've had enough on your plate, and it's not your job.'

Not technically, no, she thinks, but still. She apologises again, kneels and takes Cara's hand, tells her that if there's anything at all, anything, she just needs to ask.

She replies in staccato bursts between sobs. 'I'm scared. Really scared. That we just. Don't. Have the resources. To love. It. Properly.'

That fear again, Jo thinks. Sickness each morning. She swallows thickly to send rising acid back down her throat, withdraws a hand to wipe her own eyes. 'You will be amazing Car. You always are. You'll find a way.'

Mary's slow march with her mop is making steady progress towards them, so when Cara has dried her eyes a bit Jo helps her up and they head out onto the road. It's getting dark already and the few scattered trees are well on the turn, their leaves fallen and attempting an odd mulch with facemasks and condiment sachets.

'Yo, Miss Barker!' a guy calls over, pirouetting and waving as he turns into a block of flats.

'Hey!' she calls back noncommittally, desperately scanning the face. 'Good to see you!' There are too many shadows moving too quickly.

Cara asks who it was and she tells her that she has absolutely no idea.

'Fiver says you told his class "I'll never forget you guys!"'

She hooks her arm through Cara's and they lean briefly into one another. 'Well you *have* to tell them that, don't you?'

Up at the main road, there's a slanging match between a black cab and a cyclist. A man carrying a potted olive tree has stopped to watch, then starts throwing in his tuppence, gesturing about the markings in the bus lane. Another car honks and the cabbie leans over the other way to tell them to fuck off.

As they approach Cara's bus stop Jo holds her in a short embrace again, wary of the milling, judging eyes skirting around them. 'You'll find a way through, I know you will.' A beat before she adds. 'And that's not even one of my bullshit platitudes.' They both crack up.

'Just don't go promising you'll never ever forget me,' Cara says, and then takes her shoulders, becomes more serious. 'And *you* will get through too.'

Jo waves her onto a 31 bus, half wishing that she'd not been reminded. But no price on kindness. She turns for the station, streetlights already on, a finger of winter at her neck.

The flat is cold when she gets home. She turns the radio on in the kitchen, taking out her phone to check her messages. There's one from Cara thanking her, attached to a picture of her twelve-week scan. She stares at it, freezing for a few seconds before arachnid digits begin tapping and scrolling, scrolling further and longer now before she gets to Ben's name, hovering over the thread of his messages.

Absurd of course — she already knows each word — but she presses on anyway, rereading the entrails like an auger searching for signs missed. The mechanics of separation: arms and legs disentwined easily enough; it was hearts and guts that tore.

Don't put pressure on me. Written after she'd tried to explain things to him over breakfast in Brixton market, him stabbing the yolk in his fried breakfast, the two of them walking back to hers, him slightly ahead then slightly behind, Jo closing the door behind them, waiting a moment before following him into the lounge. She looks up, finds the place on the wall where he'd shouted and punched the wall, his other hand then moving, not to rub raw knuckles but to redo the clasp that has popped open on his rare-metal watch, this thing with a face that could withstand the pressure of over one hundred atmospheres and remain regular as clockwork in the darkest oceans.

'I'm going to change,' he'd said. A flicker of hope at this. Some self-reflection would be good. But he'd not meant it that way, grasping at his buttons, pulling at his shoes, stomping down to the bedroom to put on some running clothes.

If only things were as simple as Narnia, she remembers thinking as she'd followed him: open a wardrobe and the world is transformed. She'd tried to sew back up what she'd torn open in haste, stitch the wound before driving up to see mum. But he'd not stuck around to listen, had crawled away to the gym in his sports car.

She'd left for the hospital to visit Mum, hadn't wanted to upset her so hadn't said anything about it. Maybe she could repair things.

'Have a good week,' Mum had whispered as Jo had left the ward later that day, not realising what a week it was going to be. Things with Ben crumbling, Mum's condition worsening, case numbers spiralling, Darren's shocking test about to light the touchpaper. Anger, anxiety, pressure, ignition, combustion.

The next time she'd left for the hospital it was atop a burning missile of chaos. Darren sworn at, school walked out on, Ben gone, tumours everywhere, Jo broken open, spilling tears.

Weak and slow, with all the energy she could muster Mum had pulled herself up, reached for Jo's hand. 'Moths,' she'd rasped. 'Moths and all sorts of ugly creatures hover about a lighted candle...' A great moan of pain halting her, Jo still in raw shock at how bad things had got. 'But can the candle help it?' Each word expelled in slow agony, one of her regular quotes from *Great Expectations*.

'Careful love,' Dad had said, seeing Mum struggle and coming over, telling Jo to go easy. And that had been it. She'd gone home and the doctors had told Dad the next day: the ward was being locked down. She never saw her again. Never held her again. This grave-sized hole still unfilled inside her.

The phone in her hand goes off, makes Jo jump, pulls her back from her brooding. A second where she thinks that it might be Ben, or Sally getting back to her, but it isn't of course.

She lets it ring. She needs to gather herself, can't let Dad hear her like this. She stands, leans her head forward and shakes her hair out. Goes to the kitchen and extracts a glass of water. Takes some deep breaths before calling him back. She has good news to tell him, about Cara. Perhaps not talk about Sami's bullies being uncovered, but there are things for which she can be grateful.

'No,' she says when he asks, 'not disturbing me. Just didn't have my phone next to me.' She wants him to hear her relaxed, as if she has time, as if the sheaf of essays to be marked isn't grumbling by her feet.

'How are the kids?' he asks cheerily.

She tells him that they are fine, doesn't mention the budget crisis or her worries about what Sami might come out with in the next lesson. Doesn't talk about the constant worry that the next email might see a whole year group sent home. More work missed, more to catch up on, more damned computer systems to do battle with. She pushes it all of that away. 'Just really, really busy Dad,' she says in précis, closing a fist tight. She was about to tell him the news about Cara, but then stopped. She can still see the crack Ben's hand made. Though perhaps it was that other mark, just further on towards the light switch? Either way, she needs some filler and a pallet knife, a pot of paint. And some bloody *time*. 'Always more for less, you know.'

'Bricks without straw,' he sighs, scripture still his go-to idiom. A people brutalised. An economy savaged. God, this has turned into a cheery one, she thinks. Plagues and floods. Pillage and rape. Hundreds of thousands dead. Police still shooting black people. Ice sheets in burning sunshine. This year was about as biblical as one could get.

She remembers herself bare-kneed and fidgeting one Sunday in church, Mum's hand pressing her to be still. Dad was in the pulpit preaching about the barren woman Sarah, promised "more children than the stars." It is a happy ending as he tells it and perhaps this had made Jo want to read backwards, stories her great love even then, lifting the thick book over from Mum's lap and looking for herself.

She finds Sarah given by her husband to be taken by a King. "Taken," this odd verb that she couldn't have yet understood — her memory of this incident surely filled in retrospectively — but through the chapters it comes again and again: nieces taken by their father, a father pleading men to take his daughters, Abraham offering his wife to be taken by the Pharaoh, taken again and again, again and again, still Sarah's womb a dry desert *until they can laugh about it* and only then, only when they have learned to laugh at a woman being passed around groups of mighty men, only then does God give her Isaac, his father then tying this precious child up, placing him on a pyre, taking a knife to his throat and...

The Bible is snatched angrily away, a hard, scolding tap on Jo's knee. Enough. Mum's hands swooping in, to chastise with a slap on the leg. Nothing for her to do in the service but listen to her father whittle these words, slice them somehow into celebration. Children given and torn away at will, divine punishment and reward. A seed, yes. Each one a Pip. Fruit of the womb.

'Bricks without straw,' Dad repeats, then says something sympathetic, tells Jo not to do too much, though she feels that she is never quite doing enough. 'Looking forward to seeing you,' he says. Quiet falls, and she knows what's coming. 'Whenever you feel able.'

She contains the explosion, holds it in her stomach. Doesn't he know how little time she already has? Doesn't he understand the pressure from Jackson, that she has to get Femi into Oxford, free Sami from his bullies, belay his whole class up to grades currently *miles* of sheer face above them? Doesn't he know that she's trying to protect him, that to keep him safe she has to stay away?

'Dad...' she begins — steering herself to kindness, to patience, reminding herself that he cannot know all of this because she's decided not to tell him — but he's already smoothing over, saying not to worry and that it doesn't matter.

'DAD,' she shouts, this bursting from her mouth, the pressure behind it surprising her, surely knocking him too but the blast still coming, '*Jesus* Dad. You know it's all I want to do, but...'

'OK love,' he says. 'OK love,' he repeats more quietly.

She wants him to be a solid body, something that won't just yield to every blow, will knock her back. But just as she is about to climb down, apologise and suggest that she'll have a look for some more places that they could go to, get him some suggestions to look over, she hears a single goodbye, the slow fumble of a receiver being recradled and the line going dead.

She lets out a howl. Stares at the phone debating whether to call him back, tells herself that he's a grown-up, that he put the phone down so he should call her, that she's angry and frustrated and stressed and should wait until she can be calm and upbeat.

She will be. She will get back to that place. She has to. The world will have to. It'll just take a while. Jordan and Michael are right about that at least: her being stressed and unhappy does nothing for them. She growls in frustration, throws the handset across the room and goes in search of a wine glass, slapping the same piece of wall that Ben had hit. Her loss his loss too. Silly fucker.

15

One Friday break-time a girl in Year 7 wheels around a corner in the playground and slips on loose asphalt, a patch in need of repair, regressing from single mass into piecemeal grit. Her knee takes the brunt and through a small tear, blood begins weeping, a salty spring surfacing in her eyes at the sight of this.

Jo strides over, begins a reflex to wrap an arm around and hold her but then pulls back. The girl looks to see what she has done wrong. Nothing, just that if she needs a hug she'll need to find someone in her bubble to administer it. A quick triage is offered instead from a distance, a snap assessment, Jo asking her where it hurts, and whether she can get up. She walks her to the First Aid room saying, 'bless you, you poor love,' telling her it'll be OK. The nurse isn't there so she then tells the girl to wait on a chair outside, that she needs to be brave and dry her eyes, that Jo can't stay with her because she is needed in the hall. Someone from reception comes out and gives her a Capri Sun. She sucks greedily at the straw and looks a bunch happier.

Jo leaves her, weaves through tables on the foyer, touching the backs of chairs as she goes, pulling one or two things straight then smothering her hands in sanitiser. She's been feeling bad about her outburst at Dad but hasn't found the mental space to call him back yet. She will when she's got any better idea about whether it'd be safe to visit him. She's been daydreaming about a spa, a nice Bed and Breakfast. God, after all this she so needs it. Just needs to be away. Underwater in a pool. Sat in a steam room. Strong fingers massaging her back, without fucking gloves on.

Year 11 are being wheeled into the hall, given a motivational speech about exam success. "You can do anything," they are told, "anything you want to achieve, anything."

For a moment, they swallow it. Nelson's eyes light up, Chanel leans forward in her seat. Nishaan leans his back and tips himself onto the floor. Cara gets over, gets him up without a fuss. Jo can't work out if she looks pregnant yet. Perhaps it's just the lights, not an actual new glow. The kids will be delighted once they start to guess. She doubts it'll be long. Some crazy sixth sense they have about these things.

'You can fly as high as you like,' the speaker says once the commotion has died down. 'Come to the edge. Open your wings. Don't let anyone tell you that you can't fly.'

An ache behind Jo's breast, a longing for this to be true. Survey any group of kids on what superpower they'd want and flight will always come up top. But we can't, she thinks, we can't. We aren't angels; our lives are too heavy. Maybe before Jude, before she'd had to go to secondary school... she remembers life having had a lightness then. Swings. Deft jumps from roundabouts. Leaping on climbing frames, no thought of playground tarmac. Not that wings need opening but that burdens need removing. Find a way to let things go.

Sami is looking out of the window up at the Tower. Grades are circling, hard ground fast approaching, letters soon to be hung around their necks.

She can't tell them that this is bullshit, that if they jump there is only one way they'll go. *Don't let anyone tell you that you can't fly.* Yes, he's right in this at least. Each has to discover this truth, this loss, for themselves.

Cara straightens her back, prompting a twinge of worry, school not the easiest place in her state. Chaotic corridors, lots of stress. The season of coughs and colds, loads of asymptomatic cases surely, but who round here is getting tested? She calculates the date when Cara will be likely to go on leave. Definitely before this lot will be done with the syllabus, all of which will mean extra work. But she wants to say to Cara that she'll be really happy to step up and help in any way she can.

Another ruckus as a short *frap* is heard and the boys around Michael begin clambering away, laughing into the shirts that they are now holding over their mouths, as if this might save them from being asphyxiated. For his part, Michael is trying to act innocent, sat with his arms folded, a huge grin on his face.

'Year 11!' Jo calls, marching to the front and apologising to the speaker. But when she gets there and turns to face them she finds herself perilously close to a fit of the giggles, having to cover her mouth with her hand to try to hold it together. She shakes her head at Michael and a smile breaks cover.

'Man said you could do anything,' Jordan calls out and they all roar again, the speaker gripping the lectern and closing his eyes, repeating his mantras before pushing on with his talk. Jo wants to tell him to relax, that they don't mean anything personal by it. Nothing sacred, nothing serious. But she couldn't. No way she could trust herself to speak to him without cracking up.

16

When Year 11 arrive in Jo's lesson the talk seems long forgotten because they are already in the middle of something else. Lauren, Chanel and Safiya are a sharp spear of shoulder bags, tight hair and united purpose. Screw your plan Miss, their entrance says, sorry if you wrote it two weeks ago, but there are some lessons that need to be learned right here.

'Girls, what's going on?' Jo asks, peering out over her mask, all of them standing by their desks glaring over at Jordan and Michael, waiting, just waiting for one of them to say just one thing. In separate meetings she has said a number of things to both boys, made it clear that she expects far more. Sami is sat between the girls and these two, a wary eye on Jordan, but this seems different, is not about that.

Surprised, the girls all look at Jo as if to say: surely you know already Miss? Then Lauren tells her. Hisses, throws words like acid over the boys.

'That sack of shit Nelson walked up the stairs behind Hayley at break. Tried to put his phone up her skirt.'

Oh no. Her first thought is her own guilt. She hadn't found the time to hunt him down and discipline him properly for his part in what had happened with Sami. He might have been chastened; Hayley might have been spared. *Fuck.* She wipes her computer screen, asks Lauren what has been done so far and she tells her that Hayley's mum has collected her and Nelson has been sent home.

Jesus, she thinks. This place. Just give me one lesson where there's not some major spectacle, where she has her plan and can just get through it. She whips everyone until they sit down then lays the law down on them, the penalties for even forwarding material like that. Accusations are being swapped like gunfire, Jo desperately trying to bring some order, but it's hopeless. In her hand is *Great Expectations* but they have a real-life drama unfolding.

Anger has risen in them, and now it surges within her. As much as they want to talk, as horrible as it all is, there is nothing that can be done here about the situation. No justice can be advanced right now, only their knowledge of literature and Jackson's judgement of her capability of delivering it. In the end she has to shout — SIT DOWN — get the door closed but leave the windows open, yes it's cold but the regs demand ventilation, get caps and coats off, and go through the register. When it comes to Nelson's name they ask how long he's been put out for and she says that she has absolutely no idea.

'I don't care,' Chanel is saying, starting to preach again to her gallery, 'he is not coming back in this lesson. It's GCSEs. How can Hayley do her work when she's got *that* behind her. That is abuse. That is *abuse*. I spoke to Miss Elkins and she was well good about it.'

Cara. Of course she was.

Ade tries to make light, says, 'maybe she shouldn't dress so sket,' and it's uproar again, the boys hooting 'oh my days, oh my days,' then rounding on him too, shouting 'you can't be saying that blood, you can't,' laughing but shaking their heads at him.

Sami remains silent, shading his drawing of the fruit trees. It's grown and spread, with more detail and depth.

Jo checks in quickly with Nourin, decides Ade has been sufficiently told. 'This is being dealt with,' she calls loudly, 'so we all need to SIT DOWN and get our focus back on the lesson.' Half of her face is covered, which seems to mean half of her cues go unseen. She doesn't want to compensate with double the volume but it can be hard to know what to do.

'Miss,' Lauren complains, 'I don't mean to be rude or nothing, but you have no idea what it's like.'

Jo apparently neither fish nor flesh. Just teacher. No body to wield, no skin to be in this game. '*Please* girls, sit down. And

Lauren...' Jo says, turning to her with a wounded look, but Lauren doesn't seem to see it and cuts straight across.

'Miss, we don't *want* to sit down,' she says. The girls shout at the boys and the boys shout back and Jo wants to shout into this noise too, to tell Lauren that she *does* know, because all women know. Hands on knees, skirts pawed at, shouts from cars. Jesus, did they think filth began with the internet? She wants to ask them if *they* have any idea what it's like. To be not-young, to no longer be looked at. Could their imaginations stretch to that?

She looks at the clock, at another lesson draining quickly away. Regardless of all this Jackson is going to rule on how well she has taught them English, not on how far she might have helped progress the cause of equality.

The door is shut, the windows a sliver ajar. Every angry retort, every laugh, every threat, all of it pushes more air into the space, the whole room becoming compressed, pressurised, pushing into her. Not just the thing with Hayley but the heat still between Jordan and Sami, the feeling that Nishaan is being forgotten amongst all this, the droplets that must be flying around onto everything, concern over whether Sami knows that the boys bullying him are going to be hauled in any moment, the anxiety about what the hell he is going to say once he stands up, all this other stuff nothing compared to what he's probably gone through, but no, none of it insignificant, not for Hayley, not for Nishaan, not if you're in the middle of it.

She wants to be balanced and fair, stay positive and hopeful for each of them, not seem paranoid about every surface she touches, but most of all she wants to rip the door open, break the airlock and just walk away, *walk* from here out of London, along streets, then whatever fields, just walk all the way to Dad. Strip herself of everything as she went. Slough off each damned layer that has added itself over her. Rediscover that lightness, that adolescent weightlessness. She would, she tells herself, she would if that wouldn't mean letting so many people down, so many *children* down, and all of these forces tense and press and accelerate a single word up and out of her mouth.

'QUIET.'

It screams through the paper of her mask, lands like a banger and a brief wave of shock rolls through.

'Alright Miss, calm down,' Lauren says, rolling her eyes at Jordan, both of them then laughing into their bags as they get their stuff out.

She fumes. Feels things blaze and smoke inside of her, burning and blackening, charring and choking.

'Miss I need a new book,' Chanel says nonchalantly.

'Jesus Chanel! Really? Now?' She grabs the old one, flicks through it and weighs it. She can see that Chanel has ripped pages out, things that she'll have wanted to be rid of, marks she didn't like, comments that were critical, titles she'd messed up, leaving a thin-skinned, skeletal thing. Chanel complains about not being believed, and Jo tells her that she does believe her but the school cannot afford for people to be wasting space.

'God man this place is so brock-up,' Danny complains.

Jo goes into her cupboard, finds the box of new books empty, mumbles into the darkness for Danny to 'go fuck himself.' She comes back out and tells them that she'll have to go to the stock cupboard down the corridor, begs them to be responsible for just one minute and read quietly while she is gone, tells Sami to get his presentation ready.

Lauren and Nourin straighten their backs and open their texts, but as Jo leaves one of the boys cups his hands around his mouth, mimics another rasping fart. 'Anyone stick a phone near my backend they'll regret it,' and they're all silly young children again, howling with laughter, calling out at Michael to admit what he'd done before, him still protesting his innocence.

Making sure the coast is clear she ignores the one-way system, takes the corridor briskly, turns the key, opens the stock cupboard door, closes it behind her. She doesn't turn on the light yet, waits for the enveloping dark to smother and soothe, to put out her anger. Somewhere in here are fifty copies of *Under Milk Wood* and she lets them call to her as she waits. Sloe-black, slow, black, starless, moonless. No windows, only hunched shelves of books that mute and hush the crashing waves of commotion outside.

So calm in here. Old blackboard panels still lean in corners clinging to dust. Layer upon layer of wonderful things inscribed and rubbed out; ideas noted, smudged, erased and all this done so many times that they are cracked and pocked, no longer smooth surfaces down which white fingers of chalk could softly run. On shelves there are volumes of once-ringing poems that have been shut up, novels no longer novel, romances no longer loved, a bookshop smell that makes Jo want to lock the door and tarry — Thomas, Bryon, Dickinson, Plath — lock the door and open herself to them, give them time to speak, dance, sing their prosody. But she can't. She can't. She arrows a quick prayer to them, asking them to help her make it through.

She turns on the light, is relieved to find a box. Grabs a pack of books. Two packs. Go.

She rushes back in and at least they're not fighting, have not physically attacked each other, though they're not reading quietly and Sami is not ready to present, has not got a sheaf of notes in his hand, is not stood waiting to begin.

'Why can't you just do what you're told?' she scolds, inviting Chanel to prise a new book out of the cellophane, putting the others into her cupboard, a ball of paper in mid-air as she turns, hitting Radha on the head, Jo working back the trajectory, thinking probably Jakob, but nothing she can prove, picking up the missile, apologising to Radha, putting it in the bin as she calls them back to attention.

RIGHT. Fifteen minutes in and literally nothing has been done. But it's not *their* fault, the chorus chants at Jo. It's you, they sing loudly inside her head, *you* that isn't doing a good enough job. Cara would have been all over this. If you'd supported her better she'd probably be doing more to stay, have more reason to want to come back. Fifteen minutes, and you've got nowhere. Fail. A cast-iron fail if this an inspection.

She has promised Sami a chance to reply, and perhaps this is the thing that will save the lesson. Turn it, connect it, link it somehow.

'Going back to your homeworks,' she begins, voice still raised, lifting her hands like a minister offering benediction. 'The one on Dickens describing Pip's early life — a horrible thing that happened to him — let's take what's just happened, what we're all trying to deal with, not ignore it, but use it to understand how events shape people's lives.'

Good Teacher, they called him before he became the Christ. But she bets the crowds weren't this poorly behaved at the Sermon on the Mount, weren't even as paranoid about the unclean among them.

'So, we heard from Jordan about,' and she stops, waits again for quiet. Another ball of paper is deftly dashed back towards Jakob. Ade reaches to punch Charlie in the arm. Lauren is turned round, talking to Chanel. Danny is trying to tell a joke. Radha is trying to find Nishaan's homework in his book. 'We HEARD from Jordan,' she says again, voice rising and quietening, then becoming uncertain, not wanting to bring the fox back in, not wanting the echoes returning to the room, cries recoiling off the walls of the tower. The animal trapped. The hard glare of streetlights. Blood and fur. She dares a look at Sami to see if he is ready, nerves jangling, praying that they don't just go for him. 'I know some of you found Jordan's speech the other day uncomfortable,' she says finally, 'so it's only right in the safe space of a classroom to give people a chance to respond...' — Jordan turns to Michael and they whisper something then laugh — '...to respond in the proper way...' Jo states more loudly, looking at the two of them, one then the other, trying to pin them down. '...without degenerating into personal attack.'

There's some noise, a quick spray of discussion but then a hush, a sense that they do actually want to hear this, hear from this kid who's turned up in their manor out of nowhere, daring to backchat Jordan.

So there's quiet as Jo signals for him to come forward.

They are good kids, mostly.

There's quiet enough as he stands near the front, head bowed, holding his copy of Dickens, his little Cromwell wire-bound planner, some notes he's made perhaps, though Jo can't really see.

She pushes her hand through her hair. The sun explodes off a window in the tower. Another quick prayer for them to be kind. Sheep, not wolves.

There's quiet now as he shuffles, looks at Jo for a nod. She gives this, trying to fill a little tilt of her neck with all the encouragement and support a good mother might muster.

Quiet as he eyes the pack nervously.

Quiet as he opens his mouth to speak.

17

Sips of dirt-grey coffee. The shuffle of papers. Staff checking pigeonholes next to unread notice boards, some nibbling sandwiches, thumbing through phone screens. Some just sat, eyes closed a moment, hoping for stillness. Even in normal times the staffroom would have been a far more humdrum place than she'd imagined it would be when she'd first started teaching. Now, with strict limits on occupancy numbers and doom-laden posters everywhere, it was dead space.

But this lunchtime, a few days until half term, it is a refuge from battles on the corridors outside and in the canteen below. Alex is a cloud of gloom in the English office, so Jo and Cara have escaped. A few other bodies are scattered around constellations of catalogue-standard easy-chairs that orbit low beech tables. Along one side of the room, windows let pass what midday sun there is; people know to keep away from them in case something is seen in the playground below.

The two women hunch over a table and Cara wants to know how the lesson had gone with Sami.

Jo passes over the chaos of the lesson opening, skips the part about hiding for a moment in the stock cupboard. She doesn't mention Sami's slightly trembling hands, him looking out over the blaze of eyes, her coiled, ready to rage if they went for him. She just tells Cara that he'd begun by saying sorry.

Cara frowns, jolts her head back a touch as Jo explains that, yes, he'd told the class he was sorry if he'd sounded rude before. Jordan had lifted a hand slightly and put it back on his desk. She had listened to him with a glow of satisfaction, pride spreading at the simple dignity of his words.

'The fox hunt story, it made me angry.' Stilted, accent still strong, but so much better in just a few weeks. A move from Nishaan, his arm beginning to sweep across his desk, but Radha had reached over, slapped a hand on his table, told him to stop. She wasn't meant to do that, was meant to be keeping her hands to her own desk, though neither was Jo meant to have strayed in amongst the tables and sat herself near Jordan. But no one could keep this up, hold to every damned rule. A classroom had to be alive; learning wasn't a sterile thing. Even so, she had tried to hold her breath, avoided movement as if looking out from a hide, anxious not to disturb. 'Recently in my country, *people* have been hunted.' Jakob had snatched a glance at Ade, turned back, looked down into his desk, fiddling with the corner of his book. 'Women hurt very badly too,' Sami had continued, a little bolder in the lengthening quiet, a glance over at Lauren.

Dan from Science is part of a small circle of other teachers sitting over in the next cluster in the staffroom. Jo senses that he's listening to her tell this and raises her voice a little to make sure that they all do. Hopefully, they will see past the woman who told a boy to fuck off, see that the thing with Jackson is just procedural nonsense, understand her skill and experience, that she is getting somewhere with a group of very challenging children.

Their interest has probably been piqued by mention of Hayley. The story is everywhere of course. Dan should be feeling sorry for how he'd mocked her in the pub. *Hay-leeeeeee-ya*. Some of these young staff are fresh out of university. Lectures, unrefined banter, "pre-loading," student nights... months later and they're enforcing rules not working out how to bend them, chasing essays not begging extensions, delivering alcohol awareness and why to say no to drugs. Suddenly they've got to be grown-ups.

She has their ear for a moment, she thinks, an experienced professional explaining about this boy who had called out one of Year 11's big players. He had dared to disagree, and she had given him a chance to say his piece. Risky of course, but if these young teachers are to stay the course they have to learn that one has to work *bloody* hard, has to take the plunge sometimes, step out boldly and allow lessons to be acts of courage.

'That sounds amazing, well done,' Cara yawns as she finishes the story. 'By the way, have you spoken to Martha today?' She hasn't and now feels a bit judged, as if she'd failed to do the most important thing. 'I'm worried about her,' Cara continues, her thoughts no longer with Sami or Jo. 'I'm not sure she's coping.' She looks over at the group of staff, says that Martha would normally be with them, calls over and asks if they know where she is. They don't.

Jo makes a mental note. If some are finding it tough, she should find time to talk with them. They'll have all heard about Geoff. Like one of his keyboards: a good instrument, but not built for that kind of rough treatment. Every blackboard a coal face. Teaching was about pressure, grading and honing, mining the jewel in each child. Sat sagging in their cheap suits, picking at sandwiches, they're probably feeling cut and bruised, worn down and crumbling. Those who aren't resilient enough will go blunt, lose their edge, be inspected, removed and replaced. But she wants to help them make it.

'Jordan,' Sami had continued earlier. Jordan gave a look that warned caution. 'Jordan, you were right. The first part, before the fox, not dumb.' He had dared a smile, an olive branch, and there was Jordan's hand again, lifted slightly, accepting. 'Powerful people keeping the lid on poor people. Police. Shootings. And then a spark.' And he'd turned to Jo, raised his copy of Dickens. 'I told Miss, this book. The boy Pip stays silent, because the criminal scares him, and for this he is rewarded.' He'd then stopped, had had to take a moment to gather himself. 'But what if he had spoken about this bad man?' A look around the classroom. 'Then he is in danger. Then he has to take his family, and run.' The class had not made a sound, had let him gather the scattered pieces of himself before he'd gone on.

This is how you do it, Jo imagines telling a training session for new teachers, you take these rare moments and sharpen yourself with them.

She'd offered the class a chance for questions. No one had come forward, so she'd asked Sami if he'd found a mosque since he'd arrived. He'd looked confused, saying 'Miss, what? I'm Christian,' the class cracking up, wrong twice in a row, Ade saying ks-sake Miss what are you like, telling her she was so dumb.

No need to tell Cara that, Jo thinks, but then suddenly Cara is leaping up anyway. 'Oh shit,' she says, slopping her coffee mug down onto the table, jumping up, brushing her blouse and straightening her skirt. 'Lunchtime support for the level 4's. Totally forgot.' Jo asks her if she wants her to cover it for her but she says no, she wouldn't dream of it. She shoots off, and across at the other table there's a skirmish as some paper napkins are hurled like snowballs.

A moped whines by, out on the estate, beyond the fence. Revs and whines, revs and whines, maybe going somewhere, maybe just riding around. She has Femi and her Sixth Form class coming after lunch; she'd love to sit and chill for a bit longer but she ought to go and get on with writing a bloody assessment for Year 9.

Alex pops into the staffroom to rifle through his pigeonhole, head stuck into his phone. She feels sorry for him in a way. Head of Department. Full teaching load, staff to manage, targets to deliver and now no budget to do it with. No wonder he is so stressed.

'Hey Jo' he says, looking up and seeing her. 'Just been hearing great things from Cara about your work with Year 11.'

'Thanks Alex, that's really kind.' He lifts his head slightly, a kind of half-nod of appreciation, before heading through the door and onto the corridor.

Jo knows that she should go, but wants to bask, wait until every echo of this kindness has melted away.

When the door swings open and Jackson enters, the rest of the room seems to tighten as it looks up, but Jo takes him in with a smile. Naturally, it turns out that it's her that he's after, and as she prepares to take his praise she casts her gaze over the others. But as soon as his face moves, before words have even begun to arrive it folds into sour expression.

'Bit of a problem, Jo,' he says. 'Can I have a word?' When she doesn't immediately get up he adds, 'in my office?'

The tone and volume suddenly sound deliberate. There's an audible ruffle of attention from the young staff as Jo rises, parts of them still childish, still fuelled by gossip, scraps like these, all grist to the mill; something delicious, something sweet to keep them going through the afternoon.

Outside of the staffroom, as he marches towards the stairs, he embellishes. 'This bullying thing you'd reported. Something about you and Sami Karim?'

She halts, tells him that she'll be right down but needs to pop to the loo. He knows it would be overly petty to refuse, and with a sigh pushes through the doors and descends. Jo hurries to Cara. Cara already knows. Of course she does.

'Apparently, one of the boys you reported for bullying has now reported *you*,' Cara tells her in hushed tones while her lunchtime club work on a mind map. Jo nods, impatient. 'Said someone saw you and Sami sitting together on a bench? Outside school, in school hours?'

'How did you?' she starts to ask. She waves a child away who's sitting with his hand up.

'Jackson told me just now. I'm sorry, he was looking for you and came in. I started telling him about your lesson but he stopped me, said that there was something more serious. I didn't have time...'

Oh fuck, Jo thinks, but frowns and tries to act as if this is all ridiculous. She tells Cara not to worry, accepts a supportive clench on the arms as she turns to go, feels herself go nausea-white as she pushes out into the stairwell and heads down.

'Probably nothing,' she imagines idiots in the staffroom saying to one another, gathering their books, collecting coffee mugs, getting up to leave.

'Probably nothing...' though one will confide that they'd heard her talking about Sami a lot. That people have noticed her giving him special attention. That, what with this Hayley thing, and the current climate... Then another will whisper that they've heard it's not been an easy time. Something that kicked off the end of last year?

It *is* nothing, Jo says to herself, preparing her defence. Just a silly thing that happened even though nothing happened.

But she can almost hear them purring, each asking the other if they have heard. Feigning concern as they update her status.

18

Flustered, apologetic, Jo finally arrives at her Sixth Form lesson. They are already sat with folders out, carrying on talking amongst themselves while she gathers herself. Her desk is somewhere under little hills of paper. An urge to sweep the whole lot into the bin but there could be gold hidden, half sets of photocopies that now need to be preserved.

'How are you all?' she asks as a deflection, and they look at each other a little uncertainly, as if urging one of them to say something important, though they come back only with a roster of petty complaints. Tiredness. Too much work. Stupid regulations. Target grades. Personal Statements for University applications. Femi has already taken the plunge, applied for Oxford and is now worried that she hasn't heard back yet, wondering aloud if it was the right thing.

'Ticket out of here,' Rasheed says.

'You'll love it,' Anya adds. 'Dad will be so excited.'

Femi tries to damp this down. 'I haven't even got an interview yet.'

'Yes, but just the idea of it. If you get in he'll be telling people about it for weeks.'

Their school choices justified. Capital to profit from.

Mo rolls his eyes, smiles at Femi and shakes his head. 'And what about Daddy getting *you* an interview at his *alma mater*?' The injection of Latin surprises Jo, though she doesn't want it to. No one else blinks.

Anya bristles, tries to laugh off the accusation. 'It doesn't work like that. Level playing field these days one hopes.'

'Except it's Stamford Bridge at one end,' Rasheed says, 'and the Somme at the other.' Anya sticks her tongue out at him and Jo catches the glint of a stud through the middle of it.

'That's enough you lot,' she says, pushing around a set of quarantining books to try to find the board rubber, asking them to give her a minute. Mo sniggers at Rasheed. Jo has no idea why but feels for her skirt zip just in case, then checks her blouse buttons. Perhaps they know, she thinks, still trying to find the damned eraser, perhaps one of them saw her walking anxiously into Jackson's office, or coming out head down, eyes puffed and red as she'd marched into the Ladies.

'Bastard,' she'd hissed into the mirror, his words still searing. *A safeguarding allegation has been made so — as you know — it has to be investigated.* His voice had been calm but too smooth to be trustworthy, words offering warm support but actually holding coals to her feet.

Bastard. But her anger had mostly been turned inwards. Stupid. So *fucking* stupid. All her critical voices lambasting, the whole inner chorus in joint reprimand. *CCTV. Electronic swipe cards. You shouldn't have been so naive.* Darren saw her there. It must have been him, she'd concluded. As dangerous to her out there as he was in here.

Cara had come to find her as soon as she was free, was kind, unqualified in her support. 'Jackson has got where he's got because he'll have relished doing shit like this,' she'd said, leaning on a basin, handing her paper towels. She doesn't feel that she deserves a friend like this. 'Treading on colleagues. Enjoying the snap of bones. The rewards of psychopathy. Just ask Martha.'

'Oh dear,' Jo had said, pulling hands from her face with a look of concern. 'I was going to try to speak to her. She not doing good?' The added shame, she thinks, another weight clipped to her back. She's meant to be the experienced one here. Others should be getting the help.

'Not really. She looked so awful, so wiped out she's becoming translucent.'

They'd agree to try to talk to her together, then Cara had run to get Jo's handbag.

'You're so lucky getting out Car.' A few minutes later, time tight now but feeling better as she's patched herself up. She's reapplying mascara, a dab of blusher to add some colour.

Creating an appropriate fiction for Year 13. Makeup to make them believe. An actor prepares. 'You'd have to be a psycho to stay.'

'You're not a psycho Jo.'

'Hiding the symptoms well. Check back in a month.'

'Ha bloody ha.' The sound of the bell ringing out there on the corridor. 'Come on. It'll blow over.'

Except, Jo had thought to herself, it most likely won't. Not now. She wants to be optimistic — that lightness of being — but there's an unbearable sense of shadow deepening behind her. One thing triggers another. Stuff dominos.

'Come on. You'll be late for your Year 13s,' Cara had said, waiting patiently while she'd finished. She'd then hugged her, and it was as much as Jo could do not to cry again, to beg Cara not to let her go. The feeling of a body after all this time. To be in that state of embrace, to have someone's hands at your back, their head tight over your shoulder, no darkness could reach her then. But Cara had pulled away, had looked Jo over and pointed her to the door, beyond which were corridors and children, barking reminders about one-way systems and keeping your distance, policies and masks, back on stage again.

Walking across the crowded foyer, hurrying up the turbulent stairs, she'd never felt so removed from other people. Snagging her foot on a stray chair leg she'd had a crashing new realisation that Ben really was gone, that whatever her dad still believed she would actually *never* see or hear from her mother again. No vaccine and no end in sight. The most loving thing to do was distance. Bio-secure, but crushing her in so many other ways. She'd crossed her arms, pinched hard at a crease of skin under her arm, pain as a quick verification as she'd got to her room to teach Year 13.

Less than an hour ago she'd imagined walking in head held high, finding a way to tell them about her victory with Sami. But because she'd tried to do something good for a child and it has been dressed as grooming, now it has all turned. Stupid. She has been so stupid.

She tries to find encouragement in their trivialities. Her blouse has not malfunctioned. Her skirt has not ripped. She is a student of fiction, something of an expert in making things up. Finally, she locates the board rubber and rallies. If they'd heard rumours surely Anya wouldn't be moaning about the boiler at home packing up. She would be eyeing Jo more quietly, opening her book with circumspection, not gassing about never being so cold in her life, having to go to friends next door for baths, sob sob, swearing down that the creepy little brother had tried to peer through the bathroom door.

A blister of envy grows. Pink-skinned and sinuous, soft towels on firm, smooth flesh. A-Levels, then far away from here to study. If not Daddy's old college in Oxford then Edinburgh. Or Durham. Life back to normal by then surely, and so much to make up for. Parties and lectures. Balls and gowns and vast opportunities, her time slumming it here soon to be over, the tongue stud healed over, reduced to an alluring anecdote. All of them with their succulent lives ahead of them and Jo wanting to thrust her head down and gorge on their youth.

She grips a pen and stops herself, stands these stupid thoughts down. Thank God it's Hamlet next term, not Titus Andronicus.

'That's enough now,' — talking as much to herself as them — 'Let's get back to Forster.'

Anya tears lined paper from her pad and hands it along to the others, digs a spare pen out of her pencil case and passes it to Rasheed who nods a quiet thank you. Jo flushes a little before turning to write the date. She's explained it to them — the cuts, the lack of money — never quite saying that they'd now need to bring in their own stationery, but they'd just rolled their eyes and got on with it. Banking crises, downturns, never really known any different, Mo saying 'why should we expect school to give us paper anyway?' No one had come up with a reason. Anya had had a thick pad-full, though she's not even meant to be sharing it. Jo had bleated a weak apology, but not chastised them for breaking regs.

'We are going to be looking at the dinner party scene with Helen and Margaret.'

'Bet they got waaaasted,' Mo jokes.

'Like you did last weekend,' Femi shoots back.

'Oh, and you were sober then were you?' Anya laughs, sending Mo snorting, saying he wasn't sure how Anya could have judged anything with that guy's tongue so far down her throat. Jo scribbles a lesson headline onto the board as they sink behind her into stories about that 18th and the one that was coming tomorrow night, the meagre one hundred and four weekend days in the year nowhere near sufficient to go round a Sixth Form of nearly two hundred, every one of whom has birthdays to celebrate or parents away.

Looking down, thinking what to write, she sees in horror that there *is* a drying stain on her blouse, tears mixed with make-up, a drip of snot or something that looks worse. Back still turned, she scratches it away as best she can, waits for a blush to ebb while the class run in full flow.

'Jägerbomb!' Mo is shouting, pointing at Femi.

She ought to be taking them to task, reminding them about the huge importance of social distancing, of the dangers to other people if they didn't respect the guidance. 'And how many were at this party?' she asks.

'Six,' Mo shoots back, but Jo holds his eye. 'A few groups of six,' he concedes with a grin.

'Go out to help out,' Femi adds.

Jo narrows her eyes in reply. She wants to be warning them about the damage they are probably doing, using this as a springboard into Serious Talk about the deep purpose of literature, that Tess and Emma Bovary and Jude Fawley weren't just means to high marks and interviews at Oxford but serious interlocutors about the grave matter of how to live a good life... But she has hugged Cara, is being investigated for seeing a student outside of school, has allowed rules to slip for an easy life, doesn't live in a high-rise block.

She picks up *Howards End* as they carry on talking — interrupting, laughing, interjecting and overlapping — picks up the book and tries to find the passage about the dinner party, gets lost in the battalions of black and white type, characters taking actions in crisp, sharp lines while behind her makeup she feels blurred and smudged. She halts at a turned-down page, a pencil-mark in the margin. *Those who prepare for all the emergencies of life may equip themselves at the expense of joy.* Forster's words hit like a blow to the head. The prices they have all had to calculate. The expense of levity. The cost of all this to all of them, but these poor children more than anyone. They are seventeen years old, laughing yes, but anxious. They have all the jokes but move warily. Why shouldn't they have a drink or three to unbuckle a little enjoyment? Take a few risks, or risk a joyless life.

She's never felt a less adequate role model. She was hardly present for them over lockdown. Too dangerous to return, they said. Keep schools shut. Keep children at home. Guilt worming at her each day, a worry that caution was going too far, that they ought to be allowed to meet over Zoom, just occasionally at least. But it was too risky. What if they were in their bedroom? What if something was seen? What if someone didn't have a device, or a good enough connection. Screens conjuring images, projecting fears. The dangers of camming.

Now they are back though nothing has changed. Still this nagging worry that it had been the wrong decision. Just look at the cost, at how far behind they now were, how underprepared for their next steps. Femi's dream, trashed by super-vigilance. Could she look at Jo as an example of better choices? Where has Jo's careful life got her? Has an intimate knowledge of the classics prepared her for this, kept her running over with exuberance while the country has stumbled and fallen? Have the books she's guided Femi through given her wings or added ballast? Education as gravity, she thinks.

Is it even possible to fill a child up without weighing them down?

She flushes at the thought of the allegations surfacing. *Grooming a kid in Year 11?* The truth of it won't matter. To smoke, they'll add their own fire. They must all have seen the stained blouse, understood it as a mark of something.

'Stop it!' Anya shouts, trying to quell ribbing about a public display of affection. Alcohol, testosterone, accelerants for a youth misspent. 'He was really drunk!' She says, defensive. Raises her arms and starts waving them. 'Like an octopus.'

She can't but think of poor Hayley, not so many years since she and her friends had left their Primary, probably full of excitement about big school, hardly knowing the defences they would have to develop, the mental armour they'd have to load on — sarcasm, cynicism, guardedness, duplicity — all of it costing a little more happiness, all of this now on top of all of that, all of it needing to be lubricated. How many bottles this week? At least they're drinking to be together rather than drinking to forget they're alone.

'Shut up. Shut up. Fuck off. Stop,' Jo spits under her breath and lands with a thump back into the room.

She snatches the lesson plan from her desk, holds it with the copy of Forster. Push on. Get to half term. Take the plunge and go see Dad.

'Thank you Anya, that's way more detail than I could ever need.' She gives them the page number, directs them back to Helen and Margaret Schlegel. 'Just so we are clear: this was a society dinner party they were attending, not a Tower piss-up with call-outs for pizza.' They laugh and open their books, begin considering the question taxing Forster's dinner table: what they would each do if they had a million to give away.

Jo waves an arm at the flaking paint and creeping damp above the windows, warped and draughty in their 1950s metal casings, points down at the chewing-gummed carpet and the battle-scarred door. 'Look around this place,' she says. 'Imagine a school with endless cash at its disposal. Would everyone get great results? And even if they did, would that necessarily mean that they'd become cultured?'

There's a moment's silence while they process thoughts and formulate arguments, a moment before a torrent of disagreement erupts. Emotions rise as backgrounds and proud loyalties distort the canvas of the rational. Femi wants the money invested in high-tech new buildings, a bigger library, trolleys of iPads.

'But Forster's point is that money *doesn't* make someone cultured,' Anya complains, 'any more than having a Rolls Royce makes you a good driver.' A bitchy scoff from Femi, asking if she'd got that line from her tutor. Anya retorts, hurt. 'Femi that's not fair.'

Choppy water, but Jo is pleased with what she's animated. It's as if Forster had drawn them in caricature himself, the class falling into two warring camps, those who'd give students and teachers a vote on how it was spent, and those like Anya who'd want it to be ring-fenced, carefully accounted for and handed out in prudent portions.

'Jesus, you can be soooo patronising,' Rasheed moans, holding his book in one hand to read aloud, raising his other, palm out, to deflect the crescendo of competing voices, '"*altering poor people*"' — he slows and almost shouts this section — '"*until they became exactly like people who were not so poor.*"' He slams the book down on his desk. 'Words, right there. Rich people always thinking we aren't good enough, that we've got to be changed.'

Jo nods approval at him, feels a pulse of light returning to break the shadow. The debate catches fire, Mo raging about education being cheap. 'It's so basic it even made it onto my Sociology syllabus.' A smatter of LOLs at this, but he's serious. 'Every penny you spend in a school comes back three times.' He enumerates on his fingers. 'Less crime, better health, all that. Watch,' he says, 'watch how shutting down the youth centre last year will end up costing the council more. Guarantee it.'

Femi laughs bitterly. 'The borough is *broke* Mo. Keep the youth centre open, they'll shut a library somewhere else.'

'Plenty around here a long way from broke,' he replies quietly, drawing a sharp line under a title.

Jo quells them again, directs them to the book. 'The question you need to ask yourselves,' she says, dousing a few remaining fires of argument, 'the question Forster wants us to ask here is whether you think a poor person *can* be cultured.'

A show of hands, and they all say they're in favour, looking at each other, ensuring compliance. She strides up to the board, pen ready to strike, then the door swings open, slams against the wall.

'Sami,' she says, turning. A step back. The class don't recognise him. He is wearing a rucksack. They freeze as if in preparation to panic, have seen films, have had to do drills.

His face is all confused contortion. 'Why?' he bleats finally. Throwing this to the ground in front of Jo. 'Why, when you promised?'

Oh God. He's found out. 'Miss Elgin,' she starts to say, diverting some blame to Cara, focusing on the bullying. 'Miss Elgin saw it. Knew their names. I...'

'A boy saw us. Darren. That boy you got expelled.'

Jo splutters, aware of the audience for this explosive two-hander, searching for context, a way of explaining that it wasn't what they thought. 'That's nonsense, Sami.' She shushes him, apologises to the Year 13s, steps to herd him out of the door.

But he's not done. 'I trusted you. I said *no*. You promised,' he says, repeating this, shouting it now. 'Out there, you promised,' sweeping his hand towards the estate lying beyond the windows. 'You made it worse!' And then has no more words, no more sense he can martial into plosive glottals or fricative palatals, nothing more than a roar that barges out of his throat, no more than a twist of muscles into an ache of despair, Jo stepping further towards him but Sami turning, other voices approaching, him turning and slamming the door as he runs away, the thing bouncing on its hinges, shaking the corner of a poster free, half of Shakespeare's head disappearing.

The room has both expanded and shrunk. Jo feels small, the mass of their desks vast, the whole array of chairs and tables, of posters, pipes, windows, radiators and display boards like the innards of a machine that she has fallen into, one so complex it has left her mute.

The class have slowed, are silent, virtually still. She and they both search for something that can be said, something that will break the frost that is fast crystallising between them. But then the door cracks open again and a crumpled can of Fanta arcs through it.

'Paedo!' a voice shouts.

'Cancer mum!' another lobs in. Sounds of laughter, running feet, door handles cracking into plaster. Diminuendo as they flee but their words are still in flight, are turning and sharpening towards her and for a second she stands as if willing these arrows to pierce her.

There's a movement in her throat, a slow blink that she takes as if closing her eyes in prayer, closing them in order to see the unseen, speak to the invisible. But then she comes back, bites her lip hard as if tightening a cilice, widens her eyes and grips the desk, defences holding.

She asks if any in the class recognise who they were. Of course they don't. Of course they wouldn't. Except there is a connection, a thread that stitches them together, this class the only one she had trusted with the truth. *Just after Easter, my mum fell ill*. Truth always a dare, confession always a risk, a secret always a gift offered in good faith. All of this, now betrayed.

Anger flares, Rasheed's muffled giggles sucking the oxygen in, thoughts of them enjoying telling everyone what she'd said, fumbling over bottles of vodka, trampling out joints as they'd passed her words around, spilling them, rolling them, sending them up.

'Bang out of order Miss,' Rasheed says, trying to pull himself together.

She steps to close the door, walks back to her desk and pretends to note something on a piece of paper, trying to compose herself, lower the tempo, find harmony. 'That was both outrageous, and a lie,' she says, 'and will be dealt with most severely.'

'Yes Miss,' Anya says loyally, but Mo gives her a dirty look.

All untrue, so why should she be concerned? Why should a total falsehood spoil what they had been doing? All lies, so she can lighten the mood. Why shouldn't she?

She beams out at them. 'Moths,' she says, nodding at Anya, 'moths and all sorts of ugly creatures hover about a lighted candle.' She ejects a laugh but it is met by blank faces so she quickly feeds them the reference. 'Dickens. *Great Expectations.*' Still their stony expressions. 'Something my mum used to say to me.' Words to brighten a dark situation, meant to buoy and lift, but they drop to the floor, unattractive spoken here, unkind.

Ice forms, a sheet between her and them. She apologises, tries to get back to the text, to get the discussion lit again. 'Maybe it's not money people need in this place,' she adds quietly, 'it's a bit of bloody *aspiration.*'

Their eyes are all trained on her, widened by her expletive. She pauses, waiting for her scorching aphorism to spark and flame around them.

It is immediately extinguished. 'I'm not sure about that Miss,' Femi says, "Miss" the only nod to Jo's higher status, the rest oozing out in slow assurance, as if to an equal. 'I know Forster makes Bast poor, but he gives him a few resources too, and,' she pauses to weigh her argument, 'surely it's those things that let him aspire to anything at all, isn't it?'

Jo fixes her with a stare as she takes up her copy of the book. 'All aspiration implies Femi,' tilting her head in waspish condescension, 'if you think about the *etymology*, is that there's some air to breathe. An atmosphere in which something could grow.' Angrily holding her gaze, Jo begins to quote from the dinner party scene. *"Miss Schlegel was asked how she could ever say such dreadful things, and what it would profit Mr Bast if he gained the whole world and lost his own soul. She answered, Nothing, but he would not gain his soul unless he had gained a little of the world."*

She stands in her space by the board, contempt writ large, shame combusting with injustice. She looks out at her betrayers, Judases each one, angry words tugging at the leash to be released. Oxford? God, that would show them. But she mustn't the same mistake again. She is emotional, is under pressure, must grasp onto joy. Find a way to break the ice, to turn this to humour.

'You're right though Femi.' Concede something to her before continuing. 'Bast needed a little pure air to breathe if he was to gain his soul. But he only needs a little. And *that* lot,' she says with a sarcastic chuckle, pointing to the door, to the bastard Darren who has found a way to reach back through it and get to her, her voice cracking, desperately trying to dress words in humour before they go on stage, 'if boys like that had a *fraction* of culture between them they'd probably trade it in some Tower stairwell for an eighth of skunk.'

No one laughs. Out on the corridor voices are shouting.

'Miss,' Anya says. 'Miss, that's not fair,' the others, all eyes down.

Jo wants to rush in and fill the space, to rage about idiots in designer trainers who think they're so hard done by. A boiler breaks down and they call it suffering. They've basically sat at home for months. Not one single idea about what children like Sami have been through. No cares about the care homes ravaged, the ICU departments overrun. She makes frenzied edits, tries to keep it on the point. Blurts out sharply, 'I hope you know that every last one of you here has far more than that "little of this world" than Leonard Bast ever had, than some people coming to this country now will ever get.'

She drops her head. It is over. The quiet speaks for them: reminds Jo that she is not from round here, so how dare she. She doesn't know, doesn't live this, doesn't have cousins ordered to far-flung towns to repay dues, real street debts, more dead weight than her fucking mortgage.

She flushes with sweat, is hot with embarrassment, shame dripping off her. She knows that she should apologise, ought to right now because if Jackson hears of this... But then she looks over this edge, at the sheer drop opening up and is scared of climbing so far down.

'Get on with your essay plans,' she says finally.

'Right you are Miss Schlegel,' Femi mutters, the blade deftly thrust as Anya tries to suppress a laugh. They settle into her work, A4 pads filling with silent notes, highlighters passed back and forth, waiting until the bell goes, until they can tell everyone, put it on their stories, impatient for the next outdoor party where they'll neck their drinks and replay the scene and roar in fogs of sweet smoke as they slice her apart all over again.

19

The ringing bell starts her heart knocking again, ribs like broken wind chimes, stomach a bag of acid, swilling at the slightest movement. Year 13 talk quietly amongst themselves as they pack away, avoiding looking, averting their gaze, as if it would be cruel to watch.

'Apologies,' Jo says to them, making no eye contact. 'It's...' And that is all that will come. A writhing mass of knotted things clogs in her throat, so many threads she has no idea which to pull on to begin to unravel it, which specific thing with which to begin.

'Don't worry Miss.' Anya being the adult as they spray their tables, tearing off sheets from the industrial roll of blue tissue. 'Come on guys,' she says. 'Let's go.'

Go, and leave this woman to her prejudices, to her gradual unravelling.

Politely, they do. Everyone masks up and Jo follows to shut the door behind them. Pressing her back against the wall, palms flat behind her, she hears voices rising and falling, shouting and fading, the slap of trainers rushing past. She waits for Jackson, sure he is about to arrive, his approach surely quieter, edging the door open, asking for a word, summoning her back down. The walk that would follow. The humiliation. Word spreading like wildfire.

But he doesn't come, and when there is a knock it is just Year 7.

'Hi Miss Barker!' Kelsey calls through the door, so cheery Jo wants to weep. God love these children, she thinks, these beautiful children.

'One minute please,' and she performs emergency surgery, reaches into her breast and rearranges her innards, ties her heart down, calms her stomach. All she has to offer them is a formulaic lesson, beginning with 10 minutes of quiet reading. But sometimes that is enough, she assures herself.

When school is done she wants to get away quickly but before she can escape Alex catches her, laptop cradled as ever, another spreadsheet open.

'Sorry.' A smile that says little, offers no clues as to what he currently knows. 'Just a quick question.' He points along a coloured row. 'This kid here. Vocab score of 112 and non-verbal at 93.'

'Mo,' she tells him, wishing he'd actually use their names. 'Mohammed Mellah. Year 13.' *Alma mater*. Generous mother. She takes a long blink, cradles her heart to stop it breaking again, thinking of all that she's invested in him, prays that she hasn't just squandered it. Alex runs a finger back along the screen. 'Such an interesting kid,' she adds. 'Some very talented analysis, but he uses bravado to cover up...'

'OK. Yep,' Alex cuts in. 'But does that adaptive test score look right against the value-added he got at GCSE?' Scrolling across, cells moving, names disappearing screen-left, his nail-bitten digit marking the place.

'Possibly. It's hard to tell. Sometimes he...'

'OK. Thanks. Sorry. Bit of pressure to get these all crunched.' Preparing to feed the algorithm, just in case. Still no word on whether exams will happen. Still rumours that they might be cancelled. Or delayed. Or the content narrowed. But while no decision is made, all of these possibilities prod and poke, add to the uncertainty, the anxiety. And what about Sami? So recently arrived he has carried no bag of data with him. What will the computer do with him? What should she do with him, now that he's lost it with her, feels that she has betrayed him when all she was trying to do was help?

Alex darts away, moving to catch Cara as she comes out of her room.

She calls down the corridor. 'Jo, you seen Martha?'

She hasn't. Perhaps she should be staying here rather than trying to leave, looking after others rather than tending to herself.

Cara puts a hand out towards Alex's arm, a mime of reassuring touch, he'll have her attention shortly. 'Think she caught one this afternoon.' Jo is now walking backwards and Cara waits a moment to make sure that she is looking at her. Really looking. 'Hope you're OK too, love.' Not wanting to say any more in front of Alex. 'Go. Get out of here. Parents evening tomorrow, so go home and chill and let's catch up in the morning.'

Cara who copes. Cara who carries a child and still has the strength to support young teachers in trouble. Jo holds up a beaten-up carrier bag filled with germ-free books, a signal of appreciation.

She sets her head down and keeps it there, quickly through the foyers, out of the gates, along the scabbed and wind-whipped road out of the estate and into the welcome anonymity of the main road, thankful not to have seen Jackson or Sami or Darren or Femi or Anya, the list of characters that she wants to avoid growing by the day.

But by the time she is home she feels better. Door shut, walls around, she puts some crackers and the remains of a mild cheddar on a plate, wishing now that she'd summoned the energy to go into the shops on the way back. There's the laughter of a TV from next door, a helicopter circling above, someone thinking they can make a run for it. She refuses wine, boils the kettle for a peppermint tea instead. Some of the water spills onto the sideboard but the cloth has gone missing, probably somewhere under the pile of dishes that now needs doing. Not tonight.

Through to the lounge, she sits on the sofa and listens. The helicopter has gone. She gets the books out and starts to grind through them as quickly as she can, heart not in it and head hardly either. Tick and flick.

'Chill,' Cara had said, and she tries to obey. A cursory look at each homework and she's done. Not to the required standard, but fuck it this evening. Fuck all of it. The unendurable load of every damned thing. Walk this side of the corridor. Stay one marker away. Don't touch. Don't stop to talk. Wipe, spray, don't cough. It seems impossible that they've not had more cases. Twelve hundred kids, all those families mixing and moving, teachers hardly better than Mo and Rasheed and Anya, drinking and enjoying themselves. Managing the risk. Tasting a little joy, just to sweeten the journey. Impossible, and improbable. But how can anyone test positive if no one is testing? The rigmarole of booking, the swab down the throat, the threat of loss of work. Plus, a state that insisted on stop and search wasn't going to get far with test and trace.

But what if they'd lost their mother, were now terrified of losing their father, were told in no uncertain terms that they could not travel to a funeral? She's tried to avoid the news but everyone knows that numbers are rising like a bastard and great swathes of the north are being put under stricter measures. She thinks back to Doncaster, of hearing the cursing against London even then, this pulsing black hole far away that still reached up to order them around. There must be anger there. Life hard enough anyway, the spectre of Thatcher still absurdly strong.

Even here more shops shut each time she walks from the station, anger and stress right up at the surface of everyone, just the sapping rigmarole of having keeping away from people, not seeing people, of feeling like you're doing the wrong thing, of being judged for just walking in the street. It's bad enough having to be in school each day, feeling like you need a deep clean each evening when you get in, deciding it's best for everyone if you keep away. Teachers as super-spreaders. Heroes, but dirty. Applaud from afar.

Damn it. Fuck it. Stop thinking like this. She must try to relax. Not be so uptight. Try to stay positive — Jesus, the irony of that. She picks up an old magazine, eyes wanting to relax but finding nothing comfortable to rest on, thrusting shoulders, a tilted knee, a spread on thigh gaps that she quickly pushes past. Hair, new fashions, each piece high-grown with brambled messages. Buy this, screw like this, wear this. How to pleasure him and why to dump him. Clothes, shampoos, conditioners, exfoliators, foundations, mascaras, lipsticks, her turning the pages faster and faster until she pushes the thing away.

Does not need that in her life right now. Silence is better. The dust falls undisturbed.

But she mustn't mope. She pulls her computer onto her lap and looks again at some spas hotels she'd like to visit. She rejects an old manor house near Tring, plumps for somewhere with a bigger pool, a bigger menu of treatments, bigger rooms, bigger gardens. Three nights would be amazing. She checks through the measures, confirms that she would actually be allowed to go, would actually be able to get a massage, even if the person was dressed like a surgeon about to take her heart out. Fuck the expense, she thinks, fuck the lack of any pay rise since forever, I deserve this. We do.

She smiles as she pictures her and Dad carrying Mum's urn round with them, taking what's left of her for a pedicure and hot stone massage before driving out to finally throw her to the wind.

The ornaments stir around her, clay vessels pulling her back through walls and landing her on the hospital ward. Words nearly run dry, Mum's energies consumed by the thorny problem of how to exit a body that was torturing her. A whole evening in virtual silence. She had reached for Mum's hand as if in vain attempt to stop her leaving then and there, stroked and felt each digit, as if making a map to try to help her remember. The smallest squeeze in return had brought so many tears, tears for all that had been said, and all that hadn't, tears for that map that would dissolve so quickly.

The computer on her lap starts to whir and she breathes again. She clicks the link to confirm the booking, waits for the page to respond, a single droplet forming and spilling into a thin trail that runs down her left cheek because she cannot remember her mother's voice. She hears the words but only in her head, cannot conjure lilt or tone, feels herself grasping more desperately at phrases heard, playing them back but hearing herself say them. Touch, sight, sound, all gone. Why hadn't she kept a cardigan to smell? Anything, she thinks, just to hear that voice, to have a little more time to say what had needed to be said. A moth flutters and spasms onto the cushion next to her and with a slam of her hand it becomes dust. The screen finishes loading and a confirmation email pings through. The dam holds and she wipes the tear away, then hesitates. She wants to call Dad to tell him the good news, that she's decided to go for it, to risk seeing him, to take him away as a treat, but is wary of how fragile her levees are.

So she waits, fingers a crumb of cracker into her mouth then stands abruptly, picks up her mug, judges something wrong with the state of the lounge and pushes the scattered books back onto their shelves, straightens a throw, turns the old fruit seller around to face the wall, sits back on the sofa and inspects her nails, the ends of her hair. She forwards the email from the hotel to Dad, curses as she spies new messages on her school account. Bloody Alex, wanting target documents filled in. 930pm. Jesus.

She's about to give in and open it when her phone rings and Sally's name flashes onto her screen. She scrabbles for the handset, fumbles comically as she tries to answer, for a second thinks that she's somehow refused the call, but then Sally is speaking as she lifts it to her ear.

'Hey... Hey.'

'Hey Jo. You OK?'

'Yeah sorry, just thought I'd hit the wrong button.' Jo realises she's talking too quickly, sounding a bit desperate. She slows herself down. 'How are you, Sal? How's things?'

'Fuck,' comes the reply. 'Fuck, sorry - I've just spilt wine on the new duvet cover. Gimme a minute.' The phone is put down and Jo can hear feet padding quickly away.

Same old Sally. Life at 100mph, things are bound to get knocked over. A laugh, a shout of something, and then she's back on. 'Sorry, You were saying?'

Jo hadn't been, asks again how Sal is and she sighs and tells her she's good before firing the same question back. Stay positive, Jo thinks. Sally hasn't called to hear about your troubles. Plus, self-respect. 'I'm fine,' she says. 'Very, very busy as usual at work.'

'I don't know how you do it.'

'Nor do I,' Jo says in a voice that is darker than she'd wanted.

'Ouch. Things not good?'

She pauses before deciding on the truth. 'No,' she admits, giving up the pretence. 'Got to be honest Sal, it's not been the easiest.'

'No shit Sherlock. All of this on top of all you've been through?' A sip of wine. The sound of her rearranging pillows.

A beat before Jo realises that she couldn't know about school today, all of that crashing back and replaying at breakneck speed.

'Jo, love?' The realisation Jo hasn't replied. Sally more serious now. 'We're all amazed you made it back to work at all, especially under all these regulations.'

It's the "we" that breaks her open, this sign that people must have talked, have shown concern enough to talk about her, to ask each other how she might be doing. Thoughts hurriedly gather; still this idea that she should pretend it's all nothing, strap on her brave face. But she cannot. She needs this, needs to stop at this oasis of friendship and care, even if it's just for a few minutes, even if it won't solve anything or make anything at work more right.

She drinks in the cool kindness, doesn't flood Sally with everything, just enough to give an outline. But even with this, the knotted mass seems to ease, the threads separate a little.

'You should come over,' Sally says. 'Get some drinks down us. How about this Friday? We're still allowed to do that, right?'

A silly sense of relief that this means she can't be pregnant. Friday is the last day of half term; people would normally be going to the pub but that's not going to happen. Or if it is she should really avoid it. She says yes.

'Just you?' Sally asks.

Surely she hasn't forgotten? No. She wouldn't. Which means that she thinks that Jo might have found someone else, a thought that seems ridiculous, then diminishes into something else.

'Yes, just me,' she says with a giggle.

'Not dating then?'

'Only in the carbon sense.' Age measured in decay, in ever-decreasing levels of activity. 'Unless there's a miracle in the next four days.'

'Ha — that's the spirit!'

The spirit, she thinks, and can't help picture Dad, this holy ghost that somehow kept him aloft through so much. Stirring, lifting.

They make arrangements for Friday and catch up on a bit of Sally's news. When Jo puts the phone down it is as if air has broken into the room. Why shouldn't she find someone new? Meet someone through Sally, or even by the pool at the hotel. Not online, she thinks. It distorts. Ben *had* initially seemed wonderful but, she allows herself to admit, he *was* a bit of an inverted Tardis, big and impressive on the outside but small and very ordinary within.

She gets up, stretches, finds her little speaker and tries to turn it on, hunts around for the charger and gets it working, puts on some music, the sounds pushing the air, pressing and expanding. She opens the lounge window a moment, pushes her head out and breathes in. It is cold, cold and laden with heady carbon fractions, but it moves, drifts, refuses to be held.

She finds a gin and pours one. The tonic flat, no matter, no lemon either, no ice; the idea of it the thing. Chill out, like Cara said. She's been so tightly wound about everything that she's lost herself. She feels an ache in her chest for a physical web of people, a large circle of local friends, acknowledges this and mourns it, but reminds herself that things will change, will improve someday. The gin is too warm and watery to have had the full desired effect, but it is delicious enough. She packs her bag for tomorrow, puts her pens into her pencil case, zips it shut. She should ask for a fountain pen for Christmas. Something solid, weighty. Real ink. No plastic.

Tomorrow, Sami's class. She stops herself, reminds herself that it cannot be all about him. Don't over-invest one person. Diversify. Be good to herself. She brushes her teeth, removes her face, washes gently, moisturises, applies night cream. She really should tidy her garden, but no need right now. She marches to bed and pulls over the covers, kills the lights, turns to sleep.

As she drifts the helicopter returns, searching, yawing, the beat of its blades like the pulses of laughter. A thought of Femi and Mo, Rasheed and Anya somewhere, cracking up at her cracking up, Sami's face in pure betrayed rage, Jackson wielding a spotlight, arcing until he has her. Darren, still out there somewhere.

She turns over, but her head isn't so easily redirected. She must remain pragmatic. Much as she'd like to she cannot just chill while threats remain. No. Don't retreat just yet. Half term coming so soon now. One final extra hard push until then, just to make sure.

She makes a mental list. Apologise to Year 13. Deal with Jackson. Straighten things out with Sami. Get through tomorrow's parents' evening with Year 11.

Not as far along the road to redemption as she'd wanted, but she will make it to Sally's and have good things to share. She reaches a sleepy arm out across the mattress, opens a palm as if someone might come to stroke it in the night. Outside a siren howls and fades. Just a little more, she thinks as she drifts, just a day or so until she breaks up.

20

'Martha has quit.'

'Sorry, what? Are kidding me? Two days before half term?'

Cara doesn't wait to say hello, just lands this news as Jo strolls into the office. She is standing, bent over her desk, leafing through an old English Language textbook, efficient face on.

Jo puts her carrier bag down, then her handbag, eases off coat and gloves and mask, the weather turned chilly. 'What happened?'

'You know she had a few wobbles the past few days? Apparently, yesterday was the final straw. She texted me last night.'

Layers of implication Jo doesn't want to process. She'd come in feeling better about things, but now nerves return. 'What did it?'

'Did you know that Alex had landed a book scrutiny on her out of the blue last week?' Jo didn't. 'She says he told her not to worry about it — just a routine spot check — but then mentioned "significant failings." I mean, why the hell he's persisting with this inspection stuff while all this is going on is beyond me. Plus it turns out she'd never been given the criteria she was going to be judged on, so...'

Cara pauses while she scribbles something onto a post-it note and sticks it into a page in the book.

'Then Mark Wright said something in her lesson yesterday afternoon.' Jo frowns, needing more. 'Year 9? Brown curly hair, spots?' Still nothing. 'Kind of middle of the road kid?' Which was the trouble: only notable if they're bright or noisy, the rest too easily lost in the vast, flat sea of the unremarkable. 'Anyway, he'd asked her why she always looked so miserable, and that was it. Snapped at him, he had a go back and it all kicked off.' Cara stops for a moment, deeper in thought. 'But then last night she realised he was right. She was miserable.'

'Bloody hell,' Jo says with a long sigh. 'And she didn't want to wait until after half term?'

'Nope. Actually thought it'd be more kind. Wanted to give the school a couple of days to sort something out. I'm just setting cover now.'

'You need a hand?'

She doesn't.

Jo stands, a little awkward, redundant but unable not to feel tempted by the possibility. Giving up. Quitting. Walking out. The simplicity of manual labour, tending a bookshop. The quiet. Selling up, getting away from London. It had always been one of the fantasy conversations that circulated in the staff room and pub, contracting a mysterious illness, one that was painless but meant you *could not* come to work. A dry cough, a bit of a cold and back in March people had run into self-isolation, the fantasy not quite living up to the grim grind of the real. Too many like Geoff, she thinks, fine pieces now broken, worn out by all this, never to be restored.

Matt and Rose pop in. They have already heard, gather round Cara and then go to help her pick up some more copies of a textbook from the stock cupboard.

A sudden panicked thought. Perhaps Cara knows something again before she does, something she's not been told yet? The chorus strikes up. *Shouldn't have gone home so quickly last night, should have been brave, stuck around.* All this a drip of thoughts, sulphuric titration, concentration increasing in the swirling flask of her stomach. Burning, fuming, until she tells herself that she is being ridiculous. If they were going to act, if the school had had to, they would have done it. She needs to keep calm. Keep her head down, don't stir, let it all pass. Make it to Sally's, then away with Dad. Just two days.

She goes to her room, opens the windows but turns the radiators up. Shakespeare is only just clinging onto the display board so she fetches the staple gun and helps him back to his rightful place. She steps back, finds the effect underwhelming, a bear pit still where The Rose should be, daggers in bags, a reckoning still to come for someone.

First period, and Year 7 are in one of the ICT rooms, one way round the no-worksheet problem, each mind becalmed in front of a screen once the keyboards and mice have been sanitised. They are working through an online presentation on persuasive texts, the class not so much surfing the web as drifting gently atop it. The office chairs creak like ship-planks, mental rigging taking what little strain there is, the thirty ageing machines doubling up as radiators, pumping out warm air. Keaton is still wearing a heavy coat on top of both blazer and jumper. 'You're making me hot just looking at you,' Jo tells him before realising what she's said, pushing on quickly to tell him to get to the next article. Thankfully none of them are old enough to twist it, and she leans to open a window. In the gentle breeze the shredded blind slaps like a torn sail.

Trying not to spill or tear, she carries herself carefully to her own workstation and goes through the slides for next lesson. Pip's first meeting with Estella. The state of his boots has never troubled him before, but now — in the light of this girl — they have mutated into vulgar appendages.

She emails Cara and Alex and asks if they need any more doing to sort out Martha's classes. Alex replies and thanks her, says it's all covered, asks if Jo has all the information she needs for tonight's parents evening. Jo replies, assures him that she has. She sends this, knowing that she cannot be sure, has no idea what claims or counterclaims Year 11 parents might arrive with, what allegations they might suddenly throw or doubts they might suddenly develop about her competency. She knows that other schools have plumped for online appointments, but Jackson worries that some might miss out, that Year 11 are too important. So they have been promised distanced desks and carefully managed queues, mandatory masks and strict time limits. But it feels like a risk, one she doesn't feel like taking but doesn't feel she can challenge. Not now. For once, she thinks, I might be glad of Alex's data, a barrage of figures with which to defend myself.

It's the heating perhaps, or the fact of half term approaching, but when the lesson ends she heads back to her room and finds Year 11 moving like syrup. Charlie shouts something down the corridor to Danny but is told to pipe down by a scowling Jordan. Nishaan arrives, turns one light on and off, looks at Jo as if considering whether to ask where to sit, but decides against, and eases his bag from his back onto his desk.

She waits for the room to fill, turning on the projector and wiping the other board.

'So Miss, what's this I heard,' Charlie begins. But she cuts him off.

'Not in the mood Charlie. Sorry.'

'Innit,' Jordan says. 'Always gassing and shit. Just hole it.'

'Jordan!' Jo says, and he holds a hand up in apology before placing it back under his chin, languishing on his desk, chair pushed out behind him. In truth, she wants to thank him.

Still no Hayley. Obviously no Nelson. But no Sami. 'Is this everyone?' she asks uneasily, and a few shoulders shrug back in reply. They have been read the Riot Act this morning it seems, and for the moment it looks to have done a job. But Hayley. Poor Hayley. But why should she feel any shame? She should be here, head held high. Jo doesn't dare ask about Sami. Don't rock the boat. Just push on. She checks that everyone has their appointment time for later, and finally launches into the lesson proper.

'Dickensian England,' she begins with a flourish, throwing up the first slide, the beam of light exposing a dancing mist of dust as it sprays onto the screen. They are looking at an engraving of a rutted road and a grand-gated house, and she asks them to respond with descriptive sentences, how they might paint the scene of this world they were entering. It's sluggish work, less pulling teeth than extracting muddy boots, but she moves onto the next slide, the relevant passage of text pasted for them, Radha called upon to read.

She was dressed in rich materials — satins, and lace, and silks — all white.

Miss Havisham introduced, the jilted bride, shrunk and skeletal. Each of the girls taking over in turn, a few lines read before the next beckoned as Pip's description grows in detail. The faded lustre of the clothes. One shoe on, one on the table.

'The question here,' she offers in monotone, a few eyelids heavy towards the back, 'is whether Pip *knows* how poor he is before he is dragged up to this grand house to entertain Miss Havisham.'

A faint pop, and then darkness.

She reaches for the remote control, presses the buttons harder and points the thing more violently, looking like her Mum did when trying to work a video recorder. But it's no use, the projector bulb has gone. They stir briefly. 'This school, man,' moans Danny, and there are a few mumbled curses of agreement, reinforced by her own.

'Sorry guys. I'm sorry.' She scrabbles around for a whiteboard pen, deciding to move them onto the writing task, but the only one she can find is run out, the marks it leaves as faint and vague as the instructions she then writes with it.

'Miss man, how am I meant to read that?' Jordan calls from the back.

'I'll read it back to you,' she says and tells him to get his book open, asks others to do the same, talks slowly about imagining their own Estella, their own visit to a world far outside their own, someone who might lift them to a different place.

'Nadia Rose man,' says Michael. 'I'd go lockdown with her for *time*. That bitch is *leng*.'

'Innit,' nods Ade in lush agreement.

'Michael!' Jo barks.

'Miss it's a compliment!'

'Comparing her to an animal?'

Michael looks at Ade, then at Jo, confused.

She's about to ask them if they had learned anything at all from the whole episode with the fox, with the ways that we treat people, but then Chanel chips in. 'He ain't wrong Miss. Low-key she is well fit.'

Jo rubs her forehead. The infinite plasticity of language, curses become blessings, expletives used as praise. How did "low-key" come to mean the opposite? How did "wicked" come to mean amazing? "Bad" was now good, "the bomb" was better but "the shit" was best.

'Thank you, Chanel,' is all she can say, shaking her head, just wanting to move on. 'For this exercise, I want you to imagine someone to transport you into a totally different world.'

'Nad...' Michael begins again with a grin, but she slaps him down, tries to get them all to focus on the task.

They don't really get it and she can't summon the energy to keep them all moving. Gradually the lesson runs into the mud. They look as wearied by it as she is. Mask up. A brief circuit round, a pause to explain it again to Radha and Nishaan, then she returns to her desk.

She listens.

'This lesson is *dead*,' Michael yawns. One word that still appears to mean what it always has.

Ade looks asleep, Jakob halfway there too, Michael turned, chatting quietly to Jordan. Lauren is louder than she might be, but harmlessly dissecting some celebrity show with Nourin and Chanel in between short bursts of concentration. Charlie is in his own world, tapping a beat on the table and quietly humming some tune to himself. Kelly is looking out of the window, Danny sketching a tag. Only Jenny and Safiya properly on task, but the others are quite content. Not destroying. Not fighting. Not drawing out similes from a Dickens classic, no, but all engaged in something. All communicating. In English. Pretty much.

"Chill out. Look after yourself." Cara's words, and her the great sage right now. She looks out over the class. Why should she disturb them? The energy had popped with the projector bulb. Michael is right: it is a dead lesson, but they are resting in peace, no battles to fight.

If she does nothing they might waste the remaining twenty minutes without fuss, without stress, no one having to be kept behind. Parents Evening later. Far better to go into that without the echoes of fresh salvos, wounds still smarting. Preserve energy for when Sami returns. No reason to rock the boat, not today.

A surreptitious look at her phone and her gaze meanders, travels out beyond the windows.

'Miss.' It's Nourin. 'I've finished.'

She shouldn't really, but is so fed up with all the hassle that she doesn't put gloves on, doesn't leave the book for days to become clean, just reflexively does what she should do as a teacher, motions for Nourin to pass her work forward. She reads through it quickly. Too good for a middle set: proper attempts at sentences and punctuation, ideas well-structured into paragraphs. The spelling was pretty atrocious in places but imaginatively phonetic.

The rest of the class are entertaining themselves. Radha is helping Nishaan. She beckons Nourin to come into her taped-off teacher zone, sits her down on a chair next to her and takes her through what she's written, the writing all bubble-gum curls and loops, underlinings in pink biro. Jo asks if she's read any Dickens before, and she says she doesn't think so.

'I think you'd enjoy it. Really. He wrote soaps you know — but for newspapers. The stories didn't come out in books, they were published in bits.'

She looks up. Unrest building a bit as break approaches. A quick bark at Michael to sit down.

'Bet he didn't live round here though Miss.'

No but, by God, he'd seen much worse. 'If he was here now,' she tells her, 'he'd probably be wandering the Tower with a notebook — watching, thinking of stories.'

Nourin smirks, points out that men walking around the estate making little notes might not last long without getting beats.

They both laugh out loud at this, Jo not realising that the noise level has just escalated, that no one in the class is even close to working. Charlie and Danny have risen to dance along to Jamal's beatboxed tune and Lauren and Chanel are whooping in support.

The door swings open. Relieved to see a hand on it that can't be Sami's, there's then a moment of horror as Jackson strides in.

Silence spreads like a flame in a jar. She stands up, waves Nourin out of the teacher's space as if only just noticing that a child was in it, sat on a chair by Jo's desk, her book open between them.

'Miss Barker.'

'Mr Jackson.'

'Everything OK here?'

'Well —'

'I was just walking to the staffroom, and heard rather a lot of noise.' He turns to the children as he continues. 'I hope that everyone is doing just as you are asking them to.' He scans the room, draws a blank on names, settles on Jakob. 'You, what have you been doing?'

'Copying stuff from the board.' Sounding just as dull as it had been.

'So why the noise Year 11?' A pause, and he points at Nourin. 'You know the rules, don't you?'

She looks around for support, mumbles a yes.

'Rules that exist to keep everyone safe.' He emphasises this last word, turns to Jo to land it. 'To stop the spread of this horrible virus that — ' and he goes full teacher staccato '— Remains. A. Deadly. Threat.' Everyone fiddles with their hands, inspects their desks. 'So we do NOT shout, and we DO respect social distancing.' Another pause as he labours his point. 'So if you are being considerate to Miss Barker you will not be making such a racket. Isn't that right?' Jo agrees sternly, glaring at the class. 'Perhaps we can talk about this when we meet later?' he adds, more quietly.

She flushes with embarrassment, returns a single, subservient nod. 'Quite right,' she says to the class, 'so can we please sit down quietly, as I've been asking you to do, and get on with your work.' Eyes are rolled, heads are shaken, teeth quietly kissed. 'The bulb in the projector went,' she offers weakly to Jackson. 'And my pens had run out.' But his back is turned.

'I'm sure you'll be able to improvise,' he crows as he leaves the room without turning, withholding any affirmation; subtle, but calculated. Jo glances at Radha, desperate for any support from any quarter, but Radha looks down, away, anywhere, straightens her ruler.

She hurls stock phrases at them, hoping that Jackson might hear, but Michael can't stop laughing, one hand cupped round his mouth, the other being whipped to crack slender fingers together. 'Miss you got BOYED,' he calls.

Now she throws herself at them, shouting to silence them, eyes flaming, spitting out a barrage of clichés, threatening to go and fetch the Head again, them knowing that that would only lower her stock even further. So she begins to take it out on Michael, glowering at him, anger doubled by the accuracy of his analysis: Jackson had 'boyed' her, treated her like a child, and now she wanted, child-like, to shout something back.

But she can't. Of course she can't. Not again. Her own stupid fault for backing off, for not keeping the pressure on. If a lesson dies it is her job to resurrect it, not be glad to have a room of cadavers.

She has to regain control of them, and herself. She climbs down, hold by hold, as if from a dangerous ledge. I am a teacher, she reminds herself, and Michael is just a boy. Rude as he has been, he isn't actually wrong. Her tongue yanks at the leash, wanting to be set on him, but she manages to pull it back, hold herself back, think of the parents making their way to her this evening.

Caged behind teeth and mask her tongue is still snarling and biting as she later spirals down the stairs to the ground floor and works her way through splintered groups of tables across the foyer to the Head's office. Again. The door opens, dispatches Geoff Hand and closes behind him.

'Geoff,' she says. 'How are you?' But he doesn't acknowledge her. Sees her, but simply carries on, says nothing, edges towards the stairs down to the entrance, holding out his hand to grab the bannister, steadying himself. Over his arm is a winter coat and he stops by the doors as he puts this on, the batteries gone in his face, nothing on, nothing moving, slowly zipping up the jacket, hunching his thin frame down into it and pushing at the glass door, straining to get it moving.

'Geoff,' she says again. But still nothing. Behind her, Jackson has come out of his office.

'Come in,' he says and beckons her to follow him. She takes a seat at the large pine conference table, an oval of high gloss, a set of papers neatly arranged at one end, beyond which lies Jackson's desk, sparse, a large thin monolith of computer monitor mounted on a brushed steel arm, facing his chair like a robot head atop an angled metal spine.

'That was Geoff,' she begins, not wanting to just let this go without comment. 'Is he coming back?'

'I can't discuss that with you Jo, I'm sure you understand that.' He sits himself by the papers at the apogee.

'Yes, but is he OK? I mean is someone going to check on him? He looked terrible.'

For a split-second Jackson looks as if he has his own battles going on within. 'He did. I know.' He regains his composure. 'Of course, we'll have someone get in touch with him.'

'And what about Martha?'

He closes his eyes and rubs his temple, performing some kind of reset. 'We are here to talk about you, Jo. Please let's focus on that.'

She has decided on a strategy. Front foot, take the initiative. 'Yes, well I'm sorry if you weren't happy with what you saw earlier. With my Year 11.' His fingers form a steeple, the tips touching pursed lips. 'Unfortunate that my lesson plan was scuppered by the bulb in the projector going.'

He leans towards her, tries to smile, places his palms on the table. 'And this prevented you from keeping the class quiet? From asking a student to break the regulations that are there to keep staff safe?'

Should never have listened to Cara. *Chill out?* What was she thinking? With Sami not there she should have taken the chance to go in even harder.

She flusters. 'I needed a moment to do some focused feedback with Nourin. It was very brief.' She dares a look but can tell he smells bullshit. 'They are a challenging class,' she reminds him.

'And this is a challenging job.' He hisses with exasperation. 'I'm very sorry about Martha and about Geoff, but this is a highly stressful occupation—'

The caged muscle lurches inside her. 'So breakdown and insomnia and anxiety are just part of the terms and conditions now?' she snaps before yanking the leash back.

He watches this, opens his palms, shrugs a little and raises his eyebrows as if to concede that yes, he pretty much was saying that. 'Teaching is tough, especially now,' he says, and before Jo can say more he slaps his hands back to the table. 'Jesus Jo, in an inspection that lesson could have endangered the reputation of the *whole* school. And you know *damned well* that if we get cases and get transmission we could have the whole of that GCSE year sent home. I cannot believe, after all that's happened...' But he opts not to finish this.

She opens her mouth to offer a defence. He holds a hand up, stops her, snatches a look at a notification on his wrist. 'Look, I don't want this to take a lot of time, so let me be brief.' He takes a sheet of A4 and scans it. 'Putting aside for now today's lesson, a full report on your meeting with Sami Karim outside of the school site in school time will conclude that there isn't evidence to suggest impropriety.'

'Thank you,' Jo says, eyes shut in gratitude, as if a judge has stayed an execution. 'That's a relief.'

He drops his shoulders impatiently. 'Yes. But it will note yet another lapse of judgement on your part.'

Her face flushes. He sets the piece of paper down, adjusts it to be square with others.

'I did what anyone with a scrap of heart would do,' she says quietly. 'I tried to be kind.' He doesn't respond, so she pushes harder. 'He is a boy who may have suffered unimaginable things on his way to this country. I was simply trying to be a friendly face. Who knows where he might have gone if I'd not intercepted him.'

He snaps forward like an insect, no joy in this, no malice, pure reflex knowing that survival means attack. He clips his words as he moves to sting. 'One place he *has* been is in this office. Seeing me. We have spoken at length and I think you might be surprised at what you do not know.'

She looks confused, gives a slight shake of the head. 'He's vulnerable. It's been difficult to even get him to admit he's been bullied.'

'And he now feels worried that these allegations will only put him in more grave danger outside of school.' Then he finally does it, reaches for the dagger he's concealed, looks her blankly in the eyes and thrusts it. 'Though, when presented with a parental complaint, he agreed that behaviour in your lessons was often below expectations.'

The shock of the cold steel with which he strikes. She tries not to fall back, tries to hold herself together even as he goes to slice her apart. 'Sorry?' she says. 'There's been a complaint? From whom?' A moment as she attempts to gauge the extent of the wound. 'When exactly were you going to tell me this?'

'I am telling you now,' he says as if to excuse himself, to let her know that he is only doing what he has been programmed to do. 'Though I cannot tell you who made it.'

She looks away from him, runs her mind down the register, wondering if it is Radha, or Nishaan, the list now like the cast of a Christie novel, everyone with their own reasons to stick the knife in.

You fool, she tells herself. You shouldn't have given them this opening. She now wonders if Sami had been listening at the door to her Sixth Form lesson, had heard what horrible prejudices lay festering in places she couldn't even see. Perhaps Mo and Rasheed had gone to Alex, or to Cara?

'So I have to meet people at parents evening now and not know who has a grievance against me?'

Death in the Classroom. It almost had a ring to it. A teacher murdered, the whole class under suspicion.

He leans forward, and simpers. 'It's precisely because there's a parents evening that I feel it's best. And of course, with the incident with Darren still fresh in some parents' minds...'

That would be the plot twist: it would be the Head who had done it. Wanting rid of a failing member of their staff. Setting up a student, sacrificing them for their own purposes.

'We must focus on progress,' he says mechanically, 'try to avoid any of these incidents distracting from that.'

'Which is exactly what I was doing when I sat with Sami — focusing on his progress!'

'Though you chose to sit with him outside of school, where he was truanting. He is a student at Cromwell — ' wrapping his arguments tighter around her ' — one of over a thousand. He must follow the rules like anyone else.' He again raises a hand to stop her speaking. 'And you are a teacher at Cromwell, and must, like everyone else, follow the procedures that we have in place. Procedures that are vital to the well-oiled running of the school.'

Frictionless delivery. Productivity targets. Each cog spinning silently until it wore down, began to make noise.

'God, you make it sound like a food-processing plant,' she says, tongue up again and prowling, whipping each syllable. '*Everything* I do here is about helping these children. Years and years I have worked here, and have always focused on what is best for each child. In ten years that has never changed.'

He rears up in return. 'But perhaps education has changed,' he says. 'Perhaps Cromwell has changed. Perhaps you don't understand these boys' minds as well as you might. How they work. What they respond to.'

She reels back, aghast. 'Because I'm a woman?'

'Because...' Another gesture of silent assent, but nothing on the record.

'I'd be a better teacher if I were more manly? Less soft and feminine?'

'I mean that it is a long time since you trained Jo. Research may have moved on.'

'If you mean become more interested in a child's test scores than whether they've eaten breakfast that morning then yes, maybe it has.' She tilts her head upwards, addresses the polystyrene ceiling tiles, hopes for more humanity from them. 'Jesus, you can't stamp children out of pre-rolled sheets!' She adjusts her angle of elevation, pleads directly to him. 'Look at Hayley, or Anya and Femi.'

He frowns, doesn't appear to connect the names.

'Hayley in Year 11? The incident with Nelson? And Anya and Femi worrying themselves sick about all this data we're scraping from them every fortnight? Have you ever stopped to think if we are making them happier?'

He glares, drums his fingers on the table, then catches himself, stops, and pauses to switch tack.

'And you? Alex tells me that you aren't happy here.' She doesn't make the connection, and he selects another piece of paper from in front of him, lifts it and slowly reads a quotation. '"God I hate this job sometimes." A recent department meeting? Your response to the financial pressures we all find ourselves under.' Feedback loops. Sensors. Immediate reports of potential faults. A cold wave pours down the inside of her skin. 'A sarcastic response, when I'm sure Mr Henderson would have appreciated your support, some positive approaches, especially with new staff feeling the pressure most. Not... this.'

The machine seems hungry.

He takes a busy look at the clock, marches her towards the end, knows that he has her surrounded, framed, beaten. 'You know that my door is always open Jo. I want staff to be able to come in any time.' This said more loudly than necessary, as if for clarity on a secret tape. Jo thinks of Martha, wonders if she had sat here herself, if she'd taken up the offer, gathered her courage and come down, stepped through the jaws of the doorframe, looking for support. 'But I need staff who are on board with the vision of the school, who are fully committed to delivering it.'

'And those who disagree with some parts of it?'

'I am the Head, Jo.' Yes. No heart, no guts. 'It is up to you how you respond. Get some rest over half term and reflect on whether what we're doing here at Cromwell is something you want to put your shoulder behind.'

She says nothing in reply, waits for him to speak, to say the words that she knows now are coming.

The chorus rises in her, curses her for thinking that she could ever have eased off. Why? she thinks. Why didn't I push harder?

He stands, shows her the door and delivers the blow. 'Perhaps you should have a serious think. Ask yourself, *are you sure this job is really for you?*'

21

With the ward in lockdown nurses had done what they could to sort video calls. Tiny screens, blurred images, terrible sound. Horrendous, but she'd had to put on a brave face.

It'd been hard to tell what details Mum had understood, whether she'd known why her husband and daughter were talking to her through a computer.

Jo had had so many things she'd wanted to say, but Dad had been concerned that it was causing her stress, had asked Jo to go easy.

'You've fought so hard,' he'd told Mum as the nurse had held the tablet. 'Rest now.'

The call had been ended, the screen gone black and Jo had splintered in fury. Had Dad actually told her to give up?

Outside of Jackson's door, the ghost of Geoff not that long past, she thinks of this scene and understands a little better now the odd relief at hearing a painful message. Sometimes words don't create; sometimes they uncover that which there has been a refusal to see.

So perhaps Jackson is right. Painful as it is to hear that a parent has made a complaint, perhaps it is better to see things as they are, to stop fighting, put herself out of this misery. Having Jackson pose the question, say the actual words, ask her to consider her position... it was no more than a statement of the facts. This seed of possibility can now grow inside her, spread into each organ, infect every thought.

Tea as her chosen medicinal. That and some quiet space, alone. Hands cupped around a mug of it, she sits in her room watching the clock, waiting for parents evening to come around.

'Let's meet and have a chat after half term,' Jackson had said as the meeting had finished, walking around the table. 'Talk about what we might put in place to support you. Some things to aim towards together.' A care plan. Saying this as if it were an opportunity for regular pats on the back. But keep patting hard enough and it becomes a push, a shove, thrusting closer to the edge.

Part of her wants to be telling someone. Go to confront Alex, reveal him as a snitch. Find Cara, share the burden, unload. Talk to the school's union rep.

But then she thinks of Mum again, what it must have been like getting her diagnosis. Steered through a door, looking around to see who may have noticed. Nausea. Sweat. Attempting to act normal, to smile at people passed on the stairs, thinking that somehow they already know. There are dogs that can sniff out tumours; weakness smells.

Anger and pride, the shame of weakness, the decision not to speak up: like mother, like daughter, she thinks, knowing that it is wrong, but finding the morbid feeling of closeness inviting nonetheless. Incredible. After her first diagnosis Mum hadn't said a thing. It had been close to Christmas, she'd argued later, a busy time for Dad and a deserved holiday for Jo. Best not to trouble her or over-burden him. Deal with it in secret for a while. Resolve to redouble her resolve.

Her tea is finished. The best thing I can do, she decides, is to be strong. Just this evening and tomorrow to survive. She justifies this as she nibbles on a Custard Cream. She is angry with Alex for reporting an off-hand comment, yes, but she also has her dignity to think about, has nothing to gain from stooping to his level. Better to pull things back without going to him. Or Cara. Cara who has enough to carry.

Jo tilts her head back and expands her shoulders. There are certain things one should take on the chin. She feels more of her mother's creed spread through her. Unfashionable in this day and age, but perhaps Jackson is right. Perhaps a woman cannot so easily get into the mind of a teenage boy. She knows that it used to be monks and curates only, unheard of for women to teach boys until the Industrial Revolution. Sunday Schools and then Mr Wopsle's aunt, the doddering biddy sleeping through her evening classes, the start of education's great feminisation, the men in young Pip's life too busy labouring with iron and forging a new world. Steamships, railways, war and finance, these pounding energies unintelligible to delicate female minds. Sandra and Rose signed up as young graduates to 'Teach First,' but that was literally the way of things until not so long ago: teach first and then have children. Christ, it wasn't so long ago that you'd had to give up teaching if you got married. A child grows and nursery is the next step, young women teachers the next circle of their nurture. But then the move to learning proper, to reason, to argument, to facing down the likes of Sami and Jordan and Michael. Was it so wrong to say that they needed more strong men in their lives rather than squadrons of female teachers? Ex-army sergeants and retired Captains of Industry, that's who they're talking about recruiting these days. Iron discipline, not soft maternal pleas.

Either way, it doesn't matter which parent has made the complaint. They are right, she tells herself: she *does* need to be harder with Year 11. "Don't disturb them?" Could she get any more Wopsle? What the hell had she been thinking? Of course she had to disturb them, not offer lullabies. That was her job, what an education was: challenging boundaries and pushing children outside of their comfort zones. For Nishaan, yes maybe she had to be a port in the storm, but for the rest — for Jordan and Michael and Ade — she needed to be the storm that destroyed the port, forcing them to flee their places of safety.

Shakespeare looks down sagely on her. A tempest. Yes. She must be the tempest that drives them off their fantasy island. Be the wind that blows them out of here, that breaks the spell of the Tower — this hex that has stupefied Darren — and launches them out into the real world.

Be the tempest. Get out of these doldrums into new waters. Caliban and Ariel had stirred together, anger and hubris pressing from above and below, meeting in Prospero's warring body. High minds and base instincts had thundered into one another and — out of this maelstrom of collisions — a man had been created. Yes, this was what a school was: a weekly Genesis of dark battling light, storms and violent depths and voices demanding order, breathing into dust in hope of bringing forth life. School *was* dead, unless Jo poured her very spirit out into it.

She takes her phone and opens her photos, pauses at Ben then scrolls onwards. A beach two summers ago, a picture of her and her mother in Brighton, taken by Dad.

She enlarges it with her thumbs, swallowing, a lump rising in her throat, eyes glistening, teeth hard into lips, biting it all back. New shores. Keep pushing for this. She darkens the screen, puts it away, shuts her eyes, steels herself. Now is not the day to rest. There are snakes in the grass. There is anger and shame, the babble of voices in the shadow of a tower.

The wind moans at the windows and the metal casings strain. Fingers of rain tap and then quieten, then begin to hammer violently on the glass.

A storm, and then new shores. Bitter medicine and the flick of a knife, all of this too familiar. Perhaps mum had initially hoped that if she didn't think about it, it might shrink and go away. It would not because these things do not. She must act now before it *is* too late. A little poison to swallow, a little pain to bear, then she will be strong again.

She digs her nails into her arm, hears the clock faithfully bearing each second forward as her accusers approach, a crumb of broken biscuit on her desk so she licks a finger and raises it to her lips, a kiss of sweetness.

22

It is almost 5 o'clock. She imagines the Tower beginning to move, people pulling on coats, putting out fags, turning keys and descending stairwells, nodding hellos to neighbours, moving towards her down the cracked roadways, hobbling to meet her along uneven pavements, drawing closer along the high metal fence, past the bench towards the gated entrance.

Standing by her window she sees them below her, beginning to approach, one of them her accuser. They will all know about Darren — how she'd lost her shit and gone for a child — but perhaps the other rumours are now being shared too. An unstable woman who goes for children. Another thing to get through, just as she has got through everything else these last months. Keep fighting. Don't give up. No action to be taken by Jackson so conjure some charm, a few minutes of rough magic needed to enchant each of them, tell parents that she'll be going at the class like thunder. Do all this, get over the line into half term.

The streetlights are doing what they can, pushing back against a leaden October dusk, but rain is pressing shoulders down as parents cross the road, the air already laden with car fumes and smokes, the mulch of fallen leaves and tyre-dirt along the clogged bronchi of these streets. The flyover speeds the traffic above. Arterial roads. Bypasses. Far off in the distance, the lights of cranes reach up into the storm, signs of London's once-unstoppable swelling. Perhaps it will pause now. Take a breather. Cease multiplying.

She descends the stairs. There had been talk of plastic screens and strictly distanced queues but the early fervour of late August — worthy assurances, detailed risk assessments and strict systems — seems to have been priced out, even if now there's runaway inflation of case numbers. Some remarkable feat of government-mandated physiology: once within these walls kids don't get it, don't seem to transmit it. She should have offered to perform a comprehension exercise at Sally's wedding reception. They could have called it a school, invited 400+ guests and no social distancing. She could start a business. Weddings, birthdays. Fune…

She has to stop a minute before going in, tighten the straps that hold her in one piece. How? How could this be allowed and Mum had to die alone? She can see groups of parents laughing outside, roaring at something as they pass dripping windows. How many were buried with families kept away? Her mother's coffin, undertakers in masks, a leper's funeral, authorities in full panic, the crematorium council property, "workers had to be protected." And here she was, a couple of months later, no vaccine, numbers rocketing but fuck it, paper over it with a mask, pack the people in.

'Welcome to Parents Evening' a sign says by the door, meaning carers and grandparents too, elder brothers, an aunt who has better English, step-mums and countless other blends, a rich bouquet of those who care for these children, eyeing lists on crumpled sheets, fanning out, looking for their targets.

They are inside, taking in the newly repaired display work and the hastily swept floors. She feels like a startled creature, like she is the foreign body, sits with Lyrca looped tight around her face, eyes fixed ahead as if freezing them there on her books and data sheets would stop them in their tracks. But they are coming. Swinging bags, hacking at coughs and not giving a damn. Some dressed up a little, some wary of another meeting, another organ of the state telling them how they're letting their kids down. But coming in droves, greeting each other, neighbours laughing and joking, bejewelled handsets, bright plastic gems.

Jackson stands, prim, nervous. He greets each parent with an anxious fawning, reminds them about distancing and face-coverings though some are applying the former to the latter, just have them across beards, others leaving noses free, twin exhausts for all their droplets. Matt, Sandra and Rose are wide-eyed in best dress, chins high, backs straightened, sat at ungraffitied desks kept specially for the occasion, an extra couple of feet the only concession given to staff, that and some quickly trampled lines masking tape on the floor. A note on an empty table, directing Martha's class to see Mr Henderson. Cara is puffing her chest out, still channelling the warrior from World Book Day. Jo shrinks like Alice and has to pump herself up again, trying to fill her skin.

She watches a girl called Janine arriving. She's in Matt's class and he stands up to greet her looking confused, smiling as he goes to shake a hand in welcome before pulling smartly back. He sits them down, looks as if he is trying to work out if — behind the folds of blue paper — that's her sister Janine has brought along, an elder sister or her mum?

'Hello,' he says. 'Thanks for coming. How are things?' Janine is in Set 2, has apparently written some lovely essays, his ears blushing as whoever has come with her thanks Matt for all he's doing because Janine is loving the subject again this year. Jo wants to tell him to grab this encouragement, ferment it into something that'll keep and sustain him when tough times come. It's what you have to do, preserve and jar, hoard whatever you can.

The tang of pot wafts briefly past, loud talk, nods, smiles and greetings. She blinks hotly, swallows acid down and wishes she had more reserves to draw on herself. A group of parents are talking and bumping elbows, showing each other the appointments lists they have, checking the time on their phones. A pang of anxiety at this, reminded that they all know each other, know and talk, chat at takeaway counters and whisper in the shops. Everyone around the Tower will surely have heard everything, talked to their boys, heard the gossip from their daughters, weighing her up and pulling her apart, sucking at teeth and shaking their heads, tallying up all the ways that she'd failed their children until someone suggests writing a complaint.

Worry flips to anger as the crowds grow around her, a desire to fire questions back at them. *What is it that you expect of me?* They hand over their sons and expect her to return them home each day brighter, more balanced and better exercised. Before they ask what she doing, she wants to ask them what *they* are doing. What strategies are they using to manage behaviour? What targets have they set? What measures are they using to check whether their child is on course to meet them, and what sanctions are being used when they leave the house without the right books or uniform? They expect her to spend hours assessing homework, but are *they* checking whether any time has been spent doing it? *Why should I be the storm when you have been such a shower?* she fumes to herself. *Why should...*

'Hello? Miss Barker?' It is Nishaan's mum, him standing beside.

'Sorry, I was on another planet!' Jo scrambles to mute her soliloquy. She invites them to sit down and Mum does, Nishaan deftly drawing up his chair next to her.

'So,' Jo begins, looking at Nishaan, 'how do you think you are getting on?'

Standard tactic: deflect the issue back, hope the student does the difficult work of explaining the reasons for their poor progress. But Nishaan says nothing and his mother looks on expectantly. Is she the one who wrote to complain? Beginning her defence Jo twists papers round and nearly knocks them off the desk. Both she and mum have their chairs pushed back the regulation distance but are now trying to see the same document and she can't help think how farcical it must look, and how utterly ineffective. But what choice does she have? She feels her risk level rising, checks her mask, thinks of Dad and mutters some hex before beginning to fire rounds of data, pointing her pen at the magazine of test results starting in Year 7 and not pausing for breath. 'If we look at Year 9 and Year 10 and compare the deviation of Nishaan's mark from the mean mark in the year then we can see that, while his actual score has gone down to 35%, relative to others in the year he has perhaps done better —' She breaks down other results and throws them over the desk, gives an analysis of the aggregated data from the Year 9 national tests and their ability — if it came down to algorithmic calculation again — to predict Nishaan's likely performance in the summer, comments on his oral work and reads off a punctuality percentage before finally grinding to a halt, turning her papers back round, leaning back as far as she can and daring to look up and breathe in.

'So you think he'll be ok?' Mum says, taking her son's hands between hers.

Behind all the cells bursting with digits, this simplest question. No, it cannot have been her who'd made the complaint. But this is the one thing Jo cannot give an answer to. She shuffles in her seat, as if trying to convince herself that her body still exists, then offers a platitude, hoping that hope will be enough.

Behind Nishaan, Michael is waiting with his grandfather, a long, matted dreadlock threaded with greys and browns, and Jo turns her eyes to them, then back to Nishaan's mum, who takes the hint, thanks her deferentially and takes Nishaan elsewhere.

Jackson hovers and she begins her spiel again, Michael leaning to see what she is pointing at, puzzled at all these numbers his existence seems to have generated, his shoulders narrower, his body curled in, smaller here than when sprawled back in his chair upstairs.

'You hearing this?' the grandfather interjects, stopping Jo mid-flow, drawing his mask down as he speaks, making sure he is heard. Michael nods. 'Reading the books and doing the work?'

Michael sits back up, hands between his legs, head bowed. 'Course I am.'

'Course he is,' he parrots back with a toothy smile. 'I pity you,' he continues, lifting the mask back into place. 'Can't tell him anything, though he has plenty of lessons for me.' He opens his hands, shrugs. 'Apparently a different world now, so what wisdom could I possibly offer?' A hearty laugh at this, and before she can ask him not to he lifts Jo's copy of *Great Expectations* off the desk. 'Wonderful book. A boy given an opportunity. But imagine he didn't listen to anyone, to the advice of his elders?'

'Allow it, Gramps,' Michael says, brow furrowed in embarrassment, hands dug deep into a puffa.

'That all you have to say now, in your actual GCSE year?' Getting nothing in return, he leans back and shakes his head. 'All this SnapChat, and now your chat has snapped.' He laughs again at his own epigram, then he snaps himself, turns on Michael. 'You want to end up like your brother? All his regrets locked around his ankle? Knowledge is passed *down* Michael, that's why it's called bringing you *up*. You need to listen if you're going to learn, listen to Miss here, doing what she can to help you.'

'I told you. She can't even control the class.' This fired at the grandfather, but slapping Jo square in the face.

'Michael,' she begins to say, preparing her riposte, glad that Jackson can't hear, has been engaged in conversation with a parent. But she is cut off.

'Irrelevant. Totally irrelevant,' the man tells Michael. 'Why should someone have to control you when you should be able to control yourself? You've got to *learn* how to *learn*. These are your exams boy, no one else's. *Your* future. Your responsibility.'

Jo wishes she could run around the table and actually hug him, take his words, gorge on half now and pickle the rest. Michael sinks lower in his seat, his face even more sullen, throwing her a scowl. 'How though? Can't even afford photocopies anymore. This school is broke, man. The projector blew up yesterday.'

The grandfather looks at her for confirmation and she spies an opening. 'With everything that is going on, the Head has said costs have got to be cut. Though,' she rolls her eyes conspiratorially, 'you'll have doubtless seen the new signage outside the gates.' The man scoffs in disgust at this and she opens her hands, signalling that matters were out of them. 'These decisions can end up having an impact on delivery.'

'I'll write to the council,' he declares, and she has to explain that the council no longer run the school, this met with a blank look.

'It's run by the MAT.'

'Matt? Who is he?' he asks, reaching inside his coat for something to write with. Behind him, Jackson is prowling, over-doing the hand gestures and eye-smiles, mask matching his suit.

'Multi Academy Trust, the organisation that runs all these schools.' Silence. But she wants him to do it, put pen to paper and let Jackson have it, the school's namesake suddenly called to mind, Thomas Cromwell telling Cardinal Wolsey of the short-bladed knife, the *estoc* pushed up under the ribs, a firm twist of the wrist to make sure, a man dispatched to hell. 'You would need to write to them,' she tells him.

'Probably the same company as run the prisons now. Prisons, PPE and benefits. Jesus,' he laughs as he scribbles. 'Contracts for friends. Nothing changes. We'll have Serco running the hospital next.'

With that, it is over. He thanks her, presents an elbow as he stands and leads Michael away. She is left with empty chairs again, the hubbub of chatter, groups of parents edging past too close, peering for her name, giving one another looks, moving on, all of them talking.

She keeps scanning for Sami, wanting a chance to offer her version of events, that she is a good person, a good teacher, with his best interests at heart. After his speech to Jordan it felt as if she'd almost had him, and now it's like he's taken fright.

In front of her desk is a shifting forest of bodies she wants to retreat from, branches swaying and touching, respiring like a single organism. She wants more air, looks at the condensation on the windows, the dripping moisture pooling on the sills behind her. They shouldn't be doing this, she thinks, desperate for a long shower, for face and hands to be clean. But through the openings that bend then lean shut she keeps thinking she's seeing Sami, her longing to leave countered by this urge to stay, to face him, to win him back. A dart of skin, a glimpse of a coat and she stands and shifts but it's never him. She takes a sip from a plastic cup of tea, checks the floor around her, as if fluid might have cascaded through her insides and drained straight out like water through a parched house plant. Could I taste that, she wonders, and drinks again, feeling her forehead, swallowing to check in on her throat, wondering if she warrants a precious test appointment.

But suddenly Hayley is there, emerging from the treeline, mum steering her down into a chair, dad stood behind.

It's her but not her, a baggy top on, hood pulled up over, hair falling out through the sides. Mum sits forward, back straight, thin face, greets Jo weakly, a nod from dad. Jackson lurks and gives her a look.

'Good to see you Hayley.' Focus on her. Shut the rest out. 'How are you?' Neither parent has face coverings. She doesn't want to lean forward too much but has her arms across the table towards her, papers covered, hands together.

A smile from behind the shadows of the hood. 'I'm OK Miss.'

'Half term after tomorrow.'

'Yeah.'

She wants words that aren't words, a means of transferring meaning quietly and seriously, solemnly yet weightlessly. A quiet moment, a slow tilt of the head. Hayley looks away. 'You've got the ability to do well, you know that don't you?' Picking up her sheets, performing a thoughtful pose. 'There are all sorts of numbers I could show you that confirm that. But forget all that, I just want you to hear it from me: I believe you can do it. Get a good run together. Focus, get stuck into revision. Mocks before you know it.'

Her mum speaks into the silence. 'You're ready, aren't you petal? Ready to work hard.'

'That's good Hayley,' she tells her. 'I know it's not the easiest class sometimes and it's been the craziest time, but I'm going to do everything I can.'

'Thanks, Miss. I mean it.'

Relief at this. Get through tomorrow, reach calm waters. 'Have you had a chance to read any more of the book?' She points at the Dickens, doesn't want to pick it up, but Hayley shakes her head. 'Don't worry. Whatever work you've missed while you've been away...'

Dad, gripping the back of Hayley's chair, suddenly leans in, interrupts. 'Putting her through this. Making her miss school. I'll kill him. I'll fucking kill him,' he says in a crow-like rasp, his face a battleground in unstable truce.

'Please,' mum says, louder than she might mean to. Others have heard him and heard her too, are turning, stopping their conversations and looking. Jo watches him feel the forest crowd around him, needle him, jumpy like a boxer, head beginning to peck back and forth like a peacock, knuckles tensing white, trying to put together some combinations, not wanting to make a fist of his words.

'I mean it.' The proud and protective father. 'He tries anything like that again I will tear his fucking head off.' He turns and calls into the wood. 'Put *that* on the internet.' There's a rumble of support from a few other chestnuts.

Jo sees Hayley's discomfort. 'Mr West,' she says, 'I can assure you that the school is best placed to deal with this.'

'Is that right?' he says, dripping with sarcasm, nodding his head even more vigorously. 'Is that right? Because far as I can see it's all "follow this policy, follow that policy" while nothing actually gets done.' He stops for a moment, makes a fist and releases a tearing cough into it, sending Jo backwards as if she'd been slapped. A vein on his temple beats hot signals around his body, and he brings his arm down and round as if ripping off a restraint. 'Sweep it all away. Stop the school looking bad, that's number one here.' Hayley has buried her head inside her hoodie and, seeing this, Dad concludes. 'Your Darren had it right Hayls. Deal with it the Tower way, short and sharp.'

She can't help but draw in a palpitating, turbulent breath. The tea in her cup quivers and ripples on her desk. She pushes her chair back a little and gathers herself — physically collects her limbs closer to her core — as if in anticipation of Darren appearing. Mr West has seen her flinch and is glaring down, still gripping the back of Hayley's chair. 'Mr West, while the perpetrator certainly deserves sanction...'

He sees his prey and pounces. 'This is what I mean. THIS IS WHAT I MEAN.' His voice is rising as if new irrefutable evidence has been uncovered. 'It's all about protecting *him*.'

'Mr West,' she interjects more firmly. Her elbows are tight into ribs, knees touching, legs bent under. She looks like an animal dressed in a butcher's shop.

'Don't bother,' he snorts. 'All your fancy words. Save it for your fucking refugee boy.'

'OK, thank you,' Jackson says, alerted to the disturbance and approaching hurriedly, reflexively putting a hand to Dad's elbow.

'Get your hands off me,' he shouts, throwing himself around, knocking Jackson's arm away. 'Alright?! Don't you dare touch me.' Twisting back, turning to Jo, arcing his pointing hand, a sweep of students, teachers and other parents, his blood up, his voice raised. People are pushing back, suddenly wanting two metres. 'Keep your hands where they should be. All of you!'

Jackson is holding his forearm as if he's been shot, Alex rushing to his side to bolster him. Cara is now standing, Jo getting up to stop her, ready to protect but knocking her cup over, tea running across the desk and spilling to the floor. But it's over. Hayley has gripped her hood, got up and run, her mum following her, Dad now alone, taking one more contemptuous look at the line of staff before pushing through the gathered circle and charging away.

23

The last day of half term, Cromwell quiet as she scales the stairs. Mary is already in, pushing her mop and bucket across the foyer, hands in blue gloves, a holster of sprays at her waist. Premises staff are packing away the tables in the hall, resetting the stage for a new scene, last night's action being swept to one side. Always this hope: stack the chairs, wipe the board and clean the desks and yesterday's battles will be forgotten. Dusted, and thus done.

If only.

The rest of the evening had passed without incident, though she'd perched as if expecting one. The scrape of a chair, the slap of a book hitting the floor, the parting of bodies as someone pushed through — all of it had sent her body to the edges of things, hands to the desk, thighs to the lip of the chair. Two families, two neighbouring flats, but no sightings of Sami or Nelson. Nelson whom she now has to worry about too. She'd weighed up how to report what Hayley's dad had said, flag that Nelson was at risk. But she didn't want Jackson feeling she was criticising the school's response. Not right now. So when she'd finally left she'd said nothing to him as she'd passed him at the door. Outside, gusts had picked up the rain and chased her from the estate, heavy droplets charting their correlations down the window of the train, then jostling her through the middle of Brixton and following her to the front door. The house was a mess, but she'd stopped herself jumping in to start tidying and cleaning; time for all of that next week.

A bath behind a locked bathroom door, deep water on the verge of scalding, cleansing, dipping her head under, breath held in silence. Foam and oils. Heat, and the air pungent with lavender and jasmine, an attempt at a deeper cleanse. By the time she'd wrapped herself in a dressing gown and huddled into the sofa, she'd begun to regain her resolve.

Arrangements confirmed with Sally, she'd ignored the blinking answerphone, put on Lean's version of *Great Expectations*, the wind blowing the pages as the film had opened, Pip running past gallows, off to the church to tend the grave. Limbs creaking, set to snap and fall. Yes, she'd thought, in the midst of turmoil, become the storm. Get in early and hit them hard, a whole hour of hard labour, no mercy, no poetry, no grace. Resolute about this, she'd practised stern looks on the ornaments, silencing them with stares, intent on success as she'd lain in bed, a single slip of flesh on double sheets, rain on the window. But sleep hadn't come quickly. She'd turned and turned, straining to remember the sound of her mother's voice, wishing she'd had an hour or two more, her and Mum both turning out their thoughts, shaking the last sentences from the creases in them, everything said.

She must have slept then; a dream of fire somewhere in the night, of Pip lit by flames, of heat and pumping bellows. This is what you do, she affirms to her dreaming self, you forge pain into an offering, hammer and shape it to mean something, grind dead bones, throw the meal into pot and fire it; sorrow turned into a vessel that you carry.

And she'd woken with this, stowed it and carried it with her.

'Hey. You OK?' Cara asks as she arrives with a plastic cup of green goo.

Jo glances up from her desk, holding open her page in *Howards End*. 'Fine. You?' Any lingering shadow of yesterday's unpleasantness has been carefully masked by foundation.

Cara looks exhausted as she undoes her coat. 'I'm fine,' she tells her, but the tired slow way she unwinds her scarf seems to contradict. 'Thankful for the holiday.' She watches Jo turn to another marked section in the text, make a note and turn back. 'No let up until then though?'

'Keep the pressure on,' she says without breaking from the book. 'You going for a gentle one today?'

She sees Cara take this, weigh it, not fire it back. She sends a smile instead, undoes the lid of her drink, thinks about having some, then lowers it. 'Take it easy Jo, won't you?'

She resists a scoff. "Taking it easy" has left her looking down the barrel of a capability procedure. There is no 'easy' that can satisfy the machine. For now, survival means every moment driven hard. Overwork is what one does; sleep is what one sacrifices. Because they are children. Because meaning is made from suffering.

But she doesn't say this, just gives a thumbs up, and Cara leaves.

Period one, and Year 7 must wonder what has hit them. Looking forward to their first holiday since big school began, they cower as she demolishes a poem, tears it open, holds up its innards and then asks them to interrogate it. She does not sit, stands at the front calling down the lines of desks, no quarter given.

When Year 13 come in next period she dives straight into an apology, confesses that she'd spoken in anger last lesson, and is sorry. The mood in the room turns awkward, as if it might have been better to have just left it. Things disappear down their timelines so quickly, don't last long in the memory. Femi sighs impatiently, judders her knee beneath her desk and turns a pen incessantly around her fingers, book open in readiness to begin.

'Did you hear Miss?' Mo says, glancing at Femi. 'She got an interview. Oxford.'

'Femi that's wonderful!'

'Thanks,' Femi says quickly, returning her eyes to turning her biro, working it furiously round and round.

'Such a great achievement,' Anya adds, just as Femi loses her grip on the pen, sending it spinning onto the desk and towards the edge until she slams a hand down onto it.

'Achievement? Why?' Femi asks sharply, palm still locked over the plastic shaft, eyes still fixed on it. 'Because I'm from the Tower, right? Because I'm estate. Because...'

'Hey, come on, I didn't mean that,' Anya says, wounded, quiet. 'You know I wouldn't say that.'

She looks at no one but angles the biro towards Jo. 'Well, obviously people don't always know what it is they're really saying, so...'

'OK enough,' Jo interjects, and hands them a snap test on the background and plot of *Howards End*.

'Privilege is power, discuss,' Femi scoffs into her desk, snatching the paper.

Ignoring Femi, Mo and Rasheed hit Jo with rapid-fire complaints about the assessment, but she deflects them, refuses to retreat, says that they heard themselves that this was what the Head wanted.

'For what though?' says Rasheed. 'Just more stress.'

'To prepare us for the world of work, my friend,' Mo replies, trying to lighten the air. 'Data data data. Perform or get resigned. And that's just some jungle warehouse we'll be in fulfilling orders. Imagine these two with their Oxford ting. We're talking 24/7 online lecture stressssss.'

Anya dabs her eyes, stands, blurts a request to go to the toilet, moves to the door without waiting for assent, and rushes out.

'What's got into her? I was only having jokes,' Mo says.

'Please,' she asks. 'Please, just get on with your tests.' And they all do, but not before Femi has had the last word, scribbling her answers down, glum-faced and joyless, muttering, 'I am so ready to be out of here.'

When Anya doesn't return she instructs the others to be quiet, to not copy each other's work while she chances a look along the corridor. She can hear her before she can see her. She is sat out on a stairwell, sobbing into her sleeve.

'Anya,' she says. 'Come on.'

But the volume only rises and she starts hyperventilating, panicking loudly, looping round viciously in shock at her own state, agitating herself towards blackout.

'Calm down,' Jo tells her, not so much because she believes that Anya can, but because she is a bit frightened, has no idea what to do.

Anya does not look up, sounds like a deer at the end of a chase, her breathing like a blunt saw, the raw functions of life in desperate distress.

Jo rocks forward and then back, looking around anxiously before stepping gingerly forward, wanting to half put an arm... not around, but close by. 'Hey, come on. What Femi said was uncalled for.'

A move of the head. She wants to speak, and to do this has to gather herself a little. 'She's probably right,' she says eventually. An anguished look up at Jo, eyes red, face miserable. Between lurches of air she sobs, 'I' 'can't' 'win.' And she breaks again and Jo looks around frantically but the stairwell is completely empty, bouncing every sound right back at them. Anya buries her face in her thighs, arms tight around her knees and muffles a full-body scream of torment. A therapeutic practice she's used before, Jo thinks with eyes wide, because she then is able to gather herself, bring her breathing down enough to vent her complaint. 'If I'd gone to another school this lot would have said I was "abusing my privilege." But I came here and I'm still abusing my privilege so, what am I meant to do?'

A privilege itself to have that dilemma, but Jo holds her tongue. 'Everyone is tired and stressed I think.' Six months of high anxiety, tens of thousands dead, empty supermarkets, education in tatters. It has all been stored somewhere, will have to find a way out.

'That's the problem. It's just this pressure. This *constant* pressure. And it will never, *ever* go away.' She wipes her nose, tries to control her breathing, begins to construct an argument, still definitely Anya underneath everything. 'All these tests, all the time. And now fucking Oxbridge interviews and Dad and... God, I just want to jump off.'

Jo tenses, checks that the stairwell is safe. But Anya doesn't quite seem to mean that. 'I'm sorry if I've made anything worse,' she says.

'It's not your fault.' She growls in raw frustration. 'It's not *anyone's* fault. It's more than that. It's like *every little thing* is under stress, like *nothing* is certain now.' She mops the tears on her cheek with a paw and takes a long draw of air, a modicum of peace returning. 'When my parents went to school it was so simple. You do this amount of work and you'll get these results, that'll get you into this college then into this kind of job, be able to afford a house, live a comfortable life, and...' She breaks down again, shoots Jo a desperate look that says all she needs to. The rods and levers all broken. All the promises of her class now doubted. No guarantee of affording a roof over her head, no assurance that a degree would be worth the debt. The economy decimated. Universities like secure sanatoria. Qualifications hardly worth the paper. Even the bedrock that Earth itself would keep turning as it always had was now fracturing. Pandemics and heatwaves, nature's nerves quivering and all of her creatures feeling the tension.

She looks towards the door. The others are sat in a room with no supervision, not exactly an inspection-positive situation. She has her own pressures and they need to get back. All the workshops and policies on fostering resilience, on student mental welfare and the problems of the snowflake generation, but all of it butts up against the need to administer a test, collect some data, get this child back up and running, back on course to delivering a decent result.

'I know,' she tells her vaguely, a note of impatience just audible. In an ideal world she would spend some time with her, dig down and check if there were other issues going on. But she can't. There isn't time. 'Come on, you're going to do great.' Platitudes, but what else can be marshalled against all she has to face? League tables care about grades, not whether or not kids will do themselves harm achieving them. No footnotes allowed; two years of work will be distilled to a single letter, but she can't focus on that now. 'You just have to get on with it. Push through.' A tetchy edge to her voice. 'Come on, get up,' she orders in mock macho tone, poking Anya's leg with a toe, hoping that this comes across as friendly. Friendly and firm.

She rightly discerns that she'll have had it bred into her; Anya knows what needs to be done. She stands, wipes her eyes, pushes past and on into the classroom where she obediently bows her head and starts the first question.

Jo foregoes lunch, sits alone in her classroom to steal a march on her marking. Anya had seemed to calm quickly enough, but now her own pulse refuses to come down, her own breathing anxious as she reads their scripts, stabs into their shallow responses, punches corrections, knowing full well the damage that this can do. She handles each one tentatively, the worry that they're not clean yet trumped by the worries about falling behind with workload.

Into the office for another coffee, and Matt and Sandra are having a muted celebration for having made it through their first half term. Sandra is telling Cara that Martha sends apologies, is devastated to have let people down.

'Come on, let's raise a slice to her too,' Cara says, brandishing a knife. She delivers a supermarket cake by caesarean, tearing it from its cellophane casing, and they insist that Jo joins them for a slice. Red velvet.

'Thanks,' she says, taking a paper serviette, wary even of sharing this even though she'll be at Sally's later and God knows whether she's been going into work, going out in Soho, keeping a safe distance. But it will at least mean a proper meal, something that doesn't require plastic peeling back, stirring after two minutes, 800W. Porcelain dishes, serving spoons, multiple plates, culinary techniques beyond remove sleeve and pierce lid. Her mouth waters, feels like it's been so long. 'I'll have this in a bit. Well done you two.' Cara looks a bit deflated that she's leaving them to it, Matt tucking in with his feet on his desk, Sandra perched on the side of hers showing Cara a cottage she's heading to late tonight. Lewes, with two other couples. Not quite within regulations, but fuck it. An early bonfire party. You've got to keep living right? No one has mentioned the pub later.

'Hope it goes well,' Cara shouts ruefully.

It has to. It must.

Back in her classroom, she reads an email from Alex. More assessments he wants writing. An updated scheme of work for Year 8. The Mock GCSE paper, and can she prepare two mock-mocks, plus marking guides. She doesn't reply, doesn't remind him it's half term next week. She is in no position to fight it, feels an odd relief that she is still deemed capable enough to be given tasks to complete.

She hears her phone buzz. A message from Sally. *Go get them Jo. See you later. 8? xx*

Perfect. She can call Dad, be the grown-up, check he knows what's happening. She warms to her task, knows exactly what she has to do this afternoon.

The projector hangs from the ceiling, sophisticated but useless. But, she thinks, technology can't dazzle these boys into focus. To teach is to be a body that speaks. A voice big enough to be heard, hands strong enough to make a mark: at its core education is nothing more than this.

Two minutes later Cara catches her struggling, waddling backwards out of the stock cupboard.

'What the hell are you doing?' she asks, grabbing the door.

'Blackboard,' she tells her with a smile, short of breath, signalling for her to grab the other end. 'The bulb in the projector went. Going to use chalk instead. Thought it'd add a bit of old school authenticity. Dickens, you know.' She sits the mass of board down and puts a box of chalk onto her desk.

'God Jo,' Cara laughs nervously, brushing white dust trails off her skirt. She half opens her mouth as if to say something, but Jo suddenly lifts her end towards the spare runners to one side of the whiteboard and Cara grabs hers to help.

Taking a step back, she wipes the board and tests a stick of chalk. 'No batteries required,' she grins. 'And chalk never dries out.' Cara shakes her head as she leaves, laughs and tells Jo she's mad as she pulls the door open and steps into the corridor.

It begins to swing shut, and for a split second it's as if the hinges are squeaking... but the noise builds, builds far too fast and high, whistling, screeching and screaming. Jo twists in shock, as if all at once she knows exactly what's coming. She is already moving towards the closing sliver of door when it hits, the exploding firework taking each particle of air and filling it, thrusting it violently through the slit as she grabs at the handle.

The rocket is done but the corridor is filled with other screams now, cordite and yells and shouts and the slamming of bodies through doors, kids in hysterics as they peel themselves off the walls.

Her eyes are burning, throat tightening. Cara is leant against a display-board holding her stomach, shielding, defending, breathing out in big blows.

'Jesus, Car.'

'Sorry,' she says, 'I didn't see who did it.'

'Forget that!' she goes to embrace her then pulls back and holds her shoulders instead, looks her in the face as she feels Cara's trembles resonate with hers. 'Are you ok?'

She doesn't answer, is stroking her bump, trying to ask the same question.

'My fault,' she insists. 'Shouldn't have got you to help me.'

Danny is bopping down the corridor, hand to his mouth. 'OH MY DAYS!' he shouts. 'Miss, did you see that?' Full of excitement in the thrall of the spectacle, as if he might have also cheered for Fawkes' success, the slaughter of the entire establishment a price worth paying to witness a really decent explosion.

He cannot see the hole that it's blown in her. 'Can't you see how DAMNED dangerous and stupid that was?' Jo shouts. Facade cut open. Raw emotion. She looks at Cara, then back at him. 'Someone could have been KILLED.'

'Jeez Miss, allow it,' he says, frowning, offended. 'Wasn't me.' Trying to squirm out from under her heavy stare.

'Miss,' Cara says, struggling, urging, pleading.

'*Absolutely* unacceptable,' she hisses at him as she takes Cara's elbow. And just as she does the bell sounds, hits her right as she passes it, pounds both of their heads as they make their way into the office.

Cara says nothing. Strokes hair back from her face. Bites her bottom lip.

It is her turn to be shaken. She looks at Cara in panic, eyes wildly searching for something on which to land. 'Can I get you a tea or something?'

Cara nods at this and she hurries to boil the kettle, scoops a large spoon of sugar into a stained mug. Outside the noise is building. She places the mug in between Cara's two praying hands, kneels down in front of her. She scrunches moist eyes shut. 'This bloody place. These *fucking* children.'

'Stop, Jo,' she whispers. Her voice is unsteady, wobbles and wavers, then releases a single, broken sob. She crumples, as if everything she's been asked to carry presses all at once down into her shoulders. For a few seconds they are stooped like this. But then Cara tenses, arches and straightens her back, looks up at the clock. 'Come on. Just get through this afternoon.' She takes in a long, choking breath. 'Come on soldier. The bell's gone.'

Jo hears Alex shouting, students roaring laughter in return, others doing impressions of fireworks. 'Go,' Cara says. She can still feel her shaking. 'Go on. My lot will be fine for a minute. You go.'

Face tucked down into blouse she pushes back through the fast-running corridor to get the last things ready for Year 11, looking ready to explode at any damned child who might be responsible, ready to tear them apart for putting an unborn's life at risk, snorting air through her nostrils, daring them to cross her.

But she is too late. The whole building is writhing and shifting, shaking as they barge towards the last afternoon before the break. Word of the rocket has spread as fast as it had seared along the linoleum, any semblance of bubbles burst, heaving groups of kids all shouting BANG at one another, others shrieking in impersonation, each sound flaying, ripping, washes of bloody acid pouring from the back of her head, heart throbbing, brain pulsing as she enters the classroom.

'Truss!' Charlie says as he follows her through the door. 'That was so sick! Did you hear it?' he asks, turning to Ade, who is piling in behind, laughing, nervously looking back in case another is set off. Everyone else is thinking the same, jamming themselves, rushing into the room, slowing once safe but then being smacked, pushed onwards, the tide of them nearly taking her with it.

'Please,' she barks as she grabs for her mask and sanitiser. 'Keep some distance please.' But they don't, go full gung-ho teen and start coughing over one another, shouting that they can't breathe. 'Stop it,' she pleads. 'Guys STOP IT.'

Forget trust. No. Not now. Trust does not go betraying her to Jackson. Trust does not write secret letters of complaint. Trust does not set fireworks on its friends, put colleagues at risk.

'What is that?' Jakob asks as he is tumbled into the room by the melee.

'A blackboard, you dumbf,' Jordan informs him, launching in with a few huge shoves, no one else behind his wave of alpha pressure, making sure Jakob's ignorance didn't go unpunished. He could make a great Cromwell teacher.

Jakob absentmindedly throws some punches into those in front of him while pondering the new addition to the room. 'What's it doing here?'

'Miss got woke, innit?' Jordan says, turning to Jo, beaming, stopping the flows around him simply by planting his feet. 'That right Miss man? Enough of the whiteboard, time for the black?' He throws a fist up in a power salute, one she weakly mirrors back.

The class have taken Jordan's lead and are gradually settling behind their desks, but each new person turning through the door sends her twisting again. She can't waste any more time or there won't *be* time. She has to get this done, show Jackson that he is wrong. Show her mum that she is worthy. Get into half term with something to show for it. If she trips now they will fall and she will have failed them. She races through the register and launches out at full pelt into a comparison of Pip's early relationships in the novel with his latter ones. Dolge Orlick. Herbert Pocket. Bentley Drummle. Startop. Labourers, gentlemen, oafs, all men to nudge and prod Pip along his path.

'Date. Ruler. Margin. Copy this into your books,' she barks like a drill sergeant and begins scratching names in chalk onto the board, no quarter given, no space or time for opposition. For emphasis she slaps the back of her hand into her other palm, the noise cracking sharply, louder than she or they expect and there's a flinch on both sides, the sound of flesh hitting flesh triggering different reflexes around the room, surging then fading. But she pushes straight on, grabs the novel and starts reaching for ways that money changes Pip, getting them onto the board.

The chalk crumbles, falling faithfully to pieces as it does its work, the hypnotic tap of it as it rises between words and lands again, clutched in her fingers like a fag becoming ash as it decays into words. There is something ancient and true about this, white earth onto black surface, enlightenment in this bewitching percussion — tap, slide, tap tap, going back to dot the i's, forward again, slide, tap, full stop — a soporific spell in the warm air. She begins to calm down.

But then a metallic snap breaks the charm, the sound of a handle being worked, a rap of wood on plastic as the door hits the desk behind it. Nishaan kicks out at it, sending it slamming shut again as Sami walks by with his head down, stows his rucksack and curls himself into his desk. Mmwwaa, Mmwaa... a few sounds of kisses and chuckles from somewhere around the class.

She feels herself redden. Focus, repair yourself, address him.

'You're late,' she says loudly, curtly, turning, arm still bent at board height, the chalk still gripped in her fingers, a white nib.

He says nothing. Reaches up, pulls his cap more firmly down over his head. The bloody cheek, she thinks, him complaining about behaviour, but look at him now, flagrantly disobeying a rule.

'Sami, I cannot have people just walking in whenever they like and disturbing the lesson.' No response. He has sat with Jackson, demanded more discipline, so she will give him what he wants. 'Cap off please,' she tells him again. A navy Yankees hat, a cracked, circular sticker on the peak.

'Allow it,' he says quietly, his vernacular now quite fluent, not looking at her, reaching again for the hat, sweeping his hand round the back to check it is covering his head sufficiently.

No. She cannot "allow it." She has allowed far too much already. She will not let this go. 'Refusal to follow instructions,' she tells him, as if reading from a list of regulations. 'I'll make a note on the register; start with that,' trying to retain a note of humour. The joke escapes him.

'Miss man. I'm here innit. I beg you, just get on with the lesson,' he says, glowering at his desk. Hard to tell if it's the shadow of the peak or if he has a nasty new bruise around his eye. Someone mutters something and he turns and angrily tells them to fuck off.

'Shall I add rudeness too? Back-chat?' He flicks a look now, dark anger pent up, something of Orlick in him, rage in the blooded whites.

She has stepped to him and knows that she must not back down. Her heart beats. She swallows. She wants to scratch an itch on the back of her calf, but she can't. She knows that she must score a small victory, any small foothold of authority will do, then push on, speed on so that time won't be lost.

'It's a very straightforward instruction Sami. I'm being very polite,' she continues, motionless, a faint shrill creeping into her voice. 'You are a pupil at this school, one of over a thousand,' pulling Jackson's words out of her chest and loading them for her own use. 'You know the school rules by now, and if you want to access your education here you need to be prepared to follow them, just as everyone else does.'

But he does not move, does not pull his gaze away, a calm brutality in it, his breathing deep and even. He is far from home, needs reminding that he is just a child, a boy.

'What would your parents think of behaviour like this?' she asks, but the words putrefy in the air between them, land malicious, as if designed to hurt.

She pales as she watches him process this, his expression all disbelief at this cruelty, the slightest shake of his head. The slice of cake is still sat on her desk, steak-red. She wants it inside her now, is empty and weak but dare not glance over, feels too close to fainting. Chalk in one hand, Dickens in the other, she stands frozen, warning lights popping behind her eyes. Help, she thinks, detaching, I don't have enough blood. The rest of the class peels away, the walls darken, just her and Sami, who melts suddenly into Orlick. Dickens' villain holds a single candle, this the only light as he describes attacking Pip's sister in the forge late one night. The kitchen fire is low, her head turned towards the stove. *I come upon her from behind... I giv' it her! I left her for dead.* Springing up and savaging, not considering it his fault. *It warn't Old Orlick as did it,* the tales of bullying and beating, unfairness and prejudice, him getting off, scot-free.

'Just get on with the lesson, man,' Jordan moans. 'Innit,' a chorus of others chimes in, and the room lightens, the rest of the class back into view.

Jordan is right. She can't afford to lose the whole lot of them over one child's refusal to remove a hat. Be pragmatic. If you don't flex, you get broken. There isn't time. A deep breath.

'I quite agree Jordan,' Jo says. 'Sami's lack of co-operation mustn't stop everyone learning. We will deal with it later.'

She turns back to the board. Tap. Slide. Tap. Tap. Hitting harder and harder, desperate for the hex to be cast again as she spells out instructions for their writing task, a short essay comparing and contrasting Pip's changing social connections.

Some begin writing. Others begin talking and are quickly pounced on. Sami sits, still focused on his desk, stabbing his pen into it, agitated, book shut. She sits and breaks off a small piece of cake, brushing crumbs onto the carpet. She flicks at the book as if lining up Dickens' characters to have their say, Mr Joe reminding her of all the help she'd offered Sami, now thrown back in her face, her reputation nearly ruined. Mr Pumblechook asking why this one boy should be allowed to bend the rules, Mrs Wopsle why he needed some horrible piece of nylon to cover his head anyway. Ludicrous, Startop adds. Is his self-esteem so low he needs some branded item to bestow him worth? That's what it is, Wemmick puffs, the hat is a *brand*, a huge steaming mark burned onto him, relying on a designer label to make him feel accepted.

She is swept along in agreement. She has made a vow to teach Sami *Great Expectations* and this she will now do: show him what Pip finally learned, that being a gentleman wasn't about expensive cloth. Yes, she thinks, cleansing her hands. Take the hat. Be the storm. Prove your strength. March in among their desks. Flip it off his head and hold it as a ransom, a price on his betrayal, use it as a lever to extract some work. A victory to throw onto the table at Sally's, to tell Dad as they share a good dinner.

Quietly, she gets up from her desk and raises her mask. She walks out of her box and down the aisle towards him, nonchalantly checking other students' work as she approaches. Past Nishaan. Past Jakob. Pretending to inspect

Danny's book from a distance, heart thumping as she nears him, but repairs holding.

She is right upon him now. His eyes are down and he still doesn't seem to have seen her. *Be no weak servant of indecision!* Shakespeare tells her from his place on the wall. Do it now if you are going to.

The whole chorus propels her forward, the silent swoop of a predator, her hand reaching to grab the hat by its peak, peeling it off his head, passing it quickly to her other hand as he begins to react. The rest of her is level with him now as he twists, anger and surprise boiling over as his head is exposed.

But what the *hell* is that? There is some... *thing* on his head.

She scurries back to her taped-off area. He stands, and now she can see: it is blood, dried and scabbed around a vicious wound crudely tended with strips of plaster crisscrossing the scalp. The bruised eye is clear now the shadow of the peak has gone, a long second cut above it.

'Sami,' is all she says, as if advising him to proceed with caution.

'Give me the fucking hat.'

'Sami,' she says again, the whole class watching but her eyes fixed on him. There is no other sound.

'You happy now?' he shouts. Teaching has spread so far through her that she can't help note how much his accent has improved. He points towards the window, out towards the Tower. 'You see what they did to me? Because of you?' He is crying, bitterly, angrily. 'DO YOU?' he screams.

Old Orlick took a fiery drink. Oh God. She catches distended pupils, red and bloodshot whites. *I smelt the strong spirits that I saw flash into his face.* Perhaps he is on something. He was late because he went to get high. Has vaped something. Snorted. Smoked. Something he has bought from Darren.

'Sami,' she repeats, this time frightened, as a last-ditch warning. But it's too late. With a loud cry to rally his own armies, he runs forward, tramples the tape on the floor and launches at her. Helpless, she quarter-turns, brings her arms up to her head as he slams her into the blackboard, her face thumping hard into the surface, smearing and bouncing off.

Oh Jesus.

Like a boxer too close to an opponent he can't punch properly, flails and lashes at her head with his hands, Jo yelping high, short screams at each contact, the physical become unfamiliar, now returning with a vengeance. One animal part of her knows that she must stay on her feet and sally back, but another curls her up in defence, sliding to the floor, trying to form a hard shell from her arms, to keep her mask in place. Harder blows begin to rain down as she lies crumpled on the carpet, close enough to smell the plastic fibres, to feel the tacky areas where gum has been trodden in. In his barging struggle the slice of cake has been knocked down next to her, soft white icing splattering, flecked with the velvet crumbs. She opens her mouth to plead for help but there's no faculty for words, only the sound of wailing.

He is kicking her now. My ribs will break, she thinks. They are too frail. Forget her father's steely core, she wants a shell to withdraw into. There are blows to her stomach. Puncturing. Winding. This is it. There is no Herbert to come save her, no Trabb's boy, no Startop. The life will be kicked out of her by this child, the rest of the boys doubtless enjoying the spectacle, the girls too scared to get involved. All the shit they have been through, all the stress that they have swallowed down, now being violently thrown back up and them glad to get it out. They will have tasted sour rumours of her prejudice, weighed it with her demolition of Darren, decided that she is just getting what comes around.

Fists beat on her back, trainers lump into the side of her chest. *So now get up*, all she can think, the blows detaching mind from body, just a glint of comfort in the long literary history of beatings and kickings. Through a chink in her arm she watches him stand over her, lean back, take aim at her head. She pulls herself in and waits for the final blow.

None comes.

Detached senses return. Sami is straining and cursing, arm-locked, restrained by Jordan. Charlie and Danny, hands steady with phones, are filming.

'What the fuck you doing?' Sami shouts. 'Stop gripsing me up! Distance man, get off me.'

'Low-key part of me's wanted to swing for you,' Jordan says, a hissed calm in his voice, straining to keep hold of his prey, 'but trus', right now I'm doing you a favour.'

'*Fuck* you, man. I know where you live,' Sami snorts, but he knows he isn't strong enough. He wriggles but then relaxes, instincts telling him that when you are trapped your best chance of survival is to stop struggling. Jordan has him tight around the chest, but he is leaning Sami over Jo, still sprawled on the floor. No one in the class moves. Fists locked by his side, Sami turns to speech instead. 'I read it,' he spits at Jo cowering under him, lime white. 'Pip never even gets his money, does he?'

Michael helps Jordan manoeuvre him away.

'Government takes it, don't they?' Sami's legs go and he slips onto his knees in resignation. 'And he runs.'

Egypt. Yes. He is right. Still the reflex to wants to praise him, this pathology that wants to forgive, to get up, carry on with the lesson, focus on getting through her objectives. Half a thought of doing this, being strong, trying to climb up off the floor and begin again, when Michael swears, loud and long.

'Fuuuuuuuuck.' Out of Sami's bag he has pulled a knife. 'Man was carrying.'

Oh God.

Jo retches, face fevering, limbs shaking, heart and lungs pumping in exhausted panic. Her eyes search him, waiting for him to pounce back up and finish the job.

'No!' Sami protests, his look of terror suddenly equal to hers. 'No! For fruit. Look in my bag. Peaches!' He shrinks again, hardly needs holding now, punctured, collapsing. 'Peaches,' he says in utter defeat. 'From home.'

They are both on the floor now. She feels for her face, readjusts her mask, cannot tell if blood is flowing or if it is just sweat. Michael rummages further and holds up a brown paper bag, pulls out of it a fat, rosy fruit.

Realisation crashes on top of her. The farm. From his homework. A boy with his mother, a shaded veranda and orchards beyond, the sound of water in a sink and plates being set out, laughter of siblings from cool rooms above.

Half of the class are watching through screens, composing shots, holding steady. But there is nothing between the two of them, eyes locked momentarily together, the heat of his breath passing over her. A look grows across his smashed-up face, an understanding that dawns across the battered ground of his head. 'You thought I was him, didn't you? Thought I was Pip.'

Michael is still examining the knife, pretends to lunge at Jordan then feigns to bring the blade down onto Sami's head. Jo searches out Radha, shoots her a look of such desperation that she gets up and runs out, leaving her still on the floor, sobs beginning to break quietly from her.

'Fuck you Jordan,' Sami says, rallying a little, feeling for his own wounds. 'Where were you when it was me getting banged up?' He gets no reply, just slumps as if resigned that war has once again found a way to break in on his fragile life. 'Nobody there then, was there?' Phlegm at his mouth, sweat on his brow. 'Fuck all of you,' he says quietly over and over, covering his head with his hands, Jo unable to look anymore, unable to speak, crying into her crumpled blouse.

24

The slam of a door. A shout.

I need to get back on stage, she thinks from far inside herself, reclothe myself in my body, sit down at the controls of myself. But she is too weak to exist yet, can't help but sink back while a wan projection plays inside her head, memory currently beating reality in the battle for her thoughts.

She is thinking of her mother is telling her about finding out she had a tumour, the doctor having communicated it to her as if it were something separate. 'But no, I thought, it *is* me,' she'd told Jo from her bed. No knife delicate enough to pare apart the part that wanted life from the part that was now in open revolt against it. 'Because it *is* you, you think it will be fine.' Another gap as she'd processed. 'You think, "Surely my own flesh wouldn't rise up and rebel against me?"' She hadn't needed to add any more. The hollows of her face in deep acceptance that this is exactly what her body has done, that all deaths are a kind of suicide, that though war-talk had been refused she'd already lost, that this thing that *was* her was going to kill her, sequestrate so much that it would tear her entire frame down but have no idea why. It was never a battle because she never fought back, just gave and gave and gave until every part was laid to waste.

'Jo?' She stirs again, memories fading, reality building until she is back in the department office, mouth is like a potsherd. Tongue stuck.

'You want a tea?' Cara is asking. She then calls over to Sandra, who is fishing out a teabag. 'Plenty of milk.'

Sandra roots around in the small fridge the department keeps tucked under the desk with the kettle, pulls out a carton of long life and rattles it. 'It's finished.' She runs out to get some.

By the time the mug is administered — lots of sugar, a couple of ibuprofen — she feels a little better, though returning to her bodily self has brought hurt with it: ribs stinging, stomach like it's a mess of pulped fruit.

It's then she notices that Cara has been crying.

'Oh Car... Did you...? Your class...?'

'I tried,' she says. 'But there was this twinge so someone covered me.' Jo can't bear to ask, just throws her a look of pleading worry. 'I was going to go to the clinic but it's fine though. I think it's fine.' She takes her own mug from her table. 'Probably just stress, just indigestion.'

Sami has been hauled off to Jackson. Someone has been found to sit with Jo's class. A fresh piece of the cake and she is sitting up at her desk, Cara next to her. English teachers to the last: after the scene, the exercise in comprehension. She wants to establish the facts, understand the context, examining drives and desires. Some of her own questions are more crude. Like why had it taken so long for anyone to help? What if Jordan hadn't stepped in?

'Just horrible,' Cara says. 'What if he'd pulled that knife?'

'Peaches,' she says, as if recalling some fragment, her face newly distraught, staring into the floor. 'A bag of peaches.' Her mouth opens as if to elaborate, but no words come.

The corridor is quiet but both women know that gossip will be seeping through walls in direct messages and group chats, trickling under doors and leaching through floors, progress bars inching as videos and photos are uploaded. Cara screaming at a firework, Jo pummelled by the student she'd apparently groomed, their shame stored forever in the cloud to be reloaded, copied, sent, shared and pasted. Agony gone viral.

'It was my fault, Car,' she says finally. 'I fucked it up. Sami, Darren, everything.'

'Don't say that Jo,' Cara insists.

But she refuses this. Too many things that she should have said. She didn't fight hard enough, shouldn't have given in to rest, shouldn't have slept. You wake up and it's too late, reach out but they're already gone.

'Let's go,' she says suddenly. 'If Jackson is dealing with Sami he'll probably be up shortly and I really don't want to have to talk to him.'

'Before kids start streaming out and we're stuck here,' Cara says, grabbing her bag. 'Pub?'

It's an absurd idea.

'Who knows when we'll even be able to do it again. Level 2. Level 3. An announcement later I reckon. They'll have us in full lockdown by Christmas I swear, so we might as well make the most. Pretend we're flatmates. Or sisters.'

Jo manages a laugh. Cara can't drink and she doesn't want to, but 'yes,' she says 'yes. Come on. I'm meant to be going out later,' this offered as proof of one thing or an excuse for something else. She veils her head in her scarf, winces as she begins to move, curses as she waits for the painkillers to work.

There is a long burn mark from the firework, still the sour smell of spent powder as the two of them push through the doors and edge gingerly down the stairs, slowly past the tables and the strewn chairs, out of the back entrance, buzzing out of the security gate.

The first thing she sees is Anya ahead of them, leaving early too, walking slowly, headphones in, phone out, one thumb composing something. Jo tells Cara about her panic attack, explains that she doesn't want to have to talk to her so they hang behind and slow to a lurk. Then Anya speeds up, half a skip as she reaches Great Western Road, turning not towards home but pulling buds from her ears as she approaches a boy. He embraces her tightly, kisses her deeply before hands are held, heads gabbling away as they cross and take a side road, digging phones into their pockets.

Jo looks jealously at her, then stops dead. 'Fuck.'

Cara turns and frowns.

'Left my phone in my drawer,' she says with a defeated look.

Cara pulls out her own, then turns back towards school. 'Later,' Jo tells her. 'Don't worry, I'll get it later.'

'Yeah, I don't want...' Cara says.

'I know.' The bell. The flood of children. Year 11 among them. Sami leaving too at some point. Jackson couldn't hold him forever.

Above them cars are already choking on the Westway, red lights snaking, braking, half term traffic crawling forward towards the motorway, carrying children away to beaches and country homes, children who had carried notes into school with them, a rash of Friday symptoms, positive cases. Little white lies; mothers trying to get ahead. Jo falls a step behind, surreptitiously coughs into her elbow.

When they reach the pub it is beautifully silent, near-empty but for the smell of stale drink and fried oil. The sole barman looks defeated, pushes a cloth around the pump handles, asks them what they want, a little sigh at the order for just an orange and lemonade and a diet Coke.

Now that they are here there is nothing much to say. She doesn't want to talk about the attack. The thought is too raw, the wound still too new, still smarting if touched. Now she is seated the pain seems worse. Her body wants movement, to push on, keep walking away, get some distance, in space and time. Each sound still jolts, disturbs unstable ground, sends a fresh rockfall of images and sounds streaming. Kicks and punches, but more the desperate wailing of an animal in anguish. The pain as each hits, then the aftershock of shame.

She turns from this, twists in her chair as if to deflect it, instead tells Cara about wanting to spend a couple of days with Dad, the doubts she's now having about the wisdom of it. Parents evening, crowded corridors, too many people too close for comfort, and all that before getting pummelled.

Cara says, 'fuck it, you should go.' Then she stops, a hand slowly stroking her belly, searching for reassurance, trying to offer it.

Jo tries to feel inside her own self, but it's such a state in there that she can't decide if she maybe has a temperature. Maybe she's just flushed at the prospect of having one, of all that that will now cost. Maybe the drugs are doing weird things. She reaches into her bag and cleans her hands anyway.

They both keep an eye on the door, aware that, having come here to miss the tide of children, there'll be a river-run of colleagues before long. One last drink before the government spoils the party.

'You're going to be such a good mum,' she tells Cara, placing a cold hand over hers, knowing that she shouldn't yet desperate, touch now illicit yet more powerful for its proscription.

Cara turns her palm and wraps her fingers around. 'You're so kind.' She pauses, weighing her words, twisting her glass a quarter turn and wiping the smear of condensation that has run onto the table. 'Your mum would have been so proud of you.'

She scoffs and pulls her hand away, shakes her head, takes a slug of Coke and pushes out a laugh. 'No,' she says, shaking her head. 'No, I think all this blows any chance of that.' She pulls out sanitiser, takes a squirt and shares it. Anger erupts. 'I mean look at me. I fucked up with Darren, fucked it up with my Sixth Form and now I've fucked up things with Sami. I read it all wrong. Putting the actual "loco" into *loco parentis*.'

'You're wrong, Jo,' she says, repeating this forcefully. 'You're wrong. You're an amazing woman.'

But she won't have it. 'No. I've failed and I just need to swallow that. I've tried to fight for these kids and I've completely fucked it up, and...'

The speed with which Cara's hands move surprises her. In a flash she is holding each of her forearms, gentle but firm, leaning over the table, in towards Jo's face, eyes chasing then pinning Jo's down. There's a rasping intensity as she speaks, her voice not raised but direct and insistent. 'Now you listen here because I'm only going to fucking say this once.' The expletive slaps Jo on the cheek, not to harm or hurt but as if to wake her from a trance. 'You are a magnificent woman Jo. OK, yes, you might never be a mother, might never marry — who the fuck knows — and you might never step back into a classroom again — which no one would blame you for after today — but none of that, *none* of these things would diminish you one fucking iota.'

Her voice fills the room without intimidating it, presses without forcing itself.

'I don't know,' she says meekly. 'Maybe Jackson was right. Maybe these boys like Sami and Jordan.... I mean what happened today wouldn't have happened...'

The door of the pub opens and both of them look up to see if it's the beginning of the course of other teachers, but it's someone they don't know. Even so, Cara becomes more urgent.

'What the heck are you talking about Jo? You think these kids are here for your tits or your brain?' She stops to let this land, for a glimmer of a smile to break across Jo's face. 'You're not employed to suckle them, swaddle them, clear up their shit. You're here to *educate*. To illuminate. To share your brilliant mind. So can you *please* quit this Victorian bullshit that teaching is somehow mothering...'

And then she stops. Drops her head, her hands still holding Jo's across the table. There's the thud and squeeze of a beer pump, a pint placed onto thick wood, the ping as a card is tapped. Jo pulls an arm free to wipe a tear just as it breaks onto her cheek.

'I'm sorry,' Cara says.

A crack runs down and Jo bursts, weeping openly. The barman turns away as he works a glass cloth, Cara moves around to her side of the table and folds Jo into an embrace, leans her head into her shoulder.

'Don't,' Jo says, but doesn't move. 'I'm so scared that I've got it.' Cara holds her tighter, and then releases.

There's a bang of the door and a couple of the new teachers in biology swing through. The others won't be long.

'Drinks? You two?' one of them shouts from the bar, and they both raise hands to decline. 'Suit yourselves!' They clearly don't know yet. They soon will.

'It's been so hard...' she starts to say, but if there are words to succinctly express the pain and loneliness, the trauma of death committing a robbery while she is forced to stand away, then she has no idea where to find them. 'These next few days with Dad... we're meant to be scattering the ashes,' — she pauses, tries to fill the idea of this act with meaning but struggles not to see it crumbling into farce — 'but he's vulnerable and I don't want to put him at risk.'

'You're probably fine. Just lie about some symptoms,' Cara says. 'Go get a PCR so you can get the all-clear.' But then she sighs. 'Though you might not have a choice, what with all the rumours flying around. Half term circuit-break, all that bollocks.'

'Sometimes it feels as if it will never end.'

The door opens again and a bubble of staff breaks thirstily through, hungry for gossip and salted snacks, hurrying to the bar as if they might be told any moment that it was no longer legal to be there.

It seems impossible that the world has changed so profoundly, and even more impossible that people have accepted it so readily. Events so vast that there is nothing that anyone can do but acquiesce.

'I was expecting...' Jo begins again, but people are filling around them, hearing what had happened and sharing their anger. Cara is pulled away by Sandra; Rose gathers by Jo with colleagues she doesn't know, their sympathies laced with bitter assassinations of Sami, of Jackson, all the boys lumped together and gunned down. There should be checks. Metal detectors. It's becoming dangerous. Other colleagues form a circle at the next table, and Matt takes the tale and shares it with them. 'Terrible,' he says. 'Apparently he was carrying a knife.' Within a minute it has morphed: the knife was pulled and brandished; give it half an hour she'll probably hear that she'd been stabbed in the neck. She lowers her head in shame, wishes that she could stand to make an announcement, to explain so that everyone knows: the knife was for fruit, he was a good boy from a fine home, that she'd got him all wrong. But it's too late. The story is burning on its own now, jumping across tables, out of control.

Dan from Science has his back to her, people pressing more densely around. His tongue is running free. 'Dog eat dog,' he is saying. 'Kids smell blood.'

Animal weakness. The stench of it. Jo can't help but check her skirt and blouse for red blooms, examine arms and neck for wounds. She is fumbling, half standing, trying to put her coat on, wrapping her scarf around her neck when Cara notices.

'I can't stay,' she tells Cara. 'Just can't risk it. Just don't want to be here. This is mad. Is wrong.' Cara nods. 'Need to get my phone. Get home.'

The noise is building around them. Cara looks exhausted, but still has the energy to challenge this. 'Sure you're going to be OK?'

Jo can only nod. 'You?'

Cara nods back but then gets upset, tries to stop the others seeing, shakes her head and tells Jo she's just being silly, that Jo's the one who really got hurt today. They stand apart, aware of company, trying to communicate a tender embrace through eyes alone.

'Oh Car,' she says, 'please let it be OK. I...' Words are lodged in her, reluctant. 'Back in March,' she says, attempting to push a little further, to ease them forward.

'SCUSE ME,' Dan says, passing two dripping pints over their heads. 'Coming through!'

'I know, Jo, I know,' Cara says.

And Jo battens herself down and pulls back, reaching forward quickly and squeezing Cara's hand. 'Take care.'

'And you.' Cara draws breath.

And Jo turns and push through the doors, out into silence, out into air.

25

Having entered the pub in daytime she is surprised to now leave into night. Darkness has fallen, backdrops all greys and blacks, and what lights there are only sharpen the shadows. The flyover is snarling still, engines burning even as they stand, smoke piped out backwards, curling and rising. Perhaps people know something, she thinks. Are plotting their escapes.

She moves awkwardly, her pains still not settled into one place, still shifting and her body compensating. Waves of adrenaline wash through, turning parts of her over, squeezing her breath and sending hands trembling. She daren't look left or right from the memories, fears how perilously close she might have been to something so much worse. She knows too that this walk is not over, that there are chasms to come and Jackson still prowling.

Much of the Tower has disappeared and become one with the night, its dark mass pocked only with scattered lights. It makes the road back into Cromwell seem narrower and longer, the cold air better able to gather sounds and amplify them. With a rumble and a sharp crack a boy wheels in behind her on a skateboard, flies past close then veers, the smack of the trucks as he lands off a bench ringing loudly against high walls. She tries to roll a flinch into something smoother.

Voices echo from the ball court, laughs and shouts as goals clatter in and are immediately disputed, the splat of a soft bladder against the backboards. They'd called it a casey in Doncaster, the young estate boys she'd never much played with, who'd never asked what she was reading. From the covered porch of a low block, music thumps and rasps, the speakers of the portable box struggling to keep a small cluster of hips moving.

Two figures look down from a walkway above. 'Da hell you looking at?' one calls with menace, before both of them burst out laughing, this muffling as twin orange tips brighten and fade, voices of girls shouting and laughing behind them. 'Calm, Miss,' the other says. 'We just having jokes.' Pauses as they take another drag, faces hidden, then more friendly tones. 'It's Mo, Rasheed!'

'Turn round, go home,' a girl's voice shouts from behind them.

'Leave it Rach, she's safe,' Jo hears Rasheed say. 'She schools Femi too.'

A long kiss of teeth, a cackle of laughter. '*No one* schools Femi. She schools her own self.'

A smile found for this, though her pulse is running. To her left is the short spur of road, walled on each side, bins stored at the end. There is a smear of something on the poorly lit tarmac, kebab fat probably, or maybe animal blood, a ruptured pelt, gorged-on fur, impossible to tell. Her bearings spin. The constellations of lights above are a cheap counterfeit of the heavens, and it takes her a moment to find focus on the main school gate and push on to reach it.

The stairs are quiet save for the slow slap of mops somewhere high above, Molly a lone voice singing a gospel hymn to herself. Jo ascends on tiptoes, checks the corridor before stepping onto it. As she gets to her door she hears Alex from the open office opposite.

'Jesus Christ,' he is saying to someone. 'A total shit-show.' A pause. He must be on the phone. 'I don't know. I just don't know.' The crack and hiss of a can being opened. 'Just so fucking difficult.'

Each with their own problems — Jackson, Alex, the MAT bosses — none of them bad in themselves, she knows that. The pressure from high above pits good people against one another. Even so, those at the bottom still get hurt. She doesn't wait to hear any more.

She slips into her room, keeps the lights off. The cleaner hasn't made it yet and she presses quickly through the shadows, pulling tables straight and righting chairs, collecting the larger bits of rubbish before getting to her desk and unlocking the drawer. Below her on the carpet is the crumpled napkin, trodden icing and cake crumbs. She takes in a stuttering breath, fumbles to find her phone, tries to steady newly trembling hands as she secures it in her bag. No messages. Right, she thinks, get the fuck out of here. Patch up. Call Dad. See if she's still feeling like she's got symptoms, decide what to do about Sally's. She descends in silence, slips out of the building like a wraith.

As she buzzes out of the main gate and heads back towards the station a fizz builds behind her. Jesus Christ, another rocket. It shrieks and whizzes, sending her ducking, erupts in a bang that bounces off high walls close by, mixes with screams and the yelp of a distant dog. How are these things even legal?

She edges a look to see if people are coming for her, but from the shadows another figure leans forward, hops off a bench and stands ahead of her. An expensive-looking coat, the hood trimmed with fur, he leaves an open holdall on the seat.

Oh God.

'Darren,' she says, swallowing, pushing the straps of her bag further up her shoulder but then regretting it, hitting a bruise smack in the middle. The pain jolts her back to being on the floor again, kicks and punches coming in, a minor earthquake inside her, a few seconds of terror that she is about to be assaulted again.

'Miss B,' he replies, his face pools of white and dark as the animal-tail that frames his face curls and shifts. He flings the hood back. A slug of drink quickly taken, cigarette twitching in the other hand. Oddly this reassures her. He is putting on an act of menace, a kind of two-bit Guy Ritchie imitation, but he isn't angry. A pair of scooters rev into life, tack wildly up the road, riders crouching low in hope of greater speed, passing close and disappearing. She braces herself against them, knows that she must just hold her ground, and then they are gone. Now it is just the two of them, Jo breathing heavily, wounded, scared, but steeled for this now.

'What?' she throws at him.

Darren slowly draws and exhales, surrounding his nodding head with pungent smoke. 'Still at it, Miss,' he says with a smile that turns to a hacking cough. 'Still fucking lives up I hear. Losing kids becoming a thing with you innit?'

A flush of heat as if a fever has just switched itself on, a flashing thought of how could he be so cruel before realising that there's no way he could know. She steadies herself again though, guards against foolish reflexes, replies as blankly and neutrally as she can. 'I'm sorry you think that. Please, I need to go.' She steps to one side as if to push on. But he follows in mirror image.

'Chill Miss. My manor. We good. You safe.'

Manor. Safe. Good. So many words turned upside-down the effect is almost dizzying. She cannot chill, not with her body suddenly burning. She gathers more courage, pulls an arm to her shoulder and adjusts the bag again, narrowing her stare. If he won't let her by she'll have to talk her way past. 'And Hayley, and Nelson, and Sami? They're safe with you too?'

He considers this as he smokes. Tilts his head and takes his time. Coughs up phlegm and expels it to the ground. 'Someone had to show that prick Nelson. And yeah, I hear your boy will be needing alternative employment.' He chuckles darkly, 'told you, school is dead man,' raises his can in a cheap toast. 'All this pandemic and bullshit. Who needs it? World is fucked, innit? Choose life.'

What a life he's chosen, she thinks. If it's actually been a free choice at all. That was all that education was meant to be: an opportunity to have more choices. Guilt gushes into her like a hot tap on full. 'You're better than that.' A dismissive shake of his head, a long draw, so she pushes further. 'Sami is better than that.'

It's this this turns him, words erupting in a tumble of smoke, twisting with bitter sarcasm. 'Oh, let me guess. He should read more books? Because what, books will save him?' He spits and scoffs, then calms, pauses before delivering his line. 'Didn't save him the other night, did it? Nah, *I* did.'

She is wrong-footed by this, has no reply, an effect that seems to please him. He starts to examine the ground in front of him, test the strength of the asphalt by toeing a kick into it, looking at his box-white trainers and thinking of better of having another go. 'Got fed up of seeing the boy beat down. Called a stop.'

She watches him carefully, still a boy in so many ways. She can't see why he'd be lying about this, is both oddly proud and still horrified. 'That was brave. Thank you.'

'Yeah, well,' is all she gets initially in reply, but then he draws himself up, hunches his shoulders and fiddles again with the hood. 'And why brave? Just business. I ain't scared of no one round here.' A boy trying to wield the tongue of a man; so unlikely to end well. He drains his drink, claw marks down the can, a mix of sugar, alcohol, caffeine, crunches it and throws it to the pavement. She checks a reflex to order him to pick it up. 'You chatting shit to him about saving,' he sneers. 'Save him from what?' He waves an arm around. 'From all the terrible people here? A bit of easy money? A little protection? Seems least he deserved after all he's been through. Plus, man can always use a good soldier.'

So that's it now. Expulsion, and Darren creates a debt that takes Sami into his employ. Nausea rises inside her throat but she knows that she must fight to keep her outside calm. She tries a disinterested shake of the head, goes as if to check for a watch that isn't there. 'You have no idea who he is. That boy has more class...'

He cuts across, starts shouting, sending her arm into a judder she can't control. 'And you *never* had any fucking idea who I am either, but that didn't stop you did it?' His voice echoes loudly in the cool evening air, bounces in deft parkour off the hard walls of the flats before landing back between them.

Her job was meant to be interpretation, her skill to draw out deeper meanings from complex pages, to avoid bringing her own prejudices to the text. But Jesus, had she read Darren wrong too? She coughs three or four times into her elbow, partly in hope that it'll ward him away, partly because she does actually feel awful now, wishes she had something warmer, some more pills. She swallows, blinks to remind herself where she is, and in what potential peril. She looks determinedly into the ground. This is the reckoning, she thinks, all debts must be paid. 'I'm truly sorry for what Mr Jackson did, Darren. I didn't ask for that.' She chances a look up, but he shows no sign of accepting this. Books judged by their tattered covers. Simplified. Dismissed. 'But you still have options,' she insists. 'Get yourself over to the unit and...'

'You still don't get it, do you? *I don't care.*'

The luxury of this, the extraordinary privilege of not giving a damn. His brutal liberty is a slap in her face, his freedom to just walk away from her classroom, from school, to suffer no anxiety about how life will be — all of it a preposterous, shouted dare for her to give up her flat, sell up, move away, take up smoking and benefits, enjoy an easy life. He gives zero fucks, why should she feel any guilt?

'Darren, I've said I'm sorry,' this coming out with more anger than she meant. She stops and actually looks at him, though his gaze won't settle, jumps nervily. Wanting to find hatred, she sees a scared teenage boy again, trapped in the nightmare of his own bravado. 'I want you to know that I did care. I do care. People care about you.' Her flesh is burning. She gathers all of her battered organs, binds all the bruised parts of herself as best she can. 'I'm sorry I wasn't able to do that better for you. But there was stuff going on with my mum... you probably know... It was a shit time.'

He smokes more agitatedly now, sucking and exhaling in short, quick, strokes, the two of them locked into this series of holds that neither see another figure approaching.

'The fuck is going down here?' The voice seems to arrive before the body that sent it, but suddenly a large figure in an even larger jacket — a pristine white arctic parka — is stood with them, sending Darren's head immediately bowing.

'We cool,' Darren tells him, daring a glance up and a nervous smile, though Jo has no idea whom this first-person plural encompasses.

The man pulls a hand from his pocket and begins to turn a Mercedes key fob around his index finger.

'Darren and I,' she begins, but is immediately slapped down.

'Lady, shut the fuck up,' he tells her without taking his eyes off Darren.

'She,' Darren attempts, but this is met with even more venom.

'I said shut the fuck up,' He examines the meagre subject before him, looks Darren up and down. 'Out here hollering your voice out like you some big man. Why you hanging around chatting shit?' He stops, checks a gold watch on his wrist for effect. 'You think I'm some easy bitch you can two-time on?'

'JP I'm sorry man.'

But this is the wrong thing to say. 'You fucking ringing names out now?' He is angry, his name too sacred for speech by lesser mortals. 'I got to tear you a new hole and check you for wires now, or you just too fucking dumb for this game?' Darren cowers, opens his mouth as if to try to make amends but is silenced. 'Shut the fuck up, and do your job. Wasting my time on this shit.'

And with that, he goes as quickly as he came. A car revs high, reverses and speeds away.

Another humiliation, another lashing by a figure of power. Darren says nothing. Jo tries to express some tenderness, just a few drops to warm and offer him.

'People care about you,' she repeats. 'And Sami.' He will not look at her but she needs him to hear this, needs at least to know that she's said it. 'I know schools do a terrible job of showing it, but in the end everything in lessons boils down to that. People caring enough to try to teach. Offer something.' She fades, isn't now quite sure what she means. 'I don't know.'

But it's as if he tastes this and spits it back out, cannot stomach even a teaspoon of kindness in case it makes him soft. 'Get the fuck out of here,' he orders finally, him confident in this at least, stepping aside back to the bench. 'We calm.' She doesn't feel it and he worryingly looks far less like it than he did initially, looks as if unwelcome emotions are knocking violently at his temples as he smooths the fur around one shoulder, brushing one sleeve. Preening. 'Go!' he then screams, clubbing these thoughts back into submission. 'Get out!' he then shouts in mocking imitation of her voice. 'Just fuck off!' More manic now. 'Yeah, run bitch!' But she is not yet running. She is watching him warily as she moves. He leans down and pulls something from his bag, lights and launches it. It screams but goes nowhere, lands on the pavement to one side, crackles and explodes. 'Fuck your boy Sami. And fuck your mum,' he spits. 'FUCK HER. You think I care? You think *anyone* cares, bitch?'

He is in a rage of action now, pulling more fireworks out of his bag, aiming them at her, aiming them at anything, wanting to blow the whole place up.

Now she turns to flee, fever burning like an engine boiler, fear like steam in the heavy pistons of her legs. From behind her comes the screaming whine of another rocket, arcing over her head, drifting over towards the Tower where it lodges under a window and tries to explode.

'Ohhhh shit,' someone calls in disbelief. 'Ohhhh shit!' in dark excitement and growing alarm.

Terrified, she does not look back again, hears only his roars of rage and the fizz and crack of his barrage. Panic submerges her pains and runs her to the road, under the Westway as fast as her shoes will go. She smooths her skirt down as she slows near the station, people turning and pointing at the Tower, but her face set forwards, pushing on, aching to look normal enough to disappear but now the soreness resurfacing in every place, demanding to be attended to as she switches her bag over and pushes back her hair, locking a mask over the heat of her face.

26

The tube devours all, cares nothing, takes everyone down and asks no questions. The further from Cromwell she gets — the more distance between her and Darren and Sami and Jackson — the more she has to begin the painful process of returning to inhabit herself. In the throes of the battle there had only been general reports but, as adrenaline retreats, more details start to emerge. Which rib. Which part of her face. The kidney on the left side of her back. Grazed knees and palms now send stronger messages. She is desperate to cough but just cannot, not here, and the more she sends thistles back down her throat, the more a febrile fire heats.

Brixton ejects her, slips her smoothly up out of the bowels into the circus of Friday evening's High Street. Some energy in everyone's movements. A haste, people moving urgently to shops, out of bars. She stoops to clear her throat and wipe her brow. Her phone gasps, breathes out and begins to shake. Messages from Cara. A missed call from Dad. Ignore them until you are home, she thinks. Incense sticks on a pavement stall. A drummer drumming, two preachers preaching, she steers and weaves through them, veering away from a man unhinged, ranting, arms flailing, yelling at the voices in his head. But then he stops and turns, clicks a glowing earpiece then quietly carries on. Something is happening, a quiver through the crowds. Blue lights, sirens and sound systems, all this noise. She checks that her mask is in properly place.

She needs drugs. And drink. So instead of turning for home she pulls a hard right and walks into the supermarket, a blast of warm air as the glass opens to swallow her.

Sally's. Yes, she thinks, keep moving, worse if I stop now. Perhaps she has the bug, perhaps she doesn't. Perhaps if she has a bath and necks some painkillers she'll be symptom free, enough to get through the evening, because she needs it. The aisles are full. Someone's basket knocks on her waist and the pain rear ups. Her breathing is short, people are frantic, something is definitely not right.

She stands in front of a dizzying crowd of reds, all claiming to be suave and full-bodied, ready to deliver exotic berries, coffee beans and burned fruit right into her mouth. Ten pounds. No, fourteen. If you to Sally's, she tells herself, you don't go cheap.

There's a buggy stopped in the aisle, a woman on her phone by the crisps, her child suckling on its own device. One chubby arm reaches up, trying to turn to see mum, strapped in tight, her out of sight, the child mewling at this, their screen slipping from their other hand, over the side of the buggy onto the hard-tiled floor.

'Fuck's sake Jack,' mum says, scowling. 'Hold on babe.' Phone crimped between shoulder and cheek, she leans down, scoops the tablet from the floor, checks there's no cracks and thrusts it back firmly. 'There. Now just *hold* it.' A cartoon pig. 'Sorry babe,' she says, returning to the call. A look of longing sent upwards from the child, but she's not looking. Nothing for it, deciding to make do with the pig, thumb on touchscreen, familiar with how these things work.

She yanks the buggy to make space and Jo edges unsteadily past, aims a woozy smile at the child, comforter back in, but he grimaces and turns his face away, waiting for another episode to load.

How fucking dare you, she mouths silently at the mother, anger seeping from some inner rupture that she cannot close. Toxins ooze and speak their bile. This is how it begins, they whisper, a teacher's attention never able to make up this deficit being built from birth. She files into line to wait for a till, inching forward. *Self checkout*. Waiting for the machine to tell her where to go. *Approval Needed*. Cameras nestle on perches above, black eyes watching as she pays and leaves. How many views and shares already, her lying beaten on the floor of her classroom? Sweat on her brow, her breath hot and close and moist on her mask.

Head down as she pushes back into the street; a woman swerves and swishes to avoid her, peering out through a cotton slit across her eyes. Men from Thanet frothed for so long over cloth-folds, still bleat about being asked to cover up now. She tacks into her own road, through the main door, up the stairs, keys turning and finally she slips inside. Thank God.

Reflexes, routines, plays of normality. She puts her bag down, hangs up her coat. Nothing speaks. She hacks a proper cough out into her elbow and each thing holds its breath, nervous at her presence. The silence stands awkwardly, unsure whether to stay or go.

She begins to lean back against the door then remembers her phone and pulls forward, begins rummaging, finds it, turns it over, stumbles fingertips over the screen. Deal with it and then get herself patched up. Cara hoping she's ok. Wanting to hear she got back safe. Promising to check in over half term. A second text. *The baby is fine.* She reads it, the words pushing into her eyes as she swallows, drawing tears that she wipes away with the back of her wrist. Cleaner than hands. Her chest is building to a sob but then her handset shakes. Sally. She stares at the message, presses lips together and closes her eyes.

You seen today's briefing? The latest case numbers, London in a new level?? I'm so sorry. I was up for it but Richard being insistent we follow the new rules. Going to have to cancel :(

Her thumb hovers, unsure, even as the rest of her crumples in disappointment. Being with people. Good food. Balm after all she's been through today. The spa booking for next week. All of it collapsing slowly as the implications crash through her.

The news must be rippling because her phone wakes and trembles again. Dad. She answers but cannot speak.

'Jo?' he says into the silence that greets him. 'Jo, are you alright?' He waits, must be able to hear the pulsing intakes of breath. 'Jo, what's the matter?'

She needs to say something. To reach out, tell him what's happened. So unfair, so unjust, everything knocking her back down again, but none of this communicable. 'Dad,' is all she manages. 'Dad... I ...'

'Have you broken up?'

Anger surges and she cries out, throws the thing against the wall, grabs it and turns it off as she kneels in the hallway. No more. She doesn't want to see or hear any more. She takes the wine from her bag, twists roughly and puts the bottle straight to her lips, rim bumping on teeth, gulping as she heads to the bathroom, turning the taps on full, moving to the bedroom and beginning to strip. Deep drafts as she holds herself on the cheap chest of drawers, gingerly raising each foot, shoes off, tights off, another mouthful of wine, skirt rotated, unzipped, eased slowly and carefully away. She cradles her stomach under her top, holds palms in different places as if feeling for signs of things not being right, though now she begins probing she isn't even sure what ought to be where. Lifting the bottle again, she catches the girl with the balloons watching coldly from the dresser, howls a long scream at her, repeats it even louder as the china face remains unmoved, grabs the wine and marches back to the steaming bath.

A spill of red diffuses and blooms in the water. She stands and stares at it, an accidental Rorschach emerging in front of her conjuring one image after another until she beats a fist to her head, splashes an erasing hand through the water, curls into herself and cries.

Hunching and wincing, she lowers herself into the water. Sami's breath, hot and close. Jordan snorting and straining so close by. She's surely got it now. If she did see Dad she could kill him. She breaths in, worries about what is now working in her, latching on, multiplying. She rubs water hard around her mouth, scrubs at her fingers. Then with moistened hand she wipes her face, sees it come back chalk-smudged, slake-white. A look of shock that no one had told her. Perhaps it wasn't clear, skin so pale already it almost matches. Tears again, but under she goes, flooding them away in the mixing red water, hair floating up behind, ears and eyes submerged as if longing her flesh to disappear completely.

But a body cannot be dissolved. The hot water hits her knees and smarts, she bolts her legs, splashes back to the surface and is immediately knocked around by a coughing fit. She smells the soap, cannot tell if her senses are dulled, heart running fast. She washes her face frantically again, wipes her eyes but then can only better see the peat-black deposits that have colonised the base of each tap and calcified maps of long-dried drips fogging the shower panel. A hair around the overflow, whole fur balls evolving on the tiled floor, mixing with dust and fallen hairbands, cotton buds and nail clippings.

A look of disgust propels her from the water, a bow wave following. Filthy. Unclean. It could be everywhere. She rises out of the tub horrified that she's let things get like this. She pulls the plug, grabs a sponge and begins to scrub, drinking more then wiping away the drips of red, quite drunk now, spraying and squirting sharp creams and chemicals, burning and scouring, rinsing it all into the drain, pushing the sediment back towards the plughole, flooding water down after it.

She needs a cloth. Antiviral spray. Window cleaner for the mirror. But the kitchen seems worse than the bathroom, wine glasses crowding next to plastic trays and plates of dried remains. Rice grains like larvae, multiplying each place she looks. The sink is more than full, the bottom of it a puddle of oil and tomato pieces, a distending crust of bread, slowly dissolving. The cupboard underneath spills its cluttered guts. The dustpan falls to the floor, an empty packet of Brillo, Tupperware pots with unmatched lids tumbling out with a rubber plunger and tins of old shoe polish. With an angry swipe, she sends it spinning across the floor, reaches further in for the bottles, picks up a cloth and heads back to the bathroom.

Mirror and surfaces done, she starts to inspect the lounge. Dust upon dust on each shelf. Mugs and more glasses, empty snack packets, crumbs abandoned in the carpet. Filthy. She snarls at the china woman, jabs at her, sitting there stiffly with her fruit, stabs at her with the cloth as if it's her fault that she's clearly now infected, sending her sliding back, falling, cracking open her head.

'Shit,' she says. 'Oh shit shit shit.' She lifts a hand and bites down hard into a finger, then runs to the kitchen to get the dustpan and brush. The pan is there but the brush has taken cover. Only way to find it is to clean the kitchen, so she starts with the dishes in the sink, pulls on the plug which turns over a pan which lands on a wine glass which cannot take the weight. It breaks, shards sinking into the gunge, this slashing a hole in some inner sac, rage now flowing unchecked. The offending pan is projected into the wall above the cooker where it crashes down onto the gas rings, the noise of this joined by smashing plates and flying pots of dead herbs. She kicks out at the fridge-freezer, which stands its ground before surrendering the upper door. Toppings ketchups, pickles, mustards, mayonnaises — no actual food, just condiments, just culinary make-up — all of it now feels the full force of her levering arm as she launches them towards the sink, most not making it even close, clumping down onto the lino. An overripe tomato leaves a weak splat of juice across a Lichtenstein print.

She twists again, but objects seem to flinch and retreat. Hands by her side, still naked, hair dripping. A magazine slips to the safety of the floor. Her face crumbles in the silence. She moves with her drink to the living room, sees all her books lined up, all these novels she has torn apart and prepared for examination. Brontë. Steinbeck. Murdoch. Osborne. Shakespeare. She could dissect Hamlet's meagre psychological flesh and his anger at his mother but, from a far shelf, she hears a voice speaking back, asking: *what about this tragedy concerning yourself?* Torn from her mother at birth, kept from her in her death. All of this pain she has swallowed down, reduced in the still of her stomach to fuming spirit that has ignited and exploded. The rage that roared at Darren, that railed at Jackson, corroded the work with her Sixth Form, burned into her relationship with Ben, drove her to wreak havoc on Sami. She swigs more wine, feels only a terrible depression build. All the good she's tried to do, all the light she'd tried to bring, the things she'd laboured to carry, all of it eaten by this furious rust, all of it left cracked and weakened. And now she's infected, now her insides are filth, now she can't even see her father, can't even hold the remaining ashes of her mother.

The room is suddenly full of jeers, the shelves of the books sneering, hurling out slurs, Cara joining them with her fattening belly, Anya with her whole, rich life ahead, Ben and Darren and Sami all shouting that she deserves to suffer distance, to be locked down, separated, alone. The GCSE poetry anthology flies and hits the window. She slings novels and plays across the room, cursing all their broken promises. A Woman of No Importance. Austen. Melville. Joyce. *Especially* Joyce. More muscle behind this. Slamming him into the lounge door then finding Proust, punishing him for all the time she'd wasted. She goes for the work-weary donkey in the hall, this ornament of the beast that carried the Lord, back bowed with all its burdens. She hurls it hard against the wall. An ear gouges into the plaster before the body follows and smashes, dropping to the floor in pieces.

She sits now but her breathing is still a storm, the gusts filling and exhausting, filling and exhausting, erupting sometimes in coughs that she can't see coming. She crawls to the bedroom. Her lungs are heaving like Anya's, breath rising and falling like sacks on a rusting pulley, cries and sobs as the rope strains and creaks. No one to sit with her, to look after her. No one to cajole, to tend, to care, pull her up and help her carry on. *Suffer the little children...* but who will bear her up in her own time of strife?

She finds the young girl with her balloons, ends her on the edge of the drawers and this sharp crack of porcelain tunes her ears. So much noise. So many voices. Femi. Anya. Jackson. The open fridge is humming in the kitchen. She needs everything to stop. She charges next door, onto a chair in the kitchen, throws the main switch, the fridge fading, the imperceptible whine of lights disappearing. The flat is cast into a darkness that slowly adjusts to shadows of dim sodium reaching up from the street through the windows. A tap dares drip, and in a flash she is on it, feeling her way under the sink until the mains are shut off, out into the hall with the chair, up to the gas box, slipping the lever closed. Isolate. Lock every damned thing down.

Back towards the living room, the bottle up at her lips, in the darkness she trips on a table leg, falls into the carpet where she thrashes palms at the floor and then crumples in silence, reduced to silhouette, lost against the masses of furniture.

When she stirs again she doesn't really know how long she's been lying there. A streetlamp catches her face as she pulls herself into a seated position. She rubs her head and winces at the ache, coughs again. She is shivering and sweating.

Next to her, a dagger-like piece of the woman selling fruit. She picks it up and turns it over, wraps arms tightly around her chest, this drawing a sharp stab of pain from a still-smarting rib. The pain cracks open a fresh flask of shock, a new realisation of all that could have happened. Jackson actually firing her. Sami coming at her with the knife. Darren mauling her in a dark corner of the estate. She squeezes even tighter, strangling lungs as if not caring if she breathes again, wanting the voices to stop their taunting, blaming herself for it all. Useless teacher, unreliable colleague, discarded girlfriend, unloving daughter. A desperate look, wanting the rest done too, to finish now what has been started, kick over what remains of her life. Destined from birth to be separated, alone, so what difference would this make? She grasps the shard of pot, convulses her stomach, retches as if expelling a demon.

She stares at the sharp ceramic edge, grips it and holds it to her wrist.

An airless scream. Nothing calling into nothing. A moan from somewhere deep and primordial. She has drawn blood with the china blade. A look of surprise as she holds her arm up to the shaft of orange light, a single cherry-dark tear running down her forearm. She stares at its slow progress, this emergence of the inside of her into the out, and something about this puncture pulls her back.

Deflating, breath lulling, she lies back down into the shadows, the glazed clay head of the fruit-seller staring, glass-black pupils fixed, unblinking.

Time and again she had run infant steps to show Mum something, desperate for some affirming word, some sign of approval or delight. Time and again denied. Not a good girl. Not a good woman. Trying to carry too much, the tray tumbling to the floor. Always in the background this understanding that her birth had ruptured her mother's life. A severed cord, never quite repaired, though attempts had been made. Apron strings and thread-bound books, all latter attempts to compensate for the distance that had opened.

In the quiet of the night onto the back of her mind an understanding begins painting, familiar images in new shading. She sees her mother's depression for the first time. The self-sacrifice for her husband's calling. Her own dreams ground to dust and fired into clay; a body become hard and impenetrable. Woman as ornament.

So many things she not been able to say, the chance snatched away at the last.

'Please,' she cries quietly to no one, to no god, but there is no reply. If only she could have had that little bit more time, just the two of them, to say what had needed to be said, to hear what she's so desperately needed to hear.

She pulls to her side Mum's copy of *Great Expectations*, thinks of the chaos pulled down on young Pip's head by those who thought they knew better, of Miss Havisham going up in flames, of the thrashing of Magwitch and Compeyson in the brackish Thames, whether the boy would have been better left at the forge all along. But then, mother's books to father's, an older story forms out of this bedlam: Jacob wrestling with an angel. Sami and Jackson, Darren and Jordan. Ben with himself. Gods and men struggling and heaving, olive branches crashing and snapping, muddy splats of dust and sweat while unnoticed, unheard among their grunts, the women around them are trampled, cut to the ground.

'Mum,' she sobs, eyes fixed on the fruit seller, willing the vision to appear, reaching out a hand as if across the bed, rasping Jacob's words back at her — *I will not let you go until you bless me.*

All she asks for, just one last moment to hear Mum say it, "Jo I love you. I'm so proud of you." But no response is heard, so she calls again, louder. *I WILL NOT LET YOU GO UNTIL YOU BLESS ME.* She implores the figurine, crying and wailing, still hearing only criticism, lists of people that she has let down, things she must improve on, targets she has missed, the children she has not managed to carry, this damning chorus spilling from the china mouth before her, holding its condemning gaze until she reaches over with a last surge of rage and slams Dickens down onto the clay temples of the head.

The vision cracks, expires in a wisp of dust.

She pulls a blanket from the sofa. One last breath held in her mouth.

She closes her eyes again.

And then there is silence.

27

Uneasy, uncomfortable, her flat finally achieves something close to peace. Lights rise and fall, sounds following in phase, minutes passing, hours passing — all unnamed, unmeasured — and still she sleeps.

But then there is a knock. She stirs, wraps an arm to her stomach and rubs her head before becoming still once more.

There it is again.

Now she is awake. It is light now, almost morning. Another knock, harder, and her face flashes with panic. Not Darren? Not Sami? *I know where you live.* No, surely he'd aimed that at Jordan?

Pain returns with movement. Another sharp rap on the door and it's as if it thumps right through her. The blows to the stomach. The fists to the head. Her arms up in defence.

Her breathing quickens then stumbles into another cough.

Then a voice, a cry through the letterbox.

'Jo?'

Then another voice. 'Jo?!' A rising intonation of worry and question. From the distant anterooms of shock, it takes an age for her to gather enough breath and send a reply out and down to the hall.

'Dad? Sally?'

It is immediately them. She grabs clothes, unlatches the door and Dad bowls through it first. Before she can say anything, ignoring the mess around her, seeing just her, he reaches out and holds her, embraces her.

'Dad stop,' she cries, trying to pull away. 'I think I've got it.'

Sally is right behind, coming in more slowly.

But her dad won't let go. 'I'd rather get it than spend any more time apart,' he says. 'I mean it. Not seeing you... it's been killing me anyway.

'Don't say that Dad. If anything happened to you.' But both of them tighten their embrace.

Sally waits, and then offers an elbow, eyes smiling as she speaks through her mask. 'You had us worried there for a minute.'

Jo is both laughing and crying now, relieved and embarrassed and totally confused. 'How... Why are you two?'

Dad glances at Sally, then covers her with a loving look. 'You've got some good friends love.'

'And a Dad who worships you,' Sally adds.

His turn to look embarrassed. 'Just a little network of care. She'd got in touch back in March and we'd swapped numbers. Wanted to make sure someone was checking in on you.'

'Then when you didn't get back to me...' Sally says.

'And hung up on me,' her father adds. He puts his keys on the shelf in the hall. If he notices the disarray he does a professional job of overlooking it. 'I drove down this morning. Thank God you're ok.' A hand back onto her shoulder, and it's like a balm, like a transfusion.

It has been so long since she saw him and she's happy to be surprised. She'd expected a man reduced, pruned back, but she's the one who feels like a husk, he who has warmth to give, is supple, a melody in his voice.

He now takes in the kitchen, spies through to the lounge and the turmoil it holds, but doesn't ask. Must surely see the state of her, but doesn't press. 'How about some breakfast?' is all he says, and pulls in from outside the door a bag of groceries.

There is an awkward moment where she has to turn the water back on, the electricity and gas, start to put things back where they should be.

'I'll...' she says to them, but they won't have it, insist that she showers and gets dressed.

When she returns from the bathroom the flat is bursting with the smell of frying bacon, the sound of crackling eggs and the pop of toast. She's done a quick run around the lounge and made her bed. The ornaments she's carefully picked up, gathered the pieces of each and pushed them into a drawer. Perhaps someone will be able to do something with them.

Sally has got fresh coffee percolating and is sorting out the fridge. She says nothing as she does this, just tidies around Dad while he cooks, then returns to the cafetière, gently pushes it down and pours. The windows are open wide, fresh air rolling through.

'I've missed the news,' Jo says, fresh mask tight around her face. 'Are we even allowed to do this?'

Sally chuckles. 'I think today we're OK. Though tomorrow we might be illegal.'

Dad sighs and then smiles as they sit to eat, mutters his own quick grace then says, 'looked liked you'd seen a ghost when you opened the door.'

Jo waits before speaking, leans back and lifts her mask above her mouth as she eats, squeezes Sally's hand and thanks her again. Then slowly, through this opening, her confession comes. 'Not a good day yesterday. A boy attacked me. A kid in my Year 11 class.'

Dad puts his knife and fork down, leans back. 'Oh my love,' his face crinkling into a pained look, reaching out to hold her arm but giving space to let things be told.

And this is what she does, in short spurts tells them about Sami, about the bench and the bullying, her convinced that she could help him, the desperate need for some tangible measure of success by the time half term had hit.

'Your father's daughter.' He winces. 'Working to save the world, both of us.'

'Well I flopped,' she sighs. 'How did you do?'

He gives a quick chuckle. 'Not great either, though good data is hard to come by. Not too many come back to verify that Jesus snatched them from the jaws of hell.' He looks into his breakfast, more plaintive.

Sally refills their mugs and they sit quietly for a bit.

'Been wondering if I'm in the wrong job,' Jo tells them. 'Not sure I'm cut out for this anymore.' Then comes the truth about

Darren, the allegations, the meetings with Jackson, the ultimatum he has left her with. *Are you sure this is really for you?*

'Jesus Jo,' Sally says, drawing half a frown from Dad. She covers her mouth with her hand and apologises as she laughs before becoming more serious again. 'I'm sorry, when we spoke the other night... I had no idea it had got that bad.'

'Yeah, I just didn't want to...' Jo struggles. 'Didn't want to load you with it all, you know.'

Dad observes her across the table, looks as if questions are tugging, as if he wants to ask if she is sure and what she might possibly do instead, but whatever thoughts he might be having he holds them back, brings them to heel.

'You've had to carry so much,' Sally says gently. 'On your own too, all these crazy months. And now this.' She looks as if she is weighing things, discovering new information. 'I'm so sorry. I should have done more. And now this boy attacking you. It must have been terrifying.'

'Yes. But if I can't do the job properly, maybe it's time to move aside.'

Dad looks more worried at this. He stops, takes his mug again, waits to see if she is done. 'This is where I quote Steinbeck at you,' he says eventually. '*East of Eden* wasn't it? "Now that you don't have to be perfect, you can be good"?'

'I'm impressed,' Sally says, buttering another piece of toast. There is good marmalade, sharp and thick cut.

Jo takes the last piece. 'Very good Dad. To be honest though, I've not touched a book in months.'

'Shocking,' Sally tells her in mock teacherly tone. 'Just not good enough. What would your....' She stops. Grimaces and apologises.

'Don't be silly,' Dad says jovially. 'What would her mother think? She'd be bloody proud.' He pulls a plain jar from another carrier bag and places it on the table. It stands barely taller than the jam, looks as if it could hold homemade honey.

'Oh my God. Dad!' Jo laughs, shocked. Coffee, preserves, and the ashes of her mother. 'This is it?'

'It... Her...' he says. 'I don't know. It's... what needs still to be done.'

Jo turns the thing around, all that now remains. 'So much that was left undone,' she says quietly. 'Wish I'd tried to heal things with her sooner.'

Sally looks confused, but her dad closes his eyes slowly, absorbing, assimilating. He stretches out his hands over the table, press Jo's between his, a prayer wrapped inside a prayer. 'Your mother,' he says, flitting a look at the urn, 'was a complex woman. The kind of person who could look into a mirror and see... a mirror. She was selfless, generous, so giving.' He pauses. 'But then this habit...'

'Of disappearing,' she finishes for him. Withdrawing. He doesn't name the depression, the weight they'd all lived with. Doesn't have to.

'She heard you. I'm sure of it, even in your silence, even if you didn't get to say everything you'd wanted.'

At this Jo pulls free and begins crying, apologising to Sally as she does, Sally telling her not to be silly, putting an arm around.

'I just think of her dying on her own,' she says. 'I never got to say goodbye.'

His arms are empty but still reaching across the table. 'I'm so sorry love.' He stops again, looks pained himself, runs a hand through his black hair, just the few strands of silver. 'God this has been so hard. It's never easy losing someone.'

Jo starts shaking now, crying even more. 'Two people,' she says. 'Two people.'

'What do you mean? Jo? What do you mean?'

Sally looks worried and confused, leaning in, straining to hear the words that are broken up by great sobs. 'Two.'

'Those boys who've been expelled?' Sally offers. 'Darren, and Sami? Jo, no, you cannot blame yourself. They made bad choices. You were just their teacher.'

But she is shaking her head. 'No.'

'Ben?' Sally says. 'Forget him, Jo. He's an idiot. Not worth a moment of your grief.'

But she repeats again, 'no. No.'

Dad is trying to calm her down, asking her to explain.

'The thing I never got to tell her. Never told you. It just seemed too much, and then there was no more time.'

'Tell me now love. I don't understand.'

'The thing I couldn't carry.' She finally raises her head, tears running freely, pulls the covering from her face and looks up at him, at Sally, takes the urn into her hands. 'I was pregnant. I lost a baby, that last week before Mum died.' The words fall, thud into the floor and do not move.

Dear Magwitch, I must tell you, now at last. You understand what I say? The gentle pressure on Pip's hand. *You had a child once, whom you loved and lost.* The three of them at the table all crying now, virus be damned, arms around one another. Sally in floods, cursing herself, saying that she should have guessed, that something hadn't seemed right even with everything else. Dad saying he is so sorry, over and over, both of them telling Jo how much they love her, how they had no idea.

'Ben didn't even want it,' she manages to tell them. 'Was *pleased*. His chance to go. And how could I tell Mum? The ward locked down. Her on her own. "Oh hi I think all this worry about you has caused me to miscarry?"'

'She loved you, was so proud of you,' he sobs before gathering himself. 'Maybe,' he adds, wiping his eyes, aiming such love at his daughter, 'maybe saying it now is enough, saying it here.'

Jo's hands are still clasped around the urn. 'No,' she tells him. 'Not here, Dad. Not like this.'

—

Sally says that she's going to go, that the two of them ought to have some time. They rearrange dinner for later in the week. 'Sod Richard,' she says. 'I'll tell him that we're forming a bubble. Well, a foam.' They laugh, then share an awkward hug as she departs.

Jo asks her dad to sit, insists that he does while she finishes tidying up, restoring order. She finds her phone but decides to leave it turned off a while longer. He is on the sofa, flicking through the GCSE poetry anthology that's been rescued from the floor.

'Can I take this with us?' he asks.

'Course,' she tells him as she throws things into a bag. They've ditched the spa, have talked it over in detail, the risks and rewards, the fact of breaking the law. She will stay at Dad's for a few days. Perhaps, she thinks, there can still be a victory of sorts in all this.

Out on the road morning is still building, the night pushed back with great effort. His car is unwilling, the engine like an old man woken, slow and complaining but ultimately dutiful. He keeps the radio off, wanting to hold on to quiet, Jo next to him in the passenger seat, windows open, the urn behind them in the back, still, silent. An odd family, she thinks. Positions in the car shifted a little, but all setting off together one last time. She gives his shoulder a squeeze while they wait at some lights.

Over the Thames, Pimlico and round the palace, the streets have been swept and a few tourists are still braving the city. They circle Hyde Park and Marble Arch, push round Lords and up past Swiss Cottage then finally out onto the motorway. Moving fast, not far now. Off at Tring and into the Chilterns. Her favourite hill.

They park and begin to walk.

'You OK?' Jo shouts back having pushed ahead.

'Yes,' he calls up, stopping to speak, drawing breath. 'Just going at my own pace.'

It's chalk underfoot, an ugly soil. Ocean floor once, alive and fluid, now dead shells. Pressure and time.

'Look,' he says. There's an opening dug under the gnarled root of a tree, a sett for some creature once. 'Wonder if there's anyone home.' He stamps his foot, bends down a little, waits without much expectation. When they walk on he reaches over and takes her hand. Skin losing its tension, starting to leather, momentarily cold on first contact, then warmer as she squeezes.

'What do you think about going back? Really?' he asks.

'Cromwell?' She kicks a small stone and watches it roll and come to a stop. 'I need to,' she says eventually. She makes a mental note to call Cara, tell her everything too. Alex even. Trust them with her truth.

He stops a moment. 'I doubt they'll ever tell you, but I bet those kids adore you.'

She laughs at this. 'Maybe,' she says. What was it she'd told herself? *To teach is to be a body that speaks.* If so, be one that knows it can't say it all, accepts that it cannot work miracles. Danny would still be Danny. Nourin would still be Nourin. Jordan will still wander in a little late, part of her longing to be able to reach out to this boy — a man virtually — and embrace him, thank him for saving her. But these are odd times, and she must get things right. The best she could do would be to load her eyes with gratitude, turn to the board and begin again.

'I used to tell people,' he says as he pulls alongside her, 'that mourning is only half about the loss of what's gone. The other half is about sadness at what now can't be.' He stops and lets this settle. 'Somehow you have to give room for both. Time and space.'

Grief for futures burned down. Grief, and then acceptance. Nishaan. Femi. Hayley. Yes, she thinks, she needs to go back. Go back into battle for Sami, ask Jackson to be merciful. See what agencies she can muster to intervene with Darren. Bless him, she thinks. Bless them all. Don't let go of hope just yet. Things will change. It's been a shit year but the future will be brighter, one day. Do this with Dad, then start over. She wants to talk to Cara, get in touch with Martha and make sure she's OK.

They come to the brow of the beacon, the ground falling away steeply in front. 'Here we are,' he says. The place mum would come to blow her blues away, though today it is almost still.

He takes off his backpack, unzips it and gently lifts out the urn. 'Right. Get this done and see if some brave publican will serve us lunch? Though I'd rather have had the chest wax and pedicure.'

'Dad stop it!' she tells him with a friendly punch.

He hands it to her. It is so small. Take away the air, drain the blood, it is remarkable how little is left.

She doesn't look sure what to do, but he reaches back into the bag and pulls out a small hipflask, undoes the top with his teeth and offers it over. 'Port,' he says. 'Her favourite.' She nods and he lifts it to her lips as if ministering wine, holy, warming, binding. A breeze is blowing but he carefully pulls out the anthology, turns to a page he has folded down and begins reading.

> *Somewhere*
>   *a black bear*
>   *has just risen from sleep*
>   *and is staring*
>   *down the mountain.*
>   *All night*
>   *in the brisk and shallow restlessness*
>   *of early spring*

Spring. Mary Oliver. Jo can hear Hayley's voice. Chantel picking up from her, then Charlie, this beautiful harmony of London's children. Oh God, she thinks, I cannot leave them now.

> *I think of her,*
>   *her four black fists*
>   *flicking the gravel,*
>   *her tongue*
>   *like a red fire*
>   *touching the grass,*
>   *the cold water.*

He pauses, has to gather his voice before continuing.

There is only one question:
how to love this world.

He stops then, can't get any more words to come.

'You,' she says, taking the pages and offering the wine to him in return, then pushes the urn into his hands. 'You,' she says again.

He unscrews the top. He is crying now, tears unashamed, running free. 'I miss you,' he says as he flings dust up and around him. It doesn't move far as it falls. 'I miss you. I love you.'

He stops and passes the urn back, much lighter now. He wipes his eyes, turns to leaves her alone.

'No,' she says. 'Stay.'

She holds what is left.

'Mum, I'm so sorry.'

This dearest wound she'd kept from her.

'I lost a child,' she cries in desperate confession, 'just as I was losing you.'

To have just been able to tell her this. To have found her hands and her eyes, been held, been seen. To have been able to be there for her at the end, be there for one another. But now she must let this go, let her mother go, her unborn go, stand free of all that has haunted.

She pours some of the ash into her hands and a gust takes it, twists it away and around. Some of it falls onto her boots, some swirls back into her face.

How to love this world? Jesus, she thinks, *how* in the midst of this fucking madness? The words from the poem fly corkscrews around her. Dazzling darkness. Glass cities. White teeth. The bear down the mountain, the fox come to the city. This animal wordlessness, this great struggle that she has chosen, this blessed burden to help children wield language and speak.

No idea how, she tells herself. She just has to hope. Hope that things improve soon, that life can return. Hope, yes, but accept too that if it comes to it she must take a glorious spark from Darren's liberty, allow some of his DNA to break her long-inherited compliance. She smiles, imagining telling Jackson to *JUST FUCK OFF*, and then leaving.

Something about the disobedient ash gives her that courage now. Her mother finally free, the last parts of her falling to the earth, trodden into shit, getting into hair and up her nose, rising on the faintest breeze, disappearing, just her and her father left standing alone, this last goodbye, farewell finally to all that has been lost, all who could not be saved.

His arm is around her. 'None of it,' he is saying, 'none of it was your fault.'

She cannot agree with that, she thinks. Not yet. 'I just wish I'd been able to be there,' she says. So hard to love this world right now.

Rain threatens. They should push on.

'I'm sure she wishes she'd been able to be there for you too.'

They lock arms together, pull masks back up and turn to go.

I wish all of this, she hears the wind call after them, repenting, diminishing.

I wish all of this, it soughs, pressing weakly at their departing backs.

Because, it seems to whisper in her ear, hardly a breath now as they descend into stillness, *Because I was your mother.*

She feels a last stir of air, sees it push a faint ripple through the leaves of an elm, lifting a bough as if a hand in farewell, and then it is gone.

The characters portrayed here are entirely fictional, though everything in the novel is written as truthfully as I could make it, drawing on my experience of teaching in a variety of London schools over the past twenty years.

I am hugely grateful to all of the colleagues who have passed on their craft, and to the dazzling, funny, brilliant and inspiring students who have walked through my classroom door. *Middle Class* is dedicated to all of you.

Even before Covid hit schools so severely, there was — and remains — a pandemic of stress in our schools, one that is affecting both staff and students in devastating ways. More than an issue of workload, it is the fruit of a society that has loaded education with more demands than it can bear.

Dealing with radicalisation, personal hygiene, healthy eating, morality... as other great institutions have faded, too often all that remains in the village that raises the child is the school. It is high time that we looked again at how we raise our young people, and how we can better support those tasked with bringing them to maturity.

Although the text of *Middle Class* received very high praise from so many literary agents, all of whom were confident that another would pick it up and take it out into the world, in the end none felt able to represent it.

In the face of these rejections — however gushing — part of me thought that I should put the manuscript away in a drawer and just move on. Another part was more bloody-minded, believing that there was something here worth sharing.

If I have made the wrong choice, then accept my apologies: the fault — as with any errors in the text — is mine alone.

If you feel I made the right one, perhaps you'd be kind enough to write a review of the book, or recommend it to a friend or colleague. Thank you.

Poem on page 280 © Mary Oliver. Permission sought.

Twitter and Instagram: @kesterbrewin

Printed in Great Britain
by Amazon

82660662R00171